IT'S NOT WHAT STOCKS YOU BUY...

It's When you Sell that Counts

DONALD L. CASSIDY

VISION BOOKS
(Incorporating Orient Paperbacks)
New Delhi • Mumbai • Hyderabad

To Loura
and Michael

www.visionbooksindia.com

First Vision Books Edition 2005
Reprinted 2008, 2010

ISBN 10: 81-7094-561-5
ISBN 13: 978-81-7094-561-1

Published by
Vision Books Pvt. Ltd.
(Incorporating Orient Paperbacks & CARING imprints)
24 Feroze Gandhi Road, Lajpat Nagar III
New Delhi 110024, India.

Phone: (+91-11) 2983 6470
Fax: (+91-11) 2983 6490
e-mail: visionbk@vsnl.com

Printed at
Ravindra Printing Press
1590 Madarsa Road, Kashmere Gate
Delhi-110006, India.

DONALD L. CASSIDY is a senior research analyst with Lipper Inc., a Reuters Company. His specialty areas include closed-end funds, flows of money in mutual funds, investor psychology and behavioral finance. He was formerly a senior analyst with a regional brokerage firm based in Denver, Colorado, USA.

Mr. Cassidy is a *cum laude* graduate of the Wharton School at the University of Pennsylvania and is a member of the CFA Society of Colorado. He has lectured for CFA societies internationally and has twice served on the faculty of Harvard University's Annual Congress on the Psychology of Investing. Cassidy serves on the national speakers bureau of the American Association of Individual Investors and is program chair of its Colorado chapter.

Contents

Publisher's Note to the Indian Edition

This Special Indian Edition fulfils a critical gap in the literature available for stock market investors. The financial press is full of news of the great new shares that you ought to be buying, there is nowhere near equal emphasis on what shares you ought to be selling. This leaves the investment process stuck mid-way since the cycle is only complete once the shares you buy are sold and you fulfil the financial objectives you had set for yourself. At best, switching is sometimes recommended, i.e., sell ABC in order to buy XYZ. Donald Cassidy very strongly argues against such a strategy because, in effect, then too you are not really selling in order to make a profit but doing so only in order to buy something else.

In the case of long term buy-and-hold investors, such emphasis on buying seems to fit well with their chosen strategy. Is that really true? In fact, the buy-and-hold strategy also implies holding your shares for a certain finite period of time, not for ever. But ask any buy-and-hold investor how many scrips he has in his portfolio which have unthinkingly slipped into the "never-to-be-sold" category and chances are even he will be amazed at the number. The reasons for this widespread inability to sell are many, and all of these have been very perceptively pointed out by Don Cassdy in this book. Which is why it is an absolutely must-have component in every investor's tool-kit.

As in the case of some of the other foreign books we have made available at affordable prices for the Indian investors in the series of *Vision Investment Books,* we have made the conscious decision to retain the complete original material though in few places it varies from the Indian situation. The reasons for retaining all the material are basically two-fold: one, not to mutilate the flow of the author's thought and presentation. And, two, because Wall Street practices of today could well be the norm of the Indian stock markets tomorrow. As such, there is little harm in gaining an insight into the future. Finally, in a few instances (e.g., Commission Phobia and Tax Phobia in Chapter 2), the exact rates in the Indian context are obviously different from those in the U.S. but that in no way dilutes the thrust of the author's argument.

We hope that this book will help you sell your shares when you ought to . . . and convert your notional paper profits into solid profits Remember the old adage: a bird in hand is worth two in the bush.

Acknowledgements

A book, like any product of the human mind, is an amalgam formed from a combination of conscious and unconscious experiences that affect the author over much of a lifetime. The writer might well, therefore, acknowledge almost anyone who has ever touched his life. Publishers prefer the list be kept brief, however. This imposes a discipline at once useful and cruel. With due apologies to those numerous others whose names fell off the short list, then, I thank:

Richard Randlett, a teacher of junior high mathematics, who introduced me to investments: he will never know the horizons he opened in my mind.

Robert Scotland, a teacher of U.S. history at Wayland High School in Massachusetts: he demanded the best of good students. He allowed me to study the Great Depression as a history project and made me deliver a lecture to classmates; that experience built self-confidence.

The late Roger Spear, who founded an investment advisory firm later sold to Fidelity Management and Research Corporation: he patienctly guided and taught an impetuous young man and let him learn on company time.

Charles Kline, a finance instructor at the Wharton School: his favorite expression was simple but profound: "Everything goes in circles and cycles."

Ellen Curtiss, for many years with Arthur D. Little, Inc.: she stretched me as a researcher, editor and writer, and convinced me that it can be done.

Richard Hurwitz, formerly Research Director at Boettcher and Company: he had the confidence and vision to hire as an investment analyst a management consultant with "no previous experience," a courageous act for a manager in today's myopic corporate culture. He was a tough and, therefore, valued mentor.

Heather White, a colleague at Boettcher and a dear friend: she taught me things about brokers that otherwise would have taken years to crystallize in my mind. She also told me I was good enough to undertake the perilous task of writing a first book. Then she led me to my publisher, saving much pain and frustration.

Robert Davis of Davis-Hamilton Associates, one of several research directors I served: he has a profound sense of proportion and so maintains a cool and logical mind in crisis. He taught me much more than he thinks.

Richard Follingstad, who invited me to speak at a public seminar in 1989 about the problems of a company in Albuquerque, New Mexico: his stage provided me with a major direct exposure to how individual investors think about selling their stocks; that night convinced me this book was needed.

Scott Courts of Denver, a young broker wise beyond his years: he shared war stories, confirmed my worst suspicions, listened to and helped shape some of my concepts, and was excited for me.

Belita Calvert, who helped me in many little but important ways: from proofreading to listening to energizing and encouraging, she was always there.

Finally, and not least, Jennifer Lindsey, an author and my editor: she made a machete-like reduction of my thick draft feel as though done with a fine scalpel. This was no small task since I was accustomed to writing and editing for final publication. Her experience made the work publishable in spite of my stubbornness.

Introduction

One day an analyst was in conversation with an experienced broker to discuss the recommended sale of a certain stock, of which the broker's client held 500 shares.

"Well," said the analyst, "a sale sounds nice since the stock is up several points here. He ought to be glad to take the profit."

To his surprise, the broker replied, "I wish it were that easy. You see, this guy is funny. He really hates to pay taxes, so I have an awful time getting him to sell to take a profit."

The analyst responded that he had heard that song a few times and joked that maybe the broker should point out to the client that he ought to like paying taxes on thousands in profit rather than having a loss to worry about. The analyst then suggested offsetting other losses to close out, to help soften the tax blow and put the client's portfolio in better shape.

"Oh, no," said the broker, "he absolutely refuses to take a loss. I cannot even TALK to him about it."

In disbelief the analyst asked, "Are you saying that you have a client who is invested in the stock market but will not take a profit to avoid capital-gains tax, and who will not take a loss as a matter of pride? I'll bet you lunch that he would refuse to sell a stock unchanged because it has not done what he expected."

At that point, the broker conceded lunch because the client, indeed, held stocks if unchanged because he also hated paying commissions.

Whether the foregoing tale amuses or alarms the reader, there is a lesson in it.

Here was an intelligent man, successful in his profession, who owned a decent collection of municipals, as well as stocks and mutual funds. Not untypically, he had difficulty selling stocks whether they were up, down or unchanged. Clients like this always generate the eternal question, "Why won't he sell?"

There are many reasons why people have trouble selling their stocks. Brokers, too, have their own hesitations about getting clients to sell. In fact, selling stock is a universal problem. The inescapable conclusion is that people need help cashing in whether they are average, Main-Street investors or they are professional brokers. One of the reasons assistance is needed is that there is very little selling information in the marketplace. Much more attention must be given the art of selling out stocks whether at a gain or at a loss. And an understanding must be developed that today, many brokers are product marketers rather than investment experts. Investors need to pay attention to the psychology of selling against human nature; to individual stocks and how they behave; to how investors think and act; and to brokers and the roles they play. Overwhelmingly, most published books that deal with the stock market in any form focus on the buying transaction only and neglect the sell side of the equation almost completely. Selling may not be as exciting and it is a narrower topic; but it is absolutely necessary and has its own very interesting twists and curiosities.

This book is divided into four sections. The first describes the external and internal problems and pitfalls that investors face when confronted with a hold/sell choice. These obstructions tend to be structural in nature. The second section covers several necessary aspects of mind-set with which to approach the hold/sell decision. These problems are related to a natural avoidance of closure, which can represent with death-like finality the mortality of an investor's judgment. The third section prescribes important strategies that should be applied to smart selling decisions. The fourth section explores micro-level tactics for executing strategy more effectively and profitably.

The final chapter provides a checklist, to be used with each transaction, that functions as a learning device.

There is no difference between a long-term investor in the classic sense or a short-term trader when it comes to stock market success: anyone can profit and stay in the game, if he knows how to cash in—to sell—when the time is right.

SECTION

I

Roadblocks to Profitable Selling: Phobias, Myths & Rationalizations

C H A P T E R

1

External Roadblocks

KEYS TO INVESTMENT SUCCESS

- Understanding Today's Broker
- The Four-Letter Word: Sell
- Understanding the Importance of Changed Fundamentals
- Buying and Holding, and Other Conditioned Motivations

Today's Broker

A description of broker skills that has evolved over the past decade is not the focus of this book. However, an understanding of the broker point of view is essential in order to make investor profits in the stock market. While some of the comments about brokers may seem critical, they are intended to illustrate the broker point of view and to help the investor facilitate his or her relationship with a broker.

There are different kinds of brokers; and to compound the confusion, each brokerage firm has its own broker terminology: "account executive," "registered representative" or "investment counselor," for example. Although the title does not matter, what does matter to investors is the training, experience and basic professional orientation of their brokers no matter what they are called and no matter what firm is the employer.

This is not simply to say, "get a well-trained broker." It is a recommendation to identify the broker's orientation, to find out how he deals with the investing public.

Note that the term "stockbroker" has not been used in this book, in favor of the term "broker." The choice of words has been deliberate: most of today's brokers are not really stockbrokers in the classical, historical sense. And there are good reasons.

Fallout From the Fidelity Phenomenon

With 20/20 hindsight, it is now possible to conclude that probably the largest single factor in the gradual extinction of the traditional stockbroker was the phenomenal success of the Fidelity Cash Reserves Fund in the mid-1970s. Fidelity's success in attracting billions of dollars to its Cash Reserves Fund started a chain of events that has led, over 15 years, to the relative scarcity of the traditional stockbroker — a lamentable consequence, but not one that Fidelity's man-

Exhibit 1.1: Fidelity Cash Reserves Fund

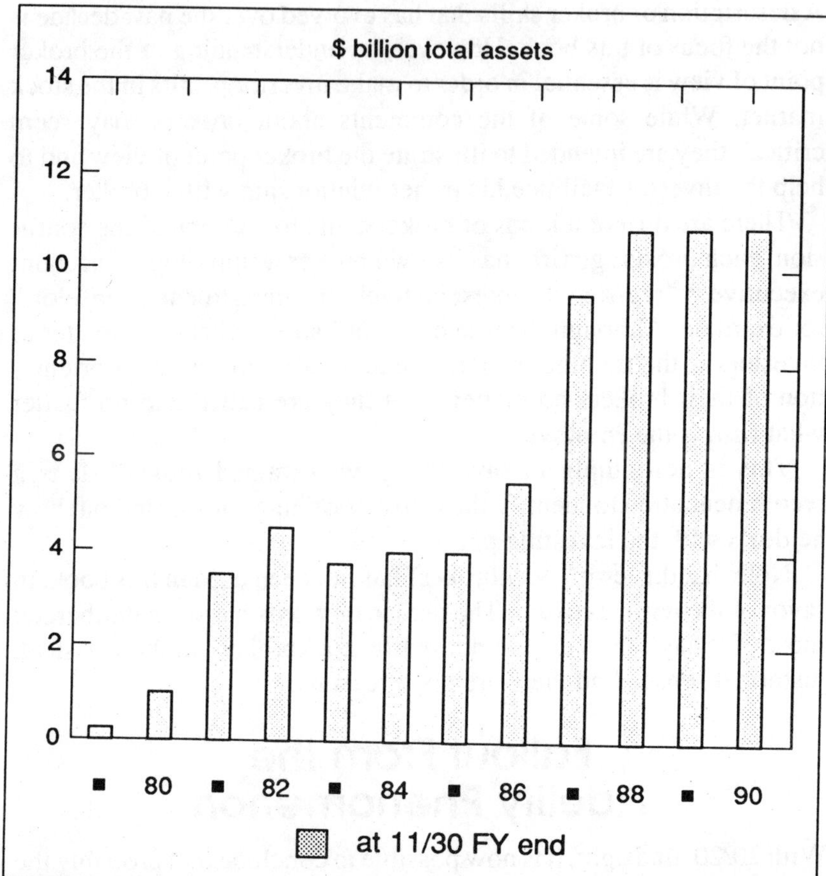

agement either foresaw or intended. The success of Cash Reserves Fund — among other funds — rippled like a pebble dropped in a pond, which widened into a series of tidal waves.

First, Cash Reserves Fund acted as a parking place for billions of dollars of investor funds during the disintermediation of the mid-1970s. When interest rates later subsided, Fidelity encouraged and educated its Cash Reserves Fund holders to transfer assets to other mutual funds within the corporate family or "group."

The effect not only was to offer the investor a better equities climate, but also — much more importantly — to demonstrate to Fidelity managers and industry competitors the success of asset gathering as a corporate strategy.

Whether or not by brilliant forward planning, Fidelity executed a strategy of gathering and maintaining control of billions of dollars in investor assets. (See Exhibit 1-1.) It was highly profitable — indeed, imperative — for Fidelity to maintain and extend its investment pool once the basic move had been made. And at the same time, it became obvious to competitors that they not only should, but indeed must, compete on equal footing by attracting their own client assets to a broad array of funds, or "products."

Asset capture, then, became a competitive necessity for every company in the industry. Had Fidelity continued playing the asset-capture game solo, it seemed plausible for it to have assembled "all" investable assets — clearly a massive threat to the jobs, egos and incomes of thousands of investment professionals in all the other firms.

Not only mutual funds were affected; all financial services providers visualized their turfs invaded and captured by the asset-gatherers. Insurance companies feared that billions of dollars would be drained from their coffers and new-policy sales choked off, as investors soaked up the mutual funds offered by Fidelity. Banks envisioned both a permanent disintermediation of deposits and a likely diversion of assets from their money-management departments. And brokerage firms saw the lure that mutual funds' professional management represented: it meant a threatened drain on the funds held by individual investors in stocks and bonds.

One-Stop Shopping

As a result of the "asset-capture game," many financial organizations became supermarkets; the department store image fits equally well. Sears, Roebuck & Co., now the second biggest U.S. department store, became a financial supermarket. Starting with a distribution base (the customer list and the walk-in traffic) and with an insurance company (Allstate), Sears added a family of mutual funds and a brokerage firm (Dean Witter), and even got into real estate brokerage and financing.

So most financial-services providers concluded, at roughly the same time, that the only survival strategy for long-term business success was to become a financial supermarket — the provider of essentially all services under one corporate or holding-company roof. By its nature, asset-gathering became an activity of prime importance because once assets were captured, they were likely to remain under management or control until the investor needed them for spending. Annual or monthly fees accruing for the management of those assets grew large as the asset base rose from tens to hundreds of billions of dollars (the amount of money funds alone, as of late 1990, exceeded $486 billion). One percent of that pie as an approximate annual management fee had become an extremely attractive prize.

So banks and insurance companies bought brokerage firms and started their own mutual funds. Mutual funds firms created insurance and annuity products, and started brokerage operations. And most significant, brokerage firms responded by marketing funds and similar products intensively.

The upshot was that individual brokers who had originally been "stock and bond brokers" now were trained to handle a variety of additional investment instruments or "products," including annuities, variable annuities, mutual funds of all descriptions, tax shelters, unit investment trusts, gold bullion, precious metal coins, and options and index futures.

Not only were existing brokers now re-educated in some or all of these new offerings, but also the standard training programs for new brokers hired by nationwide brokerage firms soon included and indeed emphasized the specialized products. Smaller, regional firms — forced to compete on as equal a footing as they could create — followed in lockstep. Thus an entire new generation of entrants into the brokerage business was conditioned to offer a full array of manufactured financial products.

Their firms became the personal analog of the financial shopping mall, where the customer never leaves the premises to satisfy any or all investment needs. Asset capture became a way of life in the investment and brokerage industry. By the mid-1980s, standard training programs for new sales personnel had relegated stocks and bonds — once the staple of the business — to literally a 10 percent or less share of time and emphasis. A stock or bond became only one of a series of financial concepts or "products" that the newly trained salesperson learned how to offer client-investors. A 1988 *Barrons* article estimated that 40 percent of the brokers in the business in 1987 had entered since 1980. Their training reflects this wholesale de-emphasis on stocks. Not only were individual stocks accorded less emphasis in training programs, but they also became palpably less attractive to the average individual investor.

This major development of the 1970s and 1980s was also, at least in part, a fallout from the Fidelity phenomenon. Huge pools of investable funds came under the control of professional money managers, whether in funds, pension plans or insurance/annuity assets. The live marketplace became highly institutionalized as an increasing fraction of each session's trading was created by professional portfolio managers, rather than directly by individuals.

Individual investors — regardless of their age or Wall Street experience — became painfully aware that they were competing as relative rookies on a playing field dominated by giant players who, right or wrong, moved the market just by playing. This realization, brought home in a series of bear markets from 1973 to 1982 and coming again as no surprise in October 1987, convinced millions of individual investors to reduce their direct participation in stocks. In large numbers they quit altogether, went into hibernation or turned their funds over to the professional managers, thereby accelerating the trend.

These packaged investments or products are *sold* to investors. They are not actively *bought* by investors. So the operational dynamic is *not* that an individual investor goes to a broker who responds by identifying a product or service to sell him. Now, in order to capture or "gather" assets in the new era, asset managers create investment products to be packaged and proactively sold to the investing public.

New Techniques in Sales

The most efficient way to sell a mass-produced product is to train a sales force in a standardized and rehearsed technique. And because in many cases certain representations must be made and certain caveats offered, the pitch is delivered essentially from a script. The extreme version is a verbatim or canned script or "pitch" that the salesperson is supposed to read from top to bottom.

The point is, that prepackaged products and rehearsed sales pitches require persuasiveness and persistence, in contrast to the choice of individual securities which required intelligence and incisive investment expertise. Played out through cold calling of fresh prospects, the sale of products results in successful asset capture. Prepackaged products also generate larger commissions than stocks and bonds.

Imagine a securities broker with a prospect or existing client whose objective is safety of principal and income. He might place $10,000 in The Consolidated Income Fund, which is professionally managed and offers a 4.5 percent commission. One or two individual income-type stocks, the alternative to the fund, pay an upfront commission of 1 percent. And at most brokerage firms, the broker's personal percentage of total commission is higher on packaged products than on stocks and bonds. Which products will the broker sell? The packaged products. Even if commissions are equal, the packaged products come with an easy, prepared script and the assurance of a proven professional management team; existing stocks do not. There is less post-sale "hand holding" with the packaged product because, presumably, it is less complicated.

There is one more important broker aspect of the asset-gathering revolution: the nature of investment sales personnel. They are paid to distribute investment products created for the benefit of management. This process usually is performed most effectively with conservative, long-term-oriented investments. The sales person of today is trained to help the client to make a decision to *buy* a product. Professional training, mind set and daily habit focuses exclusively on a relationship in which the broker suggests instruments that should be bought, which the prospect agrees to *buy*.

So the broker is not trained in the process of convincing clients that they should *sell* investment assets. This is, in effect, a structural "buy bias" — the concentration of the investment industry on the process of distributing packaged products that are designed to be *bought* by the public. Brokers are simply more practiced and more comfortable suggesting that the client buy something, not that he sell something. This evolved because brokers became channels of distribution as a result of asset-gathering, rather than sources of investment advice.

One of the ways to identify a broker's professional point of origin — asset-gathering or investment expertise — is to find out how long he has been in the investment business and what prior career he had. If he was an entrepreneur or franchisee, or — the surest tipoff — a salesman of other products or services, he is at heart a hustling sales professional and not an investment expert.

Another useful and revealing strategy is to interrupt the canned or scripted sales pitch with a question. Make the question really challenging. Ask the broker an upbeat question like, "What happens to the proposed investment if the Swiss franc rallies against the Japanese yen while the value of the dollar and gold both rise?" If the broker is an investment professional, he should have some semblance of an informed opinion. Scripted brokers will be baffled.

Because of the "buy bias," investors should expect little or no selling advice unless the broker is a traditional or classic professional from the old school. So realize that most selling activity is going to be virtually a do-it-yourself project.

There is also a psychological bias against selling stocks: all buys are made in optimism, whereas not all sells conclude successful ventures. So selling is not a uniformly happy experience for investors. And virtually every sell, unless made at the historic high eighth of a point, at least sometimes *looks* like a wrong and irretrievably completed decision. Unhappy memories of such sales prompt avoidance behavior later.

The Four-Letter Word: Sell

One of the reasons selling is a difficult proposition for a broker is the "buy bias." It is easy to appreciate the more comfortable and optimistic sense that both investors and brokers have about buying, especially when buying is contrasted with selling. As stated before, buying is, by nature, a beginning based on hope and optimism. Selling is an ending that may not conclude in optimism, and it carries a lot more "emotional baggage."

There are very important reasons why a brokerage firm almost never says "sell." All of them are logical, if viewed from the firm's viewpoint; so individual investors must center on their own profit needs when it comes to making a sell decision, not on the broker's desire for a commission or her sales orientation, and not on the profit motive of the brokerage firm. A wise investor must adopt a strong do-it-yourself attitude and discipline about cashing in when the time is right.

The necessity for this go-it-alone investor orientation is that one individual is not the brokerage firm's only client constituency, even when his business is combined with all other retail investors. Usually, a brokerage firm's most important clients are public companies. That is because the investment-banking side of the brokerage firm is in business to raise capital for these companies and it is a very lucrative business compared to retail revenues.

In fact, when an individual investor buys stock or bonds in a new issue, the broker usually points out that there is no commission on the purchase. The broker may go so far as to say, "the issuing company is paying the commission." That is correct; and except for very small orders, the investment-banking, per-share commission is well above what is paid on an aftermarket transaction.

So the level of commission dollars from companies issuing securities is high because the investment-banking side of the firm has high fixed costs (salaries, entertainment, computers, legal and accounting consultants). They need to do underwritings for these large corporate clients, or they are not profitable. That means there is an inescapable tension within the brokerage firm between the investment-banking side and the research side.

Because investment bankers need to do "deals" (i.e., bring out securities issues such as initial public offerings), naturally the firm's overall interests are best served if those stocks and bonds prove to be solid investments for the firm's clients. The firm's research analysts must make judgments on the available investment alternatives; they recommend the ones they think are best to the firm's brokers and clients through published reports and newsletters. A research analyst's job is complete only when she fully studies a company and its industry, and makes *two* recommendations: when to buy and when to sell.

Unfortunately, individual investors almost never see a sell recommendation. Why? Sale advices rarely are published because of the negative effect they could have on the relationship between the brokerage firm and its investment banking clients. Think about the implications. Suppose that in January the brokerage firm brings to market a few million shares of a company called New-Issue Industries. The firm's brokers dutifully place the stock with clients and collect commissions. But suppose something goes awry in the company's affairs shortly after the offering is made: Perhaps in March a competitor introduces a new widget or is acquired by a powerful conglomerate; or sales turn soft; or raw-material costs explode. The firm's research analyst wants to point out the potential problem to brokers and clients, suggesting that the stock be sold.

But sell to whom? Most awareness of the company is centered in the firm's retail clients. How will the clients react if they bought in January and now in March are encouraged to sell because trouble lies ahead? At the least, they will suspect their brokers are churning their portfolios for commissions. At most, they may sue the brokerage firm over alleged misrepresentation or negligence.

What happens to the relationship between the investment banking department and the corporate officers at New-Issue Industries when the research department flashes the sell flag and the stock heads south? Future business between the firm and New-Issue Industries becomes highly unlikely. If word gets around the local business community that the brokerage firm recommends the sale of stocks it brought public, other companies are very likely to use a different underwriter for their upcoming issues.

For these reasons, the S-word is absent from the lexicon of most brokerage firms. It is considered a four-letter word; although institutional clients might hear the word over the phone, it does not appear in print.

There are several dimensions to the distaste for the word "sell," and one of the most important is the reluctance of a broker to activate the sale side of a security transaction. For that reason, consider any broker assistance a gift, and do not count on that help: brokerage houses almost never say "sell," so an investor needs to know the code words brokers use when they really mean "sell."

Euphemisms

Other words for "sell," however, do appear as non-words. Brokerage firms have devised a variety of ways to describe a corporate situation that indicates a sale is the best option. One of them is to write a report covering a corporate finance client, which is labelled a follow-up to the underwriting and carries no opinion or recommendation. Follow-ups need to be read closely. Even if the official policy is to give no recommendation, the tone of the report needs to be regarded carefully. If it is less than glowing, suspect that the research analyst is not impressed with the stock and really thinks it should be sold.

Another approach is to give a recommendation other than "buy" which is kinder and gentler than "sell." The best euphemism for "sell," ironically, is its operative opposite: "hold." When an analyst does not want to say buy and is not allowed to say sell, the only option remaining is "hold." *Consider "hold" almost always as a danger sign. In fact, "hold" can be interpreted as meaning "do not hold."*

Another way of saying sell is a carefully-worded message like, "the stock is probably a worthwhile long-term holding despite some near-term uncertainties." That is translated by the cynic as "if you hold for quite a while, maybe you will not lose." All these euphemisms are signals to cash in.

Make it a point to ask a broker about his firm's rating words. For some it is "buy/hold." Others say "buy/accumulate/hold." Others may use words like "overperform/in-line/underperform," or perhaps "emphasize/under-weight." Know the range of official analyst word-choices. Anything less enthusiastic than the top choice should be interpreted as faint praise or outright damnation. If a broker does not verbally make a compelling case for the stock when the official advice is less than glowing, figure that the real message is to cash out the position.

Politics and Diplomacy

Even when there is no current investment banking relationship between the issuing company and the brokerage firm, there are important reasons why research analysts are unlikely to advise a sale. First, there is the possibility of future business, so they do not want to poison the waters. And more immediately, the analyst needs to have the continuing, cordial, constructive and prompt communication of senior management.

A sale recommendation, even if it is the correct conclusion, seldom warms up the company's management. They own shares themselves and so are never pleased by a price decline that usually follows a sale advice. Also, the analyst may have legitimate reason to fear that an adverse recommendation might stifle management's future disclosures: the worst scenario is to recommend a sale that turns out wrong.

Finally, there is the numbers game. When an analyst writes a research report advising purchase, brokers can use that report to contact every customer whose investment objective makes the purchase of that stock appropriate. That means that a buy advice has a potentially wide audience. For example, suppose that a particular electric utility seems attractive to the analyst. The recommendation to buy can be presented to every client interested in income.

But a sale recommendation has much less business-generating potential. And a sale advice applies only to those clients who already own the stock. Suppose that the analyst now believes interest rates are about to rise or that fuel costs are a problem, and decides to advise the sale of an electric company's shares. Perhaps only one in ten clients acted on the idea when a buy was advised. These people are the only audience for the sale report. Worse than that, some clients may have bought at higher prices, and their brokers are hesitant to advise taking the loss. So the sale report is not likely to be very effective in generating commissions. Research analysts are employed and compensated on the basis of the accuracy of judgment *and* on the amount of business their reports generate. So the analyst has a buy bias too.

Brokers face another dilemma when making a sale recommendation. The investor tends to blame poor results more on a sale than on a buy. Ask any broker: do clients remember the bad buy advice given but not acted on; or do they recall the bad sell advice that was acted on? Overwhelmingly, scoreboard watchers watch the stocks they owned and sold — not those they never bought. That can get the broker into trouble with the client (and the analyst into trouble with the brokers). Another way for a broker to get into even more trouble is to suggest re-deploying the funds in another stock that goes down.

In summary, there are five ways a sale advice can backfire on a broker:

1. He can offend the client who is emotionally attached to the stock.
2. Selling can close out a painful transaction (a loss).
3. The sale can be followed by a rally in the stock, which would have provided greater profit or a reduced loss if it had been held.
4. The funds liberated by the sale might be re-invested unprofitably, making the sale a double troublemaker.
5. Unless the sale price was near perfect, the broker is resented for generating a commission by suggesting the action.

It is also worth noting here that penny-stock houses *never* recommend a sell unless it is to generate funds to buy something else. The major reason is that they must buy what investors sell because they make the market in the stock. And there is a parallel to guard against in non-penny brokerage practice as well. If an investor tells a broker to sell and is given a pitch not to, this is a serious alarm signal. It may mean that the firm is concerned about the price and does not want to put pressure on the stock. Unless a broker gives solid, specific reasons to hold, insist on selling now, at the market.

The safest practice is: never wait to hear sell advice. Assume it will not be heard and plan to make personal selling-versus-holding decisions with the help of selling tools and rules that appear later in the book.

The False Security of Low Initial Risk

It has become fashionable in investment marketing circles to emphasize the avoidance of risk, particularly since the October 1987 crash. The emphasis within the industry on risk avoidance — rather than on promising the moon in growth and profits — is healthy. That the investing public is taking this advice to heart is reflected by the noticeable decline in the number of well-known penny-stockbrokerage houses, so-called boiler rooms, and other similar operations that prey on investor gullibility, greed and seemingly boundless optimism.

But even with the rebirth of emphasis on risk avoidance, the securities industry marketing effort focuses entirely on buying and virtually ignores the equally important sell side of the transaction. In most public investment seminars, the selling aspect covered most often is the stop-loss order; but rarely does the speaker adequately cover how and why to use this instrument. Although the stop-loss order is useful, routine use allows the investor (and the broker) to avoid confronting crucial selling decisions. Either the stop-loss order is triggered automatically or it is not activated at all, which neatly truncates the important selling thought-process. For brokers to advise using stop-loss orders routinely is also self-serving: if a client is stopped out of a losing position, the loss is relatively small, and the use of these orders shows that the broker exercised diligence in trying to limit losses.

Of course, if the stop-loss order is placed too close to the current price, stops are triggered often; this increases turnover in the account for defensible reasons of caution, but protects the client against major pre-commission capital loss in any one stock position.

Many investor seminars promise to highlight specific management techniques for protecting investor money to avoid risk. But managing is an active verb indicating an ongoing process. Managing a factory does not mean hiring workers, sending them through the door and walking away. In the same way, managing invested funds means buying, watching and selling. It consists of much more than an up-front, one-time allocation of assets or choice of purchases. Asset allocation — among types of investment instruments, across industries, in world regions and on a time horizon — is not a do-it-once activity. The strategies and tactics taught by many brokerage firms, however, merely list financial instruments rather than teach specific ongoing money management techniques.

The lists usually consist of mutual funds, unit trusts, insurance, annuities, bonds and stocks — none of which is a strategy or a tactic. They should be considered only the means by which to execute a strategy. The properly timed purchase *and sales* of these instruments are tactical actions. Of course, three of these six instruments are essentially one-decision (i.e., buy) investments: insurance, annuities and unit trusts. Notice that not coincidentally these are packaged products created by financial institutions to be actively sold to the public. The broker is compensated at the start to get investors to buy and there is no back-end action (selling, or deliberate cashing in) built in to the equation.

Generally, these six financial vehicles are properly described and positioned by the brokerage industry within economic cycles. But the brokerage seminars and reports focus only on identifying when a cycle is starting and how to take advantage of it by *buying* at the right time. So in the industry's eyes managing and avoiding risk becomes a function of buying good stocks and selecting the right time to buy good stocks. What this nearsighted approach ignores is that risk is constantly present in varying degrees over time; managing investment risk must be an ongoing process that does not end when a purchase is made.

So before buying, assess all the opportunities and associated risks inherent in an investment package. Look at the upside and downside (seen and unseen) carefully. Then, shift focus after the purchase from the broad to the specific: the question how becomes which stock (among many) should be sold. The notion that risk is avoided once a seemingly safe investment has been bought obfuscates the reality of future events.

The decision for proactive entry into an investment is not the only point in time when risk is assumed or avoided. By now, the investor's awareness of the one-sidedness of investment marketing should serve to heighten sensitivity to the "buy bias." Because greater external attention is always paid to buying, put more of your personal energy and work into selling. Although an investor can sit out a buy, once he owns an investment there is no way to call time out. The only way to end the game profitably is to sell.

Underestimating the Importance of Changed Fundamentals

Today's institutional domination of the market and the increased leverage and fragility of the economy require that investors pay more attention to changed fundamentals than in gentler times past. Success now requires heightened attention to fundamental news about a company — and its industry and broad environment — when an investor owns its shares. If the news is less favorable than expected, or if deterioration in the company's prospects is evident or suspected, the best action usually is to sell promptly. The reason is related to momentum: when things go wrong, it takes significant exertion of energy in the opposite direction to make them start going right again. That is true both in the management of the company's day-to-day business and also in the stock market.

In any speculative market, a snowball that starts going down hill tends to keep going. The market swings emotionally from over-valuation to under-valuation. The extent of the overshooting on each side is impossible to predict because it is driven by volatile emotions. So the investor's first job is to be smart enough to realize that the market gyrates, and then to get out of the way before the pendulum swings adversely.

While stocks do not always accelerate in decline, it is true that a reversal to upside price action requires intervention by interested buyers. And the buyers must be big enough and persistent enough, first to stop the price decline, then to stabilize the price against the trickle of further selling that results from boredom. Finally, they must overpower the sellers to push the stock price higher.

Strategies to Overcome Fundamental Problems

It is well known that running a business successfully takes a great deal of effort and attention. Few companies can be put on automatic pilot because external forces emerge or change; competitors enter the fray; or demand-side shifts require product or service changes. So management is paid to anticipate, monitor and overcome difficulties to keep the enterprise moving ahead profitably. The same is true of investing in the stock market: the investor is paid for success in anticipating, monitoring, and acting.

The investor — as well as his money — is invested in the market. So he must be on guard to keep his hopes from overruling good judgment. This strongly indicates that an investor should read more than just the annual and quarterly reports; read the 10-Ks and the 10-Qs too. Study the discussion of challenges and difficulties foreseen for the quarter or the year ahead. Compare what happened against what management's earlier projections were. Compare the content and tone of current "outlook" statements against those of three or six months ago. Pay particular attention to unfavorable changes.

Remember that in today's highly litigious climate, executives usually telegraph possible problems early on — so as to avoid being accused of withholding bad news. Listen to their warnings. If growth in revenue is slowing down, or if margins are under pressure or if costs are outrunning expansion, find out why. If the causes cannot be identified, specific remedies cannot be taken — and that is a fundamental problem. Remember that problems seldom solve themselves.

For this reason, carefully examine what a company's executives say about their corporate problems and challenges. Look for discussion of solutions and actions, not excuses. Do not be readily forgiving, because managements are paid to manage problems. If the president's report bemoans the fact that external forces are causing problems but offers no concrete corporate initiatives to reverse the difficulties, sell the stock. Fire this management team by selling the stock. Hire another team.

It is wiser to lean toward being overly harsh than overly forgiving. Be especially sensitive to the development of negative fundamentals. And paying attention just once a quarter, reading the interim report six weeks into the next quarter, is not enough. *If the price of liberty is eternal vigilance, the price of investment success is constant observation, evaluation, comparison, decisiveness and a willingness to admit a mistake and move on.*

One undeniable reason to be up to date and relatively unforgiving is that institutions moving huge amounts of money into and out of stocks, unfortunately, have become very short-term oriented. Therefore, the investor must be nimble enough to nip any potential investment problems in the bud. This investor's inclination may be to give a company the benefit of a little more time to improve. But when a professional investor with a million shares gets impatient, share price will drop even if the patient, small investor later is proven correct about an eventual turnaround.

It is apparent that taking losses quickly on important bad news or disturbing trends means falling into the pattern of short-term performance orientation. However, an investor must be realistic and do what is required in order to preserve capital. This willingness to be part of the short-term orientation if necessary falls under the broad banner of not fighting the tape. This approach means recognizing that while the market may be wrong in its approach, it is much bigger than an individual investor.

Buying and Holding, and Other Conditioned Motivations

Investors buy stocks for a number of reasons, many of which are ill-advised. Purely from an investment perspective, there are only two reasons to buy common stocks. True equities investing consists of identifying those companies with undervalued stocks in terms of future earning power, and buying them now because the projected earnings stream is expected to produce dividends. So the first objective is dividend income. The second objective is capital appreciation. Growth in price tends to occur over time if the fortunes of the underlying company improve, if interest rates do not move sharply higher and if market psychology moves from negative to positive.

Some investment purists look down their noses and call the desire for capital appreciation "speculation." It may or may not be speculation, but investors buy stocks in order to sell them at a profit in the future, whether it is intelligent speculation or investment. Whether it is speculation or investment, a successful transaction requires both buying and selling. Both are required before the transaction's final result is established.

As stated in the introduction, overwhelmingly, most published books that deal with the stock market in any form focus on the buying transaction only and neglect the sell side of the equation almost completely. Selling may not be as exciting and it is a narrower topic; but it is absolutely necessary and has its own very interesting twists and curiosities.

Dividend Income

Investors who buy stocks for dividend income should consider the total package of risk and reward more carefully than most do. It is tempting to buy common stocks of companies in which the latest year's dividends represent a high percentage of the current stock price. The buyer believes that this high apparent yield will continue. What is often not fully considered is that the collective wisdom and expectations of all knowledgeable market players set current stock prices and, therefore, an apparently high yield is usually a sign of high risk. So the buyer of a high-yield stock is taking two risks: first, that the dividend income itself may be reduced or stopped, and second, that the stock's price might decline from the buyer's level if such an adverse dividend action occurs.

Almost continuously since the 1930s depression, common stocks have provided lower current (cash) yields than either long-term bonds or preferred stocks. In this environment, if an investor requires a high current yield, he should buy senior instruments. They are less likely than common shares to suffer reduced or omitted income payments, and they usually carry covenants that make up the back cash returns in the future if those events transpire.

If an income-oriented buyer has a serious need for current income, he should not take the incremental risk of common stock ownership; instead, he should stick to senior securities. Also, the buyer of common stocks for income should concentrate not on pure current cash income alone, but rather on total return (referring to the sum of cash return plus realized or unrealized price appreciation). That appreciation, in turn, is caused by a rising level of dividends over the years. That rate of growth, expressed as a percentage per year, is added to the cash yield (dividend rate divided by stock price) to get total return. (See Tables 1-1, 1-2.)

Tables 1-1: Calculation of Annual Total Percentage Return on Investment (assumes dividend raised seven percent at year-end meeting, pre-tax)

Year End	Div Rate $	Yield Basis %	Price $	Cap Incr $	Total $ Retn	Total % Retn	Retn on Orig Cost Total %	Cash %
0 (Buy)	1.40	7.00	20.00					
1	1.47	7.00	21.00	1.00	2.40	12.0	12.0	7.0
2	1.54	7.00	22.05	1.05	2.52	12.0	12.6	7.3
3	1.62	7.00	23.15	1.10	2.65	12.0	13.2	7.7
4	1.70	7.00	24.31	1.16	2.78	12.0	13.9	8.1
5	1.79	7.00	25.53	1.22	2.92	12.0	14.6	8.5
6	1.88	7.00	26.80	1.28	3.06	12.0	15.3	8.9
7	1.97	7.00	28.14	1.34	3.22	12.0	16.1	9.4
8	2.07	7.00	29.55	1.41	3.38	12.0	16.9	9.8
9	2.17	7.00	31.03	1.48	3.55	12.0	17.7	10.3
10	2.28	7.00	32.58	1.55	3.72	12.0	18.6	10.9
	17.61			12.58	30.19	Average:	15.1	8.8

Table 1-2: Calculation of Annual Total Percentage Return on Investment (assumes dividend constant at ten percent of purchase price, pre-tax)

Year End	Div Rate $	Yield Basis %	Price $	Cap Incr $	Total $ Retn	Total % Retn
0 (Buy)	1.40	10.0	14.00			
1	1.40	10.0	14.00	0.00	1.40	10.0
2	1.40	10.0	14.00	0.00	1.40	10.0
3	1.40	10.0	14.00	0.00	1.40	10.0
4	1.40	10.0	14.00	0.00	1.40	10.0
5	1.40	10.0	14.00	0.00	1.40	10.0
6	1.40	10.0	14.00	0.00	1.40	10.0
7	1.40	10.0	14.00	0.00	1.40	10.0
8	1.40	10.0	14.00	0.00	1.40	10.0
9	1.40	10.0	14.00	0.00	1.40	10.0
10	1.40	10.0	14.00	0.00	1.40	10.0
	14.00			0.00	14.00	

Thus, a stock currently yielding seven percent with a dividend growth if 5 percent annually may provide a total return of 12 percent per year. The actual result varies as the company's fortunes change and, significantly, as the level of prevailing interest rates shifts. Major capital gains can be achieved with the use of conservative instruments such as utility common stocks in periods when interest rates are declining. In contrast, even the best in quality among utility shares decline, in some cases severely, in the face of higher interest rates.

Most investors in quality blue chips, and especially in utility shares, consider themselves long-term holders. But because of the major influence of interest-rate cycles, even blue chip stocks bought primarily for income also should be viewed as subject to sale to capture capital appreciation. So, even for those investors whose stated strategy is a long-term "buy and hold," the subject of selling should not be given ostrich treatment. Knowing how to sell is an imperative discipline sooner or later.

Capital Appreciation

As indicated earlier, the other legitimate reason for buying a stock is the projection that it will rise in price and thereby reward the holder with appreciation in capital value. Some purists argue that any basis for expecting rising value other than higher dividends amounts to the greater-fool theory. Others say that hoping to capture a swing in psychology or interest rates to increase the value of a stock amounts to speculation because the value is not driven purely by increased earnings and dividend streams from the company. Suffice to say that rises in price beyond what is driven by dividend streams *do* take place, so capturing those increases is a legitimate subject for investor study and effort.

Other Reasons

Some people buy stocks for other reasons. For example, loyalty induces many investors to buy shares of the company for which they work, or the shares of a major employer in the community in which they live. But "loyalty buys" can result in major investment losses because there is a tendency for loyalty to override common sense and, therefore, to prevent timely sales.

Other market players buy a stock because of a perceived affiliation with the members of management or because they like the products offered by the company. These purchase decisions usually are not driven or timed on a price/value basis; they are not driven by the profit motive.

Other stock purchases are made because of excitement about the concept. In many cases, either the purchaser is ignorant of investment values and just feels good about owning a company that is involved in the subject business (environmental protection, humane research on new drugs, and AIDS are forward-looking businesses) or he has purchased the stock to feel trendy. There are also many people who buy stocks for the thrill of participation in the game. They play the market because it is socially acceptable to do so. Or they believe the market can generate the thrills and emotional drama of gambling legally over a longer period of time before the money runs out.

Finally, whether their conditioning is external or self-imposed, some investors really should be called collectors. These are people who gradually accumulate a variety of stocks over a period of years. But being a collector of stocks is similar to being a pack rat: it is most unlikely that a confirmed practitioner of either art can be reformed. Western society emphasizes acquiring things, not disposing of them. This conditioning supports a buy-and-hold bias.

Financial writers, advisors, and brokers all contribute powerful external forces focused on buying. This emphasis is perhaps understandable, but it needs balance. Equal attention to selling — which nails down the profit — is required.

The balance of this book, then, is devoted to assisting investors who buy stocks for financial reasons. No remedy is offered to those who participate for less logical reasons. The book's goal is to provide guidelines about how to cash in profits when appropriate, and to limit or prevent losses. A major emphasis is placed on understanding and overcoming the inertia that causes holding rather than selling.

CHAPTER

2

Internal Rationalizations

KEYS TO INVESTMENT SUCCESS

- Overcoming Commission Phobia
- Overcoming Tax Phobia
- Overcoming Specialist Phobia (a.k.a. Stop-Order Phobia)
- Holding with a Death Grip
- Wishful Thinking

Commission Phobia

Most analysts hear the lament that investors balk at taking brokers' advice because their motives are driven by the prospect of earning more commissions. Frankly, most commission phobia is a smoke-screen that is as dangerous to potential investor profit as it is illogical.

First, look at the logic of commission phobia. Like taxes, commissions are not a surprise; therefore, paying them cannot logically be an objection at the time of sale. There is no way to sell stock without paying commissions except in five very limited exit environments:

- The company receives a tender offer so shares are sold for a net cash payment to the soliciting buyer, via its agent.
- The company conducts a share-buyback tender (a self-tender) in which some or all shares can be sold for a net cash price directly to the company.
- The company can purchase investor shares directly if the position is small (usually an odd lot). Sometimes firms solicit repurchases by mail.
- Company liquidation in which common holders receive a net cash payment.
- One individual can sell a stock certificate directly to another individual through a transfer agent by endorsing the back of the certificate.

There is one other way to avoid commissions: if the stock becomes worthless due to bankruptcy and common holders get nothing, some brokerage firms buy back the stock certificates for a nominal price. This creates a transaction for tax purposes. Absent such a transaction, investors need to amend their tax returns for the year in which the stock actually became defunct and worthless. This extreme case is a wonderful example of how an investor can be penny-wise and pound-foolish about paying commissions to cash in; it is much better to pay the exit fee and sell at a partial loss before the stock goes to zero.

Commissions are more visible in stocks, commodities and options than in most other products or services because the securities prices are publicly quoted in newspapers, on quotation machines and on television. Investors pay commissions to trade these vehicles as a way of rewarding the time or expertise of the people who actually do the trading for them. When other products are purchased, commissions are paid but they are built into the purchase price. In fact, in percentage terms, built-in commissions for goods such as cars, shoes or television sets usually are immensely higher than Wall Street stock commissions.

Investors who purchase prepackaged products from brokers, say a mutual fund, typically pay from 4.5 percent to 8 percent in commissions. Buy $10,000 in a "load" mutual fund and only $9,200 to $9,550 is working for the client; the rest is commission. Cancel a variable annuity contract and the exit fee is similar. These percentages are much higher than the typical 1 or 2 percent charged on stocks.

Investors most often display commission phobia when their investment has gone down, has done nothing or has gone up so little that its tiny price gain is more than wiped out by round-trip commissions. When their money is doubled or when XYZ Worldwide Conglomerate creates a sudden gain by proposing a takeover of the company, investors seldom, if ever, complain about commissions. That is why the phobia is a smokescreen; it masks investors' pain at admitting to a mistake that caused a loss.

One legitimate complaint about commissions, however, is the widespread gap between how much per share big institutional investors pay to play the same game. The retail/institutional commission gap is even more upsetting when individual investors lose money. Although the hurt is painful when the buying decision was their own, commission phobia is at a peak when the pain can be blamed on a bad purchase made on a broker's advice.

Effective Commission Strategies

A possible remedy for retail investors is commission discounting, with due respect to account executives and their employing firms who need to make a living.

Formula-Based Commissions

One strategy is to negotiate commissions on a formula basis with the account executive. On the buying side, a full commission is paid when the broker presents an idea the client buys. When the client makes his own selections without service or information provided by the broker, some discount is generally in order.

At selling time if the trade results in a gain, the client should pay the full standard commission without complaint. If there is a loss, a two-tiered discount arrangement can work: the deepest allowable discount should be provided if the broker suggested the purchase; if the buy was the customer's idea, a smaller discount (maybe half the deepest allowable) is granted as a consolation/courtesy and as a psychological inducement to cashing in and moving on. This strategy works best with a small or regional brokerage firm; larger firms tend to be less flexible.

If a customer and broker mutually agree to such a deal in advance, the commission problem usually can be eliminated. When clients continue to complain about commissions, however, it is then clearly a smokescreen to avoid making the decision to take a loss and move on.

Discount Firms

Besides failing to trade when it is expedient, or negotiating routine broker discounts, investors also can limit commissions by moving the account to a discount firm. But in doing this, access to research and a listening ear are given up. The one instance when a brokerage client should worry about avoiding commissions is when the broker solicits a sale for the purpose of freeing funds to make a another purchase. This is not churning per se, but it is an attempt to do two trades where one would do. And this sale generally is not suggested on fundamental or timing merits; it is only a means to enable another transaction.

Most often, however, investors should ignore commissions and sell when the time is right because the unwillingness to pay a commission in order to exit a losing situation is a self-defeating game. Unless the investor is dealing in a very small block of stock, the sale commission is likely to be a lot less than a point per share. If the stock is going nowhere or worse yet is going down, the commission saved by refusing to cash in is miniscule compared to the capital loss suffered by holding the stock.

Keep in mind that the capital losses resulting from holding too long include opportunity costs. Suppose a lazy stock is going nowhere — perhaps a utility with stagnant dividends. Resentfully, the investor refuses to sell because of the exit commission. The proposed replacement may have been a much better utility whose dividend is rising five to seven percent a year and whose stock price appreciates as a result. In this case, the refusal to pay the sale commission is very costly. Although these costs tend to be invisible compared to losses recorded on Schedule D, the effects of invisible and self-inflicted losses are, nevertheless, very real.

Tax Phobia

However investors view the economic or budgetary results of eliminating the favorable tax treatment of long-term capital gains, the Tax Reform Act of 1986 had at least one positive result: it removed an artificial excuse for not selling stocks.

Until the act legally erased the distinction between long- and short-term, many investors used the tax incentive to hold stocks for the long-term as a justification for not selling. Unless an extremely large gain was involved and/or unless the time remaining to the start of long-term status was very short (thus decreasing the likely risk of losing paper gains), these reasons for not selling were foolhardy. But over-sensitivity to tax treatment was nearly a religion for many market participants.

The converse of the hold-for-long-term-treatment philosophy on gains, of course, would have been a rule that investors should never hold a losing position beyond the short-term. As an arbitrary discipline, such an operating rule would have proven quite valuable as a capital preserver for many investors. However, this rubric seldom was observed by investors, tending to prove that selective (i.e., one-sided) attention to the long-term-gain rule was more a psychological rationalization for postponing the sale decision than a useful tax-minimizing strategy.

Unfortunately, the existence of federal and state taxation on securities gains remains a stumbling block for investors even now that the distinction between long- and short-term has been eliminated. Objectively, this reason for not selling may appear to be illogical, but experience suggests that tax phobia is still very real to many investors.

Granted no one likes to pay taxes; but paying taxes on capital gains and on such taxable investment income as dividends and interest is a reality for all investors. It is not a surprise. Nor is it a change of rules midgame. Therefore, it is illogical to balk at selling a stock at a gain just because the transaction triggers a tax liability. There are only three logical extensions of refusing to take a gain on a stock to avoid paying the income tax. The investor must have bought the stock in the hope:

1. of losing money (taxes are reduced 28 cents for only a dollar lost); or
2. that the stock's price would not change; or
3. that the stock would be held for the remainder of the buyer's life.

The first two alternatives are nonsensical and deserve no further comment. Despite tax reform, the third reason is a clever tax dodge because a legatee's basis is stepped up to the value on the date of the decedent's death. So an investor can "enjoy" the big loophole only by dying with capital gains unrealized.

The objection to paying income taxes due on realizing a gain is just another rationalization for not making a sale decision; it is especially appealing to the rationalizer because it is conveniently external to self. It can be blamed on "them," on the government or on the "system." Most other excuses for not selling also reveal logical or psychological investor weaknesses.

Tax Strategies

Income-oriented investors consciously choose among the alternatives: tax-free municipals and taxable interest or dividend generators are evaluated with advance attention paid to after-tax yields. (The tax-adjusted current yield and yield to maturity can be known in advance in the case of fixed-income instruments.)

In contrast, in the case of common stocks bought for capital appreciation, the tax outcome has to be imagined because it cannot be quantified. Therefore, an exact calculation of after-tax return is not made in advance. Because no calculation is made, the exercise of subtracting projected taxes is omitted. But the future obligation is, nonetheless, real.

Although taxes are not avoidable, they are postponable — and this is another pitfall for investors who complain about taxes. That postponability represents power. Is beating the system a source of private satisfaction that gets in the way of rational investment action? The reality is that the price/timing of a sale decision should be made regardless of tax timing. The best time to sell a stock is at its highest price point; the next best time is as close to that point as possible. The best of all tax situations is to incur huge tax obligations, which accrue only from earning an extremely large income. Maximum profit should be the goal of every transaction made by every trader and investor, so taxes should be paid cheerfully when due. Remember, also, that the amount of profit *desired* before or after tax on a given stock position is irrelevant. The amount of profit realistically allowed by the market is a better criterion for timing a sale. Similarly, the amount of profit an investor can keep always is defined as the after-tax amount, so learn to live with that reality. Ten points is ten points before taxes.

With the long-term tax distinction gone, at least half of the crutch for the non-seller has been removed. Investors must battle to remove the rest of this rationalization.

Specialist Phobia (a.k.a. Stop-Order Phobia)

One popular objection to the use of stop-sell orders is that they tip off the specialist to investor intention and so become self-defeating. In this section, that argument is examined and laid firmly to rest. There certainly is one case in which a stop-order given in advance to the specialist affects the market. That is when the stock position is so large it represents a significant percentage of an average day's trading volume. The solution is not to withhold the selling order; the solution is to avoid buying so large a position in the first place, or to sell off the holdings in a series of smaller pieces.

The Overinflated Ego

Try never to get into the I'm-too-big-to-get-out bind because, in effect, the investor who says this looks like he is not planning to sell the stock. If he buys so much he is later too wide for the exit door, he will become a collector — he is neither an investor nor a trader.

Stock collectors — people who buy but never sell — inevitably defeat themselves because they usually end up with a long list of stale losers and eventually run out of cash. They are effectively out of the game and stuck with the results of past buying decisions. In most cases, as time goes on, the original reasons for buying either do not drive the price to the desired selling point or the reasons fail to work out altogether. There are just two other possible exits for the trader or investor who accumulates a position that is too big to get out of: the takeover and tender offer (or the subcategory, the Dutch Auction repurchase offer). If an investor is big enough to accumulate a too-large block in advance of a takeover event, either he is dealing in inside information or he is already wealthy enough to forego reading books for investment advice.

Most dispassionate observers would suggest that the my-order-is-too-big syndrome is really is a disguised excuse. Most likely it is the product of an inflated ego and/or of an overactive imagination. It tends to reflect the mind-set of a trader who is never satisfied unless he grabs the last eighth of every move.

Or it can reflect a market player who is actually involved more with the excitement and action of watching the market and thinking about making decisions than with the all-important goal of taking profits in a systematic way without the burdensome intrusion of emotion, second-guessing or looking back.

The Persecution Complex

Another mind-set that masks excuse-making is also worth noting. There are investors and traders who have a persecution complex about the market (and often about much of life). For these people, the market is a very personal struggle of the hapless individual against the world. They expect to be less than satisfied every time they take action — and every time they do not take action.

They also view market mistakes not as failures of their own logic or as examples of bad luck, but rather as traps that were set with their name on them. The specialist system on the exchange floors fits their world view of conspiracy. These investors know there is a person on the exchange floor who is privileged to see many future orders for a stock. They ask in horror why they should play the game with such a trader and let him take care of their personal interests when the game is rigged.

Stop-Order Strategies

However, the mechanics of the exchange floor should be examined to understand just how likely it is, in reality, that an order will tip the buy-sell balance to work against the individual investor. The alternative tactic, of course, is to stay ever at the ready with quote machine and surprise the market with an order when the designated price is actually hit.

First, it is not advisable to enter any stop-limit sell order at a round number or at a full dollar. This positions an investor with the crowd; a stampede could develop at the round dollar level. A stop without a limit could result in a bad execution; a stop-limit could result in no execution at all if the investor is back in the line.

For example if the selling-price target on a stock is $50 per share, place the sell-stop an eighth or a quarter lower. Similar advice applies to any full dollar: instead of 18, use 17 ⅞, for example. If the target is a half-dollar level, put the order in at an eighth lower, for example at 7 ⅜ rather than 7 ½.

The guiding philosophy is this: if an investor believes that he is sharp enough to call the high on a stock's move accurately, he ought to be so concerned about getting out for sure that he would sacrifice a small amount per share as insurance against the slight chance that he is a bit off in his calculations or perhaps some others are equally smart. He should be out in this case, instead of still in and sorry for insisting on the eighth or quarter.

The only way an order above the market can affect the price is if it is so large it scares away buyers who are so tactically active that they happen to ask about it at just the right moment. In listed stocks, the specialist on the exchange floor holds the GTC (Good 'til Canceled) stop-sell (and all other) orders in his book and exercises them as market orders when they are touched off. The book is not disclosed to floor traders except in a very limited manner.

The best (highest) bid and the best (lowest) asked prices are disclosed, along with the sizes of the total orders at those levels, on electronic quotation machines. They also are quoted by the specialist to inquiring brokers standing at the trading post. But an order at a price away from the best market (even an eighth away) is never disclosed until the moment it becomes part of the best next offer (to sell) or bid (to buy).

And even in this case, remember that the market is a big game with many players. Except in very thinly traded issues, it is highly unlikely that an investor's order will be the only order on the book at any given time. When he is trying to sell 500 or 1,000 shares at 24 ⅜, there may be another 20,000 shares for sale at that price and probably a similar number to buy at 24 ¼.

Suppose that the investor buys 500 shares of XYZ at 19 and targets a sale price of 24 ½. Following the earlier suggestion to avoid 50-cent multiples, he places a sell-stop order for 500 shares at 24 ⅜. If the stock does trade up as high as 24 ⅜, his order immediately becomes a market order (without limit) to sell.

Today, the stock is finally approaching his price. It is up, say, a quarter at 24 even. The market tone remains firm. The specialist's book shows 1,000 shares bid for at 23 ⅞ and 600 offered for sale at 24 ⅛. That is the quote he provides to floor traders, and that is all. The specialist says, "23 ⅞ by 4 ⅛, 10 by 6." He does not mention that there is a bid for 7,500 down at 23 ½, or that 1,200 are waiting to be sold at 24 ¼ or that our investor has 500 for sale at 24 ⅜. None of these orders are relevant yet and so none are disclosed until they are the best orders. So our investor's order does not show until it is just an eighth or a quarter away from the last trade. Only when that time comes does his order start to show as the next limit sell order above the market.

Incidentally, he is in an advantageous position if he exercised the discipline of placing the order some time ago, perhaps when he bought the stock. Why? Stop-orders and stop-limit-orders are lined up on a first-come, first-served basis. So the longer our order has been in place, the earlier it stands in the line and the sooner it becomes a market order in the trading sequence. So if our trader's 500 shares for sale are part of a total of 3,000 or 4,000 on the book at his price, his order is filled sooner if it was among the first placed.

Having a GTC order in effect is better than putting in a day order at the same price every day until it is executed. Day orders die at the close, and the newly entered day order goes at the back of the line at its price. (Placing repeated orders also requires repeated discipline and frequent decisions.) The strong preference for stop-orders instead of stop-limit orders should be noted here. A stop-order says, "If the price reaches this level, I want to be considered a seller at market." A stop-limit order is less likely to be executed because it says, "When the stock hits this price, put me in right away as a seller, but sell me out only if you can do it at the same price. Do it right away or forget it."

So if the size of position is generally in keeping with the pattern of average daily trading (i.e., the investor is not trying to sell a whole day's worth), he will not be big enough to disturb the day's supply/demand balance. Then he should not worry that his order might stand as a roadblock for the stock and will turn back its advance a fraction short of his level.

The idea is to be objective enough to recognize that the marketplace is so much bigger than any one participant that it takes no special notice of any individual order. If an investor's ego lets her imagine that her personal 500 or 1,000 shares is going to turn the tide against the stock's advance, she is too heavily involved in her own success or failure. Place the order where it should go, and let the market operate.

"They" Paranoia

Everyone who has heard whispers about the ubiquitous "they" needs to remember that "they" do not exist in the market. This is not to say that attempted — occasionally actual — market manipulation by individuals and/or firms does not exist at all. But when "they" is cited, it is critical for investors to act against the dangerous assumption that "they" as a collective exist. Doing this is difficult because it requires leaning against the pressure of peers and brokers who give advice that is based on what "they" have allegedly decided will happen. Reject the "they" hypothesis and act in an opposite, contrarian direction.

The underlying assumptions behind the "they" myth are that everything that happens (especially if it is bad) can be explained readily; that the world, and specifically the world of Wall Street, is ruled by conspirators; that the bad guys cannot be reined in because they cannot be tracked down and brought to justice; and that the conspiracy is directed at relieving individual retail investors of their moderate wealth.

So "they" becomes a convenient scapegoat. Basically, anything that goes wrong in the plans or hopes of investors who believe in "they" is other-directed. This orientation absolves "they" believers of mistakes in judgment and poor execution of strategy, at least in their own minds.

"They" is a moving target whose identity cannot be known for sure, including at various times insiders (corporate officers), floor specialists on the exchange, corporate raiders or, lately, program traders. In late 1989, the Japanese began to take on qualities often ascribed in the past to "they" as their national investment preference jumped from one to another of the foreign-stock, open-end mutual funds, causing wide price swings without apparent logic or pattern.

What is heard most about "they" is that "they" plan to move the market in a way that will trap small investors. Typically when the market whipsaws traders, the notion makes the rounds that "they" were to blame and had laid a trap. As the story goes, "they" planned to move the market up quickly to suck investors in at the top, at which point "they" would unload the stocks in question on the unsuspecting for a neat profit. Trapped with the stocks, small investors would suffer the next price drop once "they" pulled the plug on the rally. Then investors would get discouraged and sell out at the next bottom, presumably on a drop "they" would cause by either spreading negative rumors or shorting key stocks to drive quotes lower.

At the lows, "they" would step in and take retail customers' stock away for a bargain price, once again proving that "they" are in control and that investors are their fools.

In this scenario, every miscalculation is blamed on an outside force, not on personal bad luck or — more to the point — personal lack of expertise, discipline or sophistication. It also postulates that there is an organized conspiracy to move the market. But keep in mind that the alleged conspirators would need billions of dollars to pull it off; "they" would need to trust each other totally so that none of them would cheat and step in or out at a better price than the others (or turn state's evidence later).

Strategies for Overcoming this Paranoia

The theory of "they," which neatly explains away all problems on the basis of an invincible and overwhelming outside force, has been discredited by all intelligent investors. Of course, if any rational investor really believes the game is rigged, he may question the first loss, but he would quit forever after the second. Firmly convinced that "they" have all the cards, the logical investor would see that folding his hand permanently is the only sensible course for the innocent.

Remember that, the next time someone tries to blame a reverse or a surprise on "them." And note who that someone is, to avoid giving them credence again. This someone is naive if they believe it themselves, and dishonest if they are using "them" as a scapegoat for responsibility for the loss. Even if the rationalizer played the same stock and took the same beating, what he is doing is covering his own failing by blaming it on an invisible sinister force. Fault is being offloaded.

If any doubt remains, consider these questions. If "they" truly exist and are wealthy and powerful enough to pull off market coups:

- Why would they bother? They already have more wealth and power than they need; they should buy a country!
- Why would they take the risk of being caught at it? (They have more to lose than to gain.)
- Why would they choose to prey on small investors? (Who have relatively little wealth to pillage.)
- Why is it never rumored *before* the fact that they are about to pull off a coup? (After all, major takeovers are leaked in advance on occasion.)
- When they are blamed (after the fact, conveniently, after having disappeared), why are those who blame them not able to identify the villains specifically?

If a story is spread that "they" plan to run a certain stock up (or down) before it happens, run in the opposite direction. Whoever is spreading the story has no better reason to get an investor to buy the stock — or he would give the reason. "They" theorizers are trying to unload the stock on the unwary. Sell, or sell short, rather than buy. There are three simple "they" rules to remember:

1. Do not believe people who adduce "they" as an explanation.
2. Do not accept "they" as a reason why something will happen or did happen.
3. Do not rationalize that "they" were the reason for *your* failed trade or investment, or even just bad timing.

Holding with a Death Grip

Investors tend to stretch their investment time horizons for two reasons. The first is the fact that promised or expected hot developments seldom actually take place as quickly as expected. But the second, and more indisious problem is that human beings hesitate to come to closure, to wrap things up. Selling a stock has a finality akin to undergoing a death. If the stock position is kept open, the hope for a better result is still alive. However, this hope can border on rationalization.

An example of this rationalization is a cynical Wall Street cliche that bad traders become investors. Unfortunately for legions of unsuccessful traders, this saying does not mean they have a religious experience, repent of their wasteful trading ways and turn their attention to a value-oriented investing approach. It usually means that the owners of unsuccessful stock positions — originally intended as short-term situations — hold on for a long time out of stubbornness. So these traders become investors through the back door; more accurately, they are self-trapped collectors of bad stocks.

It is important to recognize the trader-turned-investor syndrome as a classic symptom of switching objectives; this switch usually results from rationalization and fuzzy thinking. In fact, most traders do not even make a conscious decision to turn investor based on thoughtful consideration. The shift gradually creeps in through inertia.

An extreme version of the inertia and psychological baggage that can accompany losses is the investor who says, "I expect my stock could go down about 15 percent within the next month or two, but I plan to hold anyway." The comeback, of course, is to question whether, having that expectation and not yet owning the stock, the investor would buy the stock today — before the expected 15 percent capital reduction takes place. Worse yet, why not double up now for the 15 percent loss?

In other cases, the investor may not perceive any imminent specific threat to stock price or to income stream; the investment may have gone bad last month and is currently in a price-dormant phase. Or it may be a recent purchase made for a specific reason — a scenario which has not matured as expected. Doggedly refusing to accept the reality of the situation, the owner holds on; capital remains dormant, depreciates or — at best — is less successfully employed than other available opportunities allow.

This critique of the trader-turned-investor syndrome is not meant to damn the conservative, longer-term, value-oriented approach to investing, nor is it an unabashed endorsement of trading the short-term. But it does recognize that money has a time value and that investors mislead themselves dangerously if they allow a mistake or a badly timed purchase to lock up their portfolio contents until some hoped-for but nonspecific future return of better fortune bails them out.

Think about this aspect of time value and investment logic: the stubborn holder-on not only says he is willing to stand for perhaps a fifteen percent temporary capital reduction; he also says that a return just to current market value at some unknown future date is an acceptable outcome. Holding on for an imaginary non-loss is about as prudent as burying cash in the backyard. There is no return while one is risking the loss of principal.

That is not to say there is not a time to hold. Stocks should be held when market and company prospects are favorable, and when the stock would be bought today if not already owned. When the investment strategy is not working out it is usually a forceful signal to sell out because either the reasoning behind the purchase was faulty or the fundamentals of the situation have deteriorated since the stock was bought.

So if an investor would not buy the stock today, it should be sold because others who would potentially buy it are going to be in short supply if the investor is correct. This is a subtle trap for investors who like to hold. Instead of holding when something goes wrong, act like a successful business manager. Assess the situation without delay and take the warranted action. If the stock is not sold immediately, set a specific price limit, an upside goal and a time window. Then, do not deviate. Although this addresses dramatic and sudden investment problem situations, it is only part of the remedy. In addition, also review holdings periodically to catch situations that have gone dormant. For sluggish stocks a disciplined, routinized approach is needed. Keep a notebook page on which to record stock prices at regular intervals and, for comparison, the major market average of choice. Do this no less than monthly. When stocks drift, threatening to lull the inattentive investor to sleep, subject them to the tests suggested above for emergencies. This practice eliminates the cop-out, "Yeah, but I'm really a long-term investor."

Wishful Thinking

Tom Czech, in recent years the research director at Milwaukee-based Blunt Ellis & Loewi, says, "It's different this time" are the most expensive words in the investment business. They are a rationalization trap of the highest magnitude.

Recall that in the Old Testament the Lord promised Noah that never again would He cause it to rain for forty days and forty nights straight. It does not take an ecologist or an agricultural expert to presume that even half of forty days' duration would do some pretty devastating damage. Those threatened with waterlog do not focus blindly on the difference between thirty-nine and forty days; a potential drownee tries to gauge roughly how much rain would be enough to do him in.

In the same way, by trying to measure the sameness or differentness of investment scenarios with exacting precision, investors can miss the point. What is important in comparing a current situation with the past is to recognize common patterns rather than waiting to act until an exact, 100 percent repetition of the precedent can be detected. In market comparisons, close enough usually is good enough.

There are two very different aspects of the "this-time-it-will-be-different" problem in investor thinking. One is an outgrowth of the "it can't really happen to me" attitude that investors adopt when considering life's least pleasant realities. The second aspect is a logical jump from observation of very real differences to a conclusion that the implied outcome must or will be different.

Expecting "it" to be different involves a blend of reality and unreality that can be deceptive to the investor; "it" includes both the facts of a situation (fundamental news or trends) and the market's reaction to the facts. While history does tend to repeat, perfect replications hardly ever occur.

So even if it is literally true that "it" will be different this time, investors should not be lulled into complacency by differences. To focus on the divergences while failing to note the similarities is to miss the big picture. By not seeing important similarities to past events, investors can make an erroneous decision to hold based on misfiltered information.

Confronting Reality

Although business situations are seldom if ever identical, success in business can be analyzed; patterns of managerial behavior are recorded, categorized, and taught in graduate business school classes. In the same way, there are common contributors to failure which are discernible in deteriorating investment situations. Following is a list of some of the danger signs:

- Heavy promotion of the stock by management or agents
- Projections of unusually strong/lengthy growth
- Use of round numbers for predictions (e.g., 50 percent growth, or a "$10-billion market")

- Questioning the motives or expertise of reasonable doubters
- Strong claims to being the best, unique or exclusive in a business
- Defining the market narrowly so that, by definition, one is the leader
- Ready excuses faulting outside forces when performance falls short
- Lateness in reporting earnings (against either prior practice or SEC filing deadlines)
- Change in outside auditors
- Change in lead banker without improvement in interest cost and/or size of credit facilities
- Substantial insider selling of the stock
- Resignation of key officers or of directors
- Sales or margins trends diverging negatively from competitor trends
- Inconsistent management statements
- Identical (seemingly rehearsed) management statements
- Stonewalling when trouble is obviously present.

Faced with some combination of perhaps three or four of the above, an investor reasonably and prudently can conclude that something is wrong and should get out of the stock. To insist that a particular combination of adverse events as seen in another situation can be fully repeated before concluding the stock is in trouble is naive, and probably costly.

As already indicated, things do not get better by themselves. When a company's affairs appear to be deteriorating, even if certain negative events have not been reported, investors are well advised to assume the worst by projecting that the situation is likely to continue worsening.

The point is, investors should be looking diligently for disturbing similarities to other problem situations rather than watching for comforting differences. The objective is to detect trouble as early as possible, thereby preventing or limiting loss of investor capital. There is an analyst's cliché that the first earnings disappointment will not be the last. Similarly, be suspicious at the first signs of any type of trouble. Unless a neutral or skeptical observer can be convinced that all is well, exit before things have a chance to become worse. Ask dispassionately whether, in light of today's facts, it is a good idea to buy now.

As indicated earlier in this chapter, there is a real but subtle difference between the "this-time-it's-different" rationalization and "this can't be happening to me." If what is going wrong is like something that went wrong once before, there is probably a reason. Putting it bluntly, the same mistake has been made again. Wishing something would not have happened again, however, is just across the reality-denial border from "this is not happening." This indicates a need to deny that anything is wrong, a blocking of the pain caused by a mistake. And, of course, when a mistake is public knowledge (the broker knows, and at year's end the tax accountant will know, too) the distaste is all the more deep and embarrassing.

What usually happens in these situations is that the investor focuses in the wrong direction; he turns subjective and inward. But the reality is that whatever is happening (collapsing earnings, a dividend cut, executive stock sales or resignations) is happening to the company — not the investor — in the objective plane, entirely unconnected causally to this particular investor's current ownership of the stock. It is happening, period.

The personal internalization that says "it is happening to me" and eventually "this can't be happening to me" is a rationalization. Sometimes an investor grasps at the discernible differences from a disastrous past investment experience and uses them to tell himself shakily that it will be alright, it is not at all the way it looks.

Instead of rationalizing, sell the stock at the point in time when trouble strikes the company and reassess the situation from a cooler distance. Remember that things do not right themselves. And realize that some serious buying power from other investors will be required to get the stock back up to higher levels.

A smart investor asks this key question: if I did not own the stock, with today's knowledge would I be a buyer now? When trouble first appears, prepare for the worst. This includes developing a mental scenario of what other shoes might drop, how long it all will take to play out the situation and how the market will react to the problem. The most important aspect of performing this mental exercise is to examine prior situations in search of their similarities rather than differences. Then from a big-picture standpoint, remember that history does repeat.

SECTION

II

Developing the Proper Mind-Set for Profitable Sales

CHAPTER

3

Acknowledging Mistakes

KEY TO INVESTMENT SUCCESS

- Record Keeping
  - Investor Mistakes Checklist
  - Stock Reassessment Checklist
  - Sale Checklist
  - Buy/Review/Sell Evaluation
  - Master Tally Sheet

How an investor handles mistakes is more important than how many mistakes she makes, or even how extreme they turn out to be. There are three guidelines to remember when contemplating inevitable investing mistakes:

- Expect to make mistakes and learn to live with them.
- Mistakes can have a greater or lesser net cost in the long run, depending on what an investor does or fails to do with them.
- Make the most of mistakes by turning them into learning experiences; keep detailed, real-time records of every transaction from start to finish.

It is axiomatic that all investors have to learn to forgive themselves for the mistakes they inevitably make. That is because the object of the game is to be right more often than wrong, and to be right big and wrong small. The corollary to this axiom is to keep mistakes under control and in perspective. Put ego aside by remembering that the competition is not the market, the broker or the guy next door — it is the investor's own record.

If an investor can learn to perform better over time, his performance record improves almost automatically precisely because he is learning not to make the same mistakes repeatedly. He also learns to control and channel his intensity, to concentrate on the stock at hand. Another principle that must be learned in order to profit consistently is not to let market results have an enduring effect; if one can avoid the emotional scars of mistakes, subsequent moves can be made rationally and more skillfully.

The beginning of mistake wisdom is to acknowledge and take ownership of investment errors, and then let go of them. As in all of life, we must forgive ourselves or be unable to live with ourselves. In investing, of course, the object over time is to make fewer mistakes in proportion to total transactions and, if possible, to make mistakes less costly and successes more profitable.

People who are accustomed to winning consistently because of their brilliance and hard work are likely to be frustrated in a very fundamental way by the stock market; intelligence and diligence are helpful but not sufficient for the achievement of market profits. Examples are "A" students, successful lawyers and corporate executives. In the same way, people who succeed by precision or by rules are likely to be disappointed that investing cannot be totally controlled or predicted. Examples are engineers and civil servants.

On the other hand, people who have routinely felt the ups and downs of life are, by conditioning, psychologically better prepared for the realities of a mix of winning and losing on Wall Street. Sales people, for example, know the frustration of bad weeks and do not expect perfection; their understanding that winning means just a higher-than-average success rate — not 100 percent perfection — gears them more effectively on an emotional level for the stock market.

Once the psychological art of living with mistakes is mastered, those mistakes must be turned into sources of opportunity if an investor is to profit from them. In fact, mistakes *must* be used as building blocks for the next transaction. Think of each buy and sell transaction, both gain and loss, as the tuition required to make progress in the learning process. An investor always pays tuition; the important question is whether he pays attention in class and gets his money's worth by learning something.

Investment success can be built on both right and wrong past moves; those behaviors that result in pain need most to be understood so they can be changed. One of the most costly sources of error is the tendency to repeat mistakes. And the most costly and troublesome mistakes are those of which the investor is unaware.

Unfortunately, brokers and investment advisors are too often unwilling or unable to help investors become aware; they should be considered only technical experts in the market and not behavior-modification teachers. They may run money better, but they do not teach clients how to do it. So investors are on their own with the challenge of learning from past mistakes. And they need to overcome rationalization and avoidance behavior in order to focus on this learning opportunity.

Following are the two most important steps investors can take to analyze their own investing behavior:

- Face up to errors instead of ignoring or minimizing them.
- Categorize mistakes and work toward avoiding repetition.

Record Keeping

The most productive way to face errors is to record all investment behavior, analyzing what worked and what did not work. In this way, personal behavior patterns emerge that can be changed. It is helpful to create a notebook and record every transaction, even computerize the data, for future analysis. If honest, real-time records are not kept scrupulously — saving confirmation slips until tax time does not count — the tendency is to overlook the learning potential in mistakes. In effect, the investor who is unaware of his mistaken behavior is still flying blind.

Note the suggestion that records be kept *in real time*. This has four positive effects. First, memory tends to fail when it must process mistakes, so recorded facts are a necessary component for accuracy. Second, real-time records eliminate cumbersome back-checking, a big task which can be an extremely effective barrier to keeping the analysis up to date. Third, real-time records preclude fudging or minimizing errors, which tends to occur when an investor wants to look back through rose-colored glasses. And finally, if an investor actually writes answers to specific questions he asks both himself and a broker about tactical mistakes, it is easier to identify mistakes before he makes another ill-conceived move.

Following is a worksheet that is geared specifically to catching the most common investor mistakes. The questions are shortened to emphasize key words that identify the most common points in time when mistakes are made. It may be helpful to photocopy this worksheet into a notebook and add blank pages for lengthy answers.

Record the following information when each stock is bought:

Investor Mistakes Checklist

- ☐ Whose idea was the purchase (mine, broker, advisory letter, friend)?
- ☐ How long was the stock actively studied before taking action?
- ☐ Why is the stock expected to perform as projected?
- ☐ Is the general market in a major uptrend or downtrend?
- ☐ What was the prior-day closing level of the Dow-Jones Industrials?
- ☐ What was the execution price of the stock purchase (excluding commission)?
- ☐ What was the prior-day closing price of the stock?
- ☐ What was the month-earlier price of the stock (was it a case of chasing strength)?
- ☐ What was the week-earlier price of the stock (was it a case of chasing strength)?
- ☐ What is the price objective for the stock, including the implied P/E?
- ☐ What is the time of expected workout (date, and number of months from now)?
- ☐ What is the implied return in percent/year?
- ☐ What is the actual or mental stop-loss price point?

As indicated by the questions above, it is very important to establish not only a price objective for each stock holding, but also an associated timeframe. To record this data, mark a calendar or tickler file at the projected workout date. Do it when a stock is purchased.

This creates an effective reminder to look at that time at every position and reassess it.

At the tickler or projected-workout date, record in real time the following information:

Stock Reassesment Checklist

- ☐ What is the closing level of the Dow-Jones Industrials?
- ☐ What is its percentage move since the buy date?
- ☐ What is the stock's closing price?
- ☐ What is the percentage move since the buy date (compared to DJIA)?
- ☐ Is the overall market still in a bull, bear phase?
- ☐ Is the stock in a major uptrend?
- ☐ Has the stock not moved to the established price goal? Why?
- ☐ Why continue holding the stock? Cite specific reasons, not wishes.
- ☐ What is the new price target (and implied P/E)?
- ☐ What is the new workout date (put in tickler file again)?

When the stock is sold, record the following in real time:

Sale Checklist

- ☐ What is the DJIA at sale date (compute percent moves from buy and review dates)?
- ☐ What was the sale price (compute percent moves from buy and review dates)
- ☐ Did the purchase rationale come true?
- ☐ If not, when did failure become apparent?
- ☐ How long was the time between failure and sale date?
- ☐ Was the stock held for a longer/shorter time than planned?
- ☐ What was the high price of the stock while it was held (compute the percent down from that point to the price at which it was sold)?

- ☐ What was the low price of the stock while it was held (compute the percent down from the price at which it was bought to that low)?
- ☐ Did the stock ever sell above the price target while it was held?
- ☐ If yes, why was it not sold then?
- ☐ Was an above-market GTC sale order ever placed?
- ☐ Was a stop-loss order ever placed and then removed or lowered?
- ☐ Was the sale execution planned or impulsive?
- ☐ Was the stock sold on strength, weakness, boredom, company news, or general market action?
- ☐ Whose idea was the sale?

The investor who truthfully answers all the questions in the checklists above can expect to be uncomfortable. Good! The questions that cause the most discomfort usually identify where the most common mistakes are made or where performance is less than optimal. In order to learn from prior mistakes, note these portions of the investment sequence and review them the next time a purchase is made. In fact, highlight the problem questions on the checklists and refer to them often before, during and after subsequent positions are in place.

Then tally the most common mistakes on a master sheet (see page 62) and check the box for each mistake. For example, a tendency to hold longer than planned, or a pattern of selling from boredom. A cluster around the most resistant problem areas will emerge. That is where to concentrate improvement efforts in order to become more profitable in the market.

While analyzing mistakes, it is important to disregard the delusion that any investor can ever "bat a thousand;" but do believe that improvement in performance is possible, indeed likely, if systematic effort is applied to noting and correcting mistakes.

BUY/REVIEW/SELL EVALUATION SHEET

Complete this section at the time of purchase:

Stock ____________________

Buy date ____________________

Study period ____________________

Whose idea? ____________________

Reason bought? ____________________

Major market trend? ______ DJIA prior-day close? ______

Stock prices:

Buy price ____________________

Prior close ____________________

Week ago ____________________

Month ago ____________________

Was this sale a case of chasing recent strength? ______

Price objective:

$ ____________________

P/E ____________________

By date ____________________

Elapsed months ____________________

Implied return per annum as a %? ______

Stop-loss point? ______ Mental/actual? ______

Complete this section at the tickler/review date:

DJIA close? ______ Change since buy date (%)? ______

Stock close? ______ Change since buy date (%)? ______

Satisfied with relative performance? ______

Major trend:

Market? ______ Stock? ______

Was the price goal reached? ______

If yes, why held? ______

If no, what went wrong? ______

BUY/REVIEW/SELL EVALUATION SHEET (continued)

Revised target:
$? ____________________
P/E? ____________________
By date? ____________________
Why holding? ____________________

Complete this section at the time of sale:

Date? ____________________
Was hold period longer/shorter than planned? ____________________
DJIA close ____________________
Change from buy date (%)? ____________________
Review date (%)? ____________________
Sale price ____________________
Change from buy date (%)? ____________________
Review date (%)? ____________________
Satisfied with relative performance? ____________________
Did buy reason happen? ____________________
If no, when apparent? ____________________
Time between visible failure and sale? ____________________
High price while held ($)? ____________________
Giveback to sale price (%)? ____________________
Low price after buy ($)? ____________________
Percent overpaid (%)? ____________________
Reached target while owned? ____________________
Why not sold if not? ____________________
Used GTC target order? ____________ Used stop? ____________
Stop pulled/lowered? ____________________
Sale planned/impulsive? ____________________
Sale trigger/circumstances? ____________________
Whose idea? ____________________

Master Tally Sheet

At Buy Date:															
Stocks Scored to Date	1	2	3	4	5	6	7	8	9	10	11	12	13	14	15
Whose idea	☐	☐	☐	☐	☐	☐	☐	☐	☐	☐	☐	☐	☐	☐	☐
Good reason	☐	☐	☐	☐	☐	☐	☐	☐	☐	☐	☐	☐	☐	☐	☐
Study period	☐	☐	☐	☐	☐	☐	☐	☐	☐	☐	☐	☐	☐	☐	☐
Market trend	☐	☐	☐	☐	☐	☐	☐	☐	☐	☐	☐	☐	☐	☐	☐
Chased strength	☐	☐	☐	☐	☐	☐	☐	☐	☐	☐	☐	☐	☐	☐	☐
P/E target	☐	☐	☐	☐	☐	☐	☐	☐	☐	☐	☐	☐	☐	☐	☐
At Tickler Date:															
Major trend	☐	☐	☐	☐	☐	☐	☐	☐	☐	☐	☐	☐	☐	☐	☐
Exit-at-goal failure	☐	☐	☐	☐	☐	☐	☐	☐	☐	☐	☐	☐	☐	☐	☐
Stock trend	☐	☐	☐	☐	☐	☐	☐	☐	☐	☐	☐	☐	☐	☐	☐
Conviction re-holding	☐	☐	☐	☐	☐	☐	☐	☐	☐	☐	☐	☐	☐	☐	☐
At Sale Date:															
Held too long/short?	☐	☐	☐	☐	☐	☐	☐	☐	☐	☐	☐	☐	☐	☐	☐
Relative performance	☐	☐	☐	☐	☐	☐	☐	☐	☐	☐	☐	☐	☐	☐	☐
Scenario right?	☐	☐	☐	☐	☐	☐	☐	☐	☐	☐	☐	☐	☐	☐	☐
Decisive at failure?	☐	☐	☐	☐	☐	☐	☐	☐	☐	☐	☐	☐	☐	☐	☐
Percent given back	☐	☐	☐	☐	☐	☐	☐	☐	☐	☐	☐	☐	☐	☐	☐
Percent overpaid	☐	☐	☐	☐	☐	☐	☐	☐	☐	☐	☐	☐	☐	☐	☐
Exit-at-goal failure	☐	☐	☐	☐	☐	☐	☐	☐	☐	☐	☐	☐	☐	☐	☐
GTC order at target?	☐	☐	☐	☐	☐	☐	☐	☐	☐	☐	☐	☐	☐	☐	☐
Stop tactics	☐	☐	☐	☐	☐	☐	☐	☐	☐	☐	☐	☐	☐	☐	☐
Sale planning	☐	☐	☐	☐	☐	☐	☐	☐	☐	☐	☐	☐	☐	☐	☐
Circumstances/trigger	☐	☐	☐	☐	☐	☐	☐	☐	☐	☐	☐	☐	☐	☐	☐
Whose idea?	☐	☐	☐	☐	☐	☐	☐	☐	☐	☐	☐	☐	☐	☐	☐

C H A P T E R

4

Keep a Clear Head

KEYS TO INVESTMENT SUCCESS

- A Case Study — Recognizing Crowd Psychology
- Taking Time Out

Winning on Wall Street is a difficult game. Following the secondary crash of October 1989, a survey taken for *The Wall Street Journal* indicated that the majority of the investing public sees the deck stacked against them: insider trading is perceived as an institutional advantage over individual investors; market manipulation is widely-suspected as a result of the scandals and prosecutions of recent years; and program trading by huge investing institutions (and brokerage firms for their own accounts) is viewed as an investment barrier for the little guy.

Whether an investor is right or wrong about a stock or about market motivation, multi-billion-dollar investors do move the market the way they think it will go simply by acting. So investing is a difficult game for individuals, even when they play on a relatively even playing field and even if information is fully and equally available to all market participants.

The reality is that not every investor functions in the stock market with equal efficiency or earns equal returns. The disparity in market performance generally boils down to how well each investor — individual or institutional — can invest against his emotions. So keeping a clear head means the difference between profits and losses. It means staying clear-headed when everyone else is not, especially during market swings from panicky lows and price despair to manic euphoria.

Statistically, it is known that most market participants in one cycle stay around for the re-enactment of the drama the next time around. Almost incredibly, a majority fall prey to the same mistakes in the subsequent cycle. So it pays to remain emotionally clear-headed.

It is the nature of all speculative markets that they move from one extreme to the other. For example, in a recession, the U.S. economy might show a 3 percent to 5 percent drop in real GNP. Corporate earnings may slide 25 percent. But the major stock averages might fall 30 percent to 40 percent in a year, as if economic life were about to disintegrate.

In this scenario, some individual stocks will fall 80 to 90 percent — and that includes only the survivors; some other companies inevitably go out of business and their stocks become expensive wallpaper.

Crowd Psychology

What takes hold of investors in this kind of extreme market movement is crowd psychology. What should govern is an awareness of the pattern of each individual investor's most recent market experiences, and the reason is simple. The degree of recent success or failure has a powerful influence on the success of subsequent market plays. Success enables more success, to a point. Failure takes its toll in future failures generated by mistaken thinking.

A Case Study

To illustrate, following is a hypothetical stock chart on which are overlaid the buying, holding and selling decisions — and emotional reactions — of a hypothetical investor who should be considered realistic. In fact, this investor is so real in composite, as to be the force that moves the stock on the chart the way it is illustrated. (See exhibit 4-1.)

The actions and reactions demonstrated, multiplied by thousands of active buyers and sellers in millions of shares annually, create the type of price gyrations seen below. The chart follows XYZ Corporation and the time scale is assumed to cover several years from the start of one bull market to the bottom of the following bear market. The price scale is in the typical range for many actively-traded common stocks. Given the volatility of individual issues in recent years, the relative rise of 200 percent followed by nearly a 70 percent collapse is not at all misrepresentative of reality.

Specific price points on the chart are marked with the letters "A" to "Z," capsulizing the hypothetical composite investor's thoughts,

Exhibit 4-1: XYZ Corporation (The Emotional Roller-Coaster)

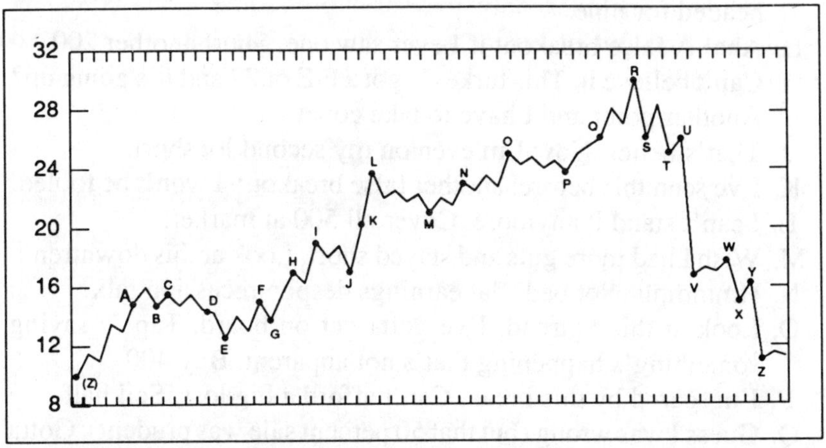

feelings and actions in the comments that follow. Trace the price movement from one letter to the next, moving from the beginning of the price action to letter "A" for example, and then read the comment corresponding to that letter.

Then observe price movement point B and look at the relevant comment. In that way, the thoughts and feelings generated by a typical stock action can be followed in a telescoped view.

A. Looks like a winner; up 50 percent from the panic lows. Good relative performance. Buy 500 shares at market.
B. Just a little consolidation. The earnings-per-share forecasts are good. Not worried; plan to hold.
C. Alright! Back to original cost. Now it's really ready to go.
D. Glad I sold here. It both broke down and triggered the stop. That's two strong signals and I didn't miss them.
E. Knew I was right about that dog. Glad I'm out.
F. I've seen this price before. The stock isn't worth it. Short 300.

G. See, I knew it! Now I've got this one figured out. This baby is headed for nine.
H. Aha! A false breakout if I ever saw one. Short another 200.
I. Can't believe it. This turkey's got a P/E of 22 and it's going up? Another point and I have to take cover.
J. That's better. Now I'm even on my second lot short.
K. I've seen this before: another false breakout. I won't be fooled.
L. I can't stand it anymore. Cover all 500 at market!
M. Wish I had more guts and stayed short. Look at this downtrend.
N. Hmmmph. Not bad: flat earnings despite recession talk.
O. Look at this uptrend. I've gotta get on board. Tape's saying something's happening that's not apparent. Buy 400.
P. I'm scared by this break. Can't afford a big loss. Sell half.
Q. Guess I was wrong (but that 50 percent sale was prudent). Gotta buy back that 200 shares since the market is firmer again.
R. Terrific! $30 and going north. I'm not greedy: 32 and I'll be gone. That's a 20 percent profit.
S. Just a correction. Darn market's off 120 points. But there's gotta be a fifth up-wave. I'll take 30 when it gets back there.
T. Well, it makes no sense to see the price here. Look how high the yield is. That'll support the price. It just can't go lower.
U. That's better. The market's stabilized too. We've seen the worst.
V. Dividend cut 60 percent? Who could have seen that coming? Can't sell now. Too big a loss.
W. Guess the worst is over. I'd average down if I had the cash. No, on second thought this one's hurt me enough. Can't trust it.
X. Margin call? Sell half. I love this stock at these prices but just can't put more cash into the market.
Y. Glad I didn't sell it all. Should have met the margin call and held it for the rally.
Z. Here we go: down again. I can't stand it anymore. Get me out; sell at market.

This hypothetical chart reflects a very confused investor, it is true. And the sequence may seem too long to represent any single investor/ stock relationship that had gone so badly. But many an individual investor tends to make several, if not all, of these flip-flop mistakes before quitting, and for three reasons:

- He has made a profit on the stock before, which generates an affinity for playing it again.
- He feels he understands the company or the industry, and so believes he understands the stock as well.
- He wants to get even, or reach breakeven before letting go here to play another stock.

All of these mind-sets are representative of unclear thinking. Not only do many investors dig in their heels and insist on coming out of the stock "relationship" whole; the bad feedback creates more confusion, which makes them dig in their heels even deeper.

The comments associated with the chart include five highly significant reactions to price behavior that indicate typical investor mistakes when emotions take over:

- Swings back and forth between fundamental and technical explanations and rationales,
- The tendency to follow and mentally project continuation of the recent trend,
- The tendency toward extremes of emotional reaction,
- The belief that the market is out to trap the individual investor,
- Prior bad experiences with the stock create damaging and confusing effects on the investor.

Taking Time Out

One useful way to short-circuit the negative thinking spiral listed above is to quit playing a stock after one or two losses. Whether or not there is unfavorable chemistry between the stock and the investor, playing again only deepens the destructive pattern and imposes more risk of additional mistakes. In the same way, if there is a pattern of consecutive losses or whipsaws across several stocks, quit all of them for a period of time.

This does not mean selling everything (long-term positions that are working well and would be bought again today need not be disturbed). Just stop trading and clear the mind. Draw up lists of the stocks that are most solid and those that are shaky, and describe why. Set price targets. Write down firm resolves not to sell on weakness or buy on strength. This pause in the play allows an investor to control his actions before a return to the market; his tendency to follow the crowd will be diminished.

This pause, however, is best accomplished when some selling has taken place and a cash cushion exists. If an investor stops while fully committed, there is an urgency about getting back to the action because there are still positions causing active worry. A key question to ask is: if action absolutely could not be taken for a month, which stocks would be most comfortable to own?

Also note that it is a mistake to take a head-clearing pause after every loss. But when there is a run of mistakes, say three or more, seriously consider calling a halt. Those errors count whether in the same stock or across several. Then ask a broker to take a dispassionate look at current positions and make independent suggestions with which to compare. Ask him to mail a copy of his suggestions on a specified date. If the broker has difficulty helping in this way, the investor has received a useful warning about the broker's usefulness.

The clearest heads do prevail in the market. A losing streak that the investor does nothing to correct can become self-sustaining as personal confusion gains the upper hand over reason. So call a halt before the downslide sets a precedent for future trading failures.

CHAPTER

5

Transform Denial Into Action

KEYS TO INVESTMENT SUCCESS

- Learning from the Manville Corporation Case
- Denial Prevention

The process of deciding to sell a stock is a difficult one at best unless an investor has developed a methodology and adheres to it mechanically in order to avoid inevitable internal mental battles. When a loss is involved, the sell decision is even more difficult because the issue of pain-avoidance is now present. It is human nature to seek self-preservation, and pain is a phenomenon that indicates a danger to well-being. Some investors are obsessed with safety, but most are reasonably balanced in their tolerance of the risk involved in earning a profit. But every investor has some threshold at which pain is avoided, sometimes at ridiculous cost.

One of the most convenient ways to avoid the pain of loss — or even of profit squandered — is denial. Dealing with an investment or trading loss involves not only financial pain, but also ego pain. A majority of shareholders at some point attempt to avoid both pains by failing to deal with the reality of their losses. They prefer not to think about it, or they minimize it. When specific stock positions go bad, the pain-avoider becomes a longer-term holder who is more accurately a collector of stocks. He has no real investment motive or astuteness of value judgment and is, in fact, simply denying the pain of potential loss.

Unfortunately, most investment brokers are of virtually no help to their clients in dealing with losses — they are unwilling or unable to break down client denial or avoidance behavior. Part of the broker's inability to help stems from the bias of his training; he is oriented toward persuading clients to buy, not sell, securities. But the broker problem goes much further.

The broker, too, as a human being is a pain-avoider. The broker needs to remain on cordial and constructive terms with clients. A successful sales person must listen to the customer and act on feedback. So, naturally, when the customer indicates an unwillingness to deal with losses, the broker hears that message loud and clear — and heeds it. An unspoken contract between the investor and the broker develops: "I will not complain about my problem if you will do me the favor of not reminding me of it."

There are several rationalizations that investors use to deny losses, or the importance of their losses. One relies on the rubric of the U.S. tax code. Investors are well aware that, for tax purposes, no loss is recognized as having occurred until a closing transaction actually takes place (and the 31-day "wash-sale rule" is not violated). Using this tax reality as a psychological crutch, many investors actually talk themselves into believing that they do not have a loss until they actually take one. On objective examination, of course, such reasoning is absurd. It is possible the price might recover and today's paper loss might be reduced or recovered — or might even become a paper (or real) profit in the future.

But the truth is that if the stock is quoted below what was paid, there is a loss of capital because wealth is measured by the current value of assets less liabilities. Liquidate investments under duress, value an estate, or switch investments to obtain maximum current income from available assets and reality prevails. A stock is currently worth only what it can be sold for now — not what it was bought for, what the owner wishes it would be or what he thinks it should sell for. If price is below cost, a loss exists. Period.

If an investor is too smart or too logical to attempt self-deception with the "paper-loss-isn't-real" farce, he may rely instead on a less disprovable assertion: the stock will come back with enough patience. Hope springs eternal; and once in a great while, a loss does reverse and rise from the ashes. Then, the investor who has sold out at a loss and later sees the price recover says, "See, if only I'd been smarter or more patient and followed my instinct and had held on, I would not have had that loss."

So taking the loss on a final basis (the confirmations and the Schedule D entry are lasting souvenirs) sets up a second source of pain by being "wrong again:" watching the stock move higher without being on board for the recovery. This horror can be avoided by refusing to take the loss in the first place, says the denier.

What psychologists call denial is, in the investment arena, an umbrella description for a variety of rationalizations and self-deceptions. All are designed to allow the possessor of a losing investment to justify doing nothing about it.

There are several variations on the denial theme. One springs from the memory of the purchase price, or from the memory of the highest price ever reached, or the best achieved as a holder. That price level is a high-water mark that becomes a once-was, a could-be-again, a should-be, then a will-be and sometimes a gotta-be. It does not matter how many months or years ago the high-water mark was made. It does not matter that the company's fundamentals or general market psychology have been eroded seriously. It does not matter that a rise of several hundred percent from current prices may be necessary for full recovery. To avoid accepting and dealing with the loss, the denier waits (and waits, and waits...) for recovery, denying the long adverse odds.

The Manville Corporation Case

A specific example of how extreme and irrational the predisposition to denial can be is in order. In 1988 after more than six years under Chapter 11 protection, Manville Corporation announced that it would complete its reorganization soon and, in the process, issue a very large number of new common shares to settle the claims of creditors and asbestos-injury victims.

Official company documents filed with the SEC indicated that the exiting holders' equity would be diluted 94 to 97 percent. Following local media coverage of the good news that Chapter 11 status would end, Manville common (old) stock rose from $2.00 to $3.00 on extremely heavy trading volume.

The company even took the unusual step of issuing a statement, in response to market action, in which it repeated previous written warnings that its stock involved a high degree of risk.

Part of the reorganization was to be a reverse split on a one-for-eight basis. (Reverse splits are designed to cut the number of shares outstanding and to return a stock's price to a respectable level.) The long and very consistent history of declining value following reverse splits compounded the prospective negative effects of massive dilution from the bankruptcy settlement.

A local brokerage analyst issued a very strong, urgent recommendation to brokers that they contact all clients who owned Manville common shares to sell the old stock at market without delay. A dual trading market existed in Manville shares. The old stock retreated a few days later to $2.00 per share. But the post-split shares were trading at the very same time on a when-issued basis at $8.00 each.

There were technical, mechanical reasons internal to the market's rules — not relevant here — why such a spread in prices could exist. In fact it did exist. The simple fact was that an investor holding the old stock would see a certain loss of 50 percent in capital: 800 shares currently worth $1,600, for example, would in a few weeks become 100 shares worth $800. It was like being able to read a future *Wall Street Journal* and check the quotations in advance. A holder of the old stock had the opportunity to sell the existing shares, simultaneously replace the position with one-eighth as many when-issued new shares and pocket the difference in cash.

Neglecting to sell, therefore, indicated the knowing acceptance of a certain penalty to capital: not a tiny marginal loss but a whopping 50 percent loss! To the broker community's amazement, some clients could not be convinced to sell the stock even to avoid absolutely certain losses. Some said, "I've held the stock for a long time and see no reason to abandon hope now." Others did not want to create a wash sale even if it would preserve half the capital involved. One client wanted $2.50 per share and would not sell for less. One client repeatedly swore he "didn't care" about the loss.

Denial Prevention

The Manville Corporation example shows that it is important to understand that investors must set up their own ways of dealing with reality, even if that requires what seem like unnatural or artificial devices: stop-loss orders entered at purchase, rigorous periodic reviews of each position, even filling out a questionnaire to justify continued holding.

Another denial-prevention strategy is to sell one stock periodically — perhaps quarterly to avoid too much churning — whether it is needed or not, just like routine auto maintenance. Do it regularly and in the process mediocre stock holdings can be sloughed off much more easily. The practice in making sell decisions will make future ones easier.

Recall the virtual chaos and the near-paralysis on Wall Street after the crash of 1987. Many brokerage firms were far behind in calculating margin calls to clients; therefore, investors had an unusual opportunity to assess their positions and take action before they were forced to. One of the more insightful client thought processes went something like this:

1. I expect the world to go on.
2. I expect to remain an equities investor.
3. The decline has created some wonderful values right here at today's prices, so I do not want to quit now and return later.
4. I will face a margin call. I do not have the courage (or the cash) to put up extra money, so I will need to do some selling.
5. It is in my best interests to keep those stocks whose prospects seem best from current levels.
6. Therefore, to raise the needed cash the only logical move is to sell those positions that I would least likely buy again today.

A self-imposed thought process or exercise something like this, developed for an imaginary crisis such as a possible future crash, can be helpful by forcing the reluctant investor to focus quickly. It helps him recognize which stocks are not going to profit. Those are the ones to sell. After going through this exercise several times in a period of months or a year, losses generally can be dealt with more easily. The first time through, do it on paper. Then pick up the phone and issue the sell order to a broker. Eventually, it will improve investment results as tired dollars are repositioned into more promising situations.

CHAPTER

6

Require Realism to Support Hope

KEYS TO INVESTMENT SUCCESS

- Fundamental Psycho-Mechanical Realities
- Understanding the Aftermath of the Crash
- The Hold Decision

It is true that a positive attitude helps produce positive results and, conversely, that believing something to be impossible can be a self-fulfilling prophesy. However, while wishing may be a necessary component of success in endeavors over which the investor has some degree of control, in itself it is not sufficient. In the stock market, where an individual is too small to exert a meaningful influence over price for very long, wishing simply will not make it so.

Thousands of investors — optimistic by natural temperament and encouraged in their "buy bias" by brokers — spend more energy in hoping than in logical and cool-headed analysis. Their continual wishing is actually counterproductive: in baseless optimism, they deceive themselves and ignore reality by holding a stock that is not working out.

Fundamental and Psycho-Mechanical Realities

There are two reasons that hoping against hope fails: one reason is fundamental, the other reason is psycho-mechanical (as distinguished from a technical reason, or the conventional market contrast to fundamentals). See Exhibit 6-1.

Exhibit 6-1: Stock Price Driving Factors

Psychology	Fundamentals: *Good*	Fundamentals: *Bad*
Positive	Price Up	Price Perhaps Even
Negative	Price Likely Down	Price Down Sharply

If a company is not producing expected results, profit disappointment sets in. Fundamental results — an expected product announcement, a technology breakthrough, patent award, sales increase, earnings turnaround or dividend boost — must occur to generate profits. If this does not happen, the stock loses supporters and, eventually, the price takes a deep decline (particularly if positive expectations had been high and/or had persisted for a lengthy period).

When fundamentals fail, the implication is very clear: sell the stock, do not hold it. It can always be bought back later if the fundamentals do come through. If disillusionment becomes major, early signs of fundamental progress will be disbelieved, thus providing time to buy back not too far up from the lows. That's the good news.

The bad news, ironically, is that fundamentals might actually be going according to plan, which naturally encourages optimism. But even though fundamentals may be good, the market may not be willing to pay for the fundamentals. All too often, investors are lulled into misguided overconfidence because the company's story works out as anticipated. Therefore, they expect the stock to respond favorably, which sets up a trap.

An old market proverb says stocks fall of their own weight, but it takes buying pressure to boost them up. At first, it may seem obvious why technicians say that for a stock to remain strong it must rise on increasing volume, and that a price advance occurring on declining or low volume is suspect.

But there is a second and more profound implication about the difference between fundamental realities surrounding the company and the psycho-mechanical forces or factors that drive its stock price. Do not assume the two operate in the same direction.

Back to the distinction between technical (which describes a stock's price and volume action) and the term "psycho-mechanical." The latter encompasses the nonfundamental factors actually operating in the stock market in real time — the things that drive investors to place buy or sell orders for the stock. This difference must be explored to understand why a stock can go down while its fundamentals are positive.

A logical investor sells unless a positive decision can be justified to buy the stock. This is supported by the contention that stocks always should be presumed suspect and constantly subject to sale unless there is positive justification for actively deciding to buy. Holding can be logical only if others reasonably are expected to buy.

Why hold a stock at all? There are only two income-based objectives: dividend potential and interest rate volatility. With an income objective, hold the stock if its dividend is secure and/or it is subject to increase. With interest rate changes, hold only if interest rates will not move adversely enough (i.e., sharply higher) to reduce the market value of the expected dividend stream.

If the objective is capital appreciation and not income, the only justification for holding is a belief that price will begin to rise or will continue to rise. Just expecting a stock not to decline is not a good reason to hold it. That is the equivalent of putting money into a checking account and leaving it there. Actually it is worse, because the stock expectation might prove overly optimistic and the stock could decline anyway; but the (insured) bank deposit is presumed risk free.

This leads to the key element: hold a stock only if it is expected to rise (enough to compensate for opportunity cost and risk). Then logically examine the basis for any bullish expectations by envisioning realistically the stock's positive psycho-mechanical factors. Only the psycho-mechanical factors — added to positive fundamental news — drive the price higher, so both are required for a price rise. One alone is not enough, except briefly near runaway tops.

The Aftermath of the Crash

Now, several years after the 1987 market crash, it has become clear that there is a need for positive upward (buying) pressure ("sponsorship") in order to keep a stock's price from falling. The market for a stock is not like the market for food, for example. Stock demand is psychological, not based on necessity. To compound the effect of a lack of compelling stock demand, there tends to be an ongoing supply of shares which, if not matched, pushes prices lower over time. Included are unending sources of selling pressure: settling an estate, retiring and living on one's assets, paying for a college education, vacations, medical expenses, raising capital for a business or to buy other stocks, boredom and disappointment — all of these create a supply of shares. If this supply is not met by equal demand, prices decline.

The central issue then, is the source of buying power or demand for a stock. It is true that at some point a stock can become so compellingly cheap that it finds support. But the problem is that a cheap price level may not yet even approximate yesterday's closing price. Thus a logical corollary: do not hold a stock unless it would be a prudent purchase today. If an investor is not willing to buy it for his own portfolio, who else would? If he buys it anyway, this is the greater-fool theory at its worst.

So look objectively at how purchase decisions favoring a stock are likely to be generated. Think in terms of sponsorship for the stock. For sponsorship to exist, it is necessary that corporate management be involved in the process of providing information to the professional investing community and to the public. This does not mean an investor should look for a company that is actively and aggressively promoting its stock; in fact, those situations are suspect and usually are best avoided. Sponsorship is executives giving their time to research analysts who want to follow the company and may wish to recommend the stock to their clients, or place or keep it in managed portfolios.

Remember, demand for a stock does not occur in a vacuum. With the exception of a magazine story or news event, themes that catch the public's attention (pollution or AIDS) or word-of-mouth recommendations, most retail demand for stocks is generated by stock brokers who call clients and suggest reasons to buy. With so many other prepackaged products to recommend, most brokers today do not find their own stock stories; they rely on research-department recommendations for ideas. So the clients of these brokers buy stocks that have sponsorship. Other stocks are neglected.

This description of stock sponsorship might seem to be useful as a screening device for identifying promising stocks to buy. But remember that the focus here is on how to make decisions about holding or selling a stock already owned.

Although the Dow Jones Industrials in late 1988 were above 2000, it was a dreary period for common stocks. As a result of the 1987 crash, many individual investors quit the market altogether and remained too leery to return. Large numbers of those who remained had losses and refused to take any action because they felt "locked in." The result was a very low level of participation by individual investors. The minimal speculative tendency that did exist was centered on takeovers when the news seemed palpable, and the reason to buy was based on more than hope or theory.

Starting at that time, many brokerage firms reduced staffing and many brokers left the business due to declining customer activity. Even more important was the reduction in research coverage. This meant the public was far less prodded to buy stocks. Those analysts who remained employed generally concentrated more heavily than ever on large-capitalization issues. The reason is clear: an analyst's time costs the firm money. And that expense must be justified by trading activity that generates commission revenue dollars.

So because the investing public tends to be timid, it trades now in familiar names more than in smaller, fledgling enterprises. As a result, many stocks have narrower brokerage sponsorship than before the 1987 and 1989 crashes, and some others have lost all research coverage. The research department's reasoning goes, "If clients will not buy it, why should we bother to recommend it? And if we don't plan to recommend it, why should we even continue to follow it?"

The resulting near-term implication for stocks is apparent: increased urgency surrounding the hold/sell decision, especially in smaller-cap issues and low-priced stocks, listed and O-T-C. It was widely noted (although roundly denied by brokerage firms) during and just after the 1987 crash that the trading market in many unlisted stocks virtually disappeared for a day or more. Market-making firms reduced their exposed capital, causing a lack of depth in the market. While the problem has become less acute with the passage of time, it remains present.

The penalty suffered by low-priced issues is compounded by margin rules (and to some extent by investors' caution as well). Most brokerage firms extend credit (margin) of up to 50 percent of the purchase price on stocks priced at $5 per share or higher (some firms have adopted a $3 standard). When a stock declines below the stated level, it becomes worthless for purposes of calculating margin-account equity.

Therefore, a price decline through these levels snowballs down hill. The decline triggers margin calls, causing further selling. Aware of this, market makers became wary of carrying O-T-C inventory, and tactically savvy investors relinquished their lower-priced stocks. Further into a risk-averse climate, most brokers understandably became hesitant to call clients and suggest that they buy low-priced, more speculative stocks.

This illustrates psycho-mechanical factors in the market which, together with fundamentals, determine stock prices and trends. Part of the aftermath of the October 1987 crash is a real change in the mechanical inputs that constitute the market for individual stocks. Simply put, stocks now have less sponsorship than previously. Therefore for any given disappointment in fundamentals (or general market hesitancy), the resulting decline in share price is likely to be more sudden at first, more substantial in extent, and more extended over time than would have been the case before the crash.

Today, the number of active, risk-taking investors is down. And the number of brokers and analysts offering buy advices also is down. As a result, hoping against hope is more dangerous than ever. In addition to assessing whether fundamental news supports an advancing price (remember, just staying even is not good enough), also judge whether the psycho-mechanical forces in the market allow the price to advance. In the negative, cautious post-crash environment, lean more heavily than ever toward a "guilty until proven innocent" attitude. The burden of positive proof must now lie on the stock.

Remember that stocks fall of their own weight, but it takes buying pressure to move them higher. One way to judge a stock's prospects is to look at recent price charts: if the price is not in an uptrend — particularly if it has broken down — assume that demand has weakened. If that is the case, the holder's invested capital will shrink if the stock is held.

Be coldly objective: *is* there going to be buying pressure to move the stock up? Where will it originate? If the sources of support cannot be identified (as distinguished from the reasons why the stock "ought" to go up), a decision to hold will lose money. If there is no specific reason for continued optimism (on price action as well as on underlying fundamentals), an investor is literally hoping against hope.

In these circumstances, not to sell is to make a wager against the odds. And remember, a decision to hold is like a decision to buy again today — it is a reinvestment for another day in the same stock without paying commissions. The hold action is more subtle and does not involve a phone call to a broker or a transaction cost. But that decision to hold should be a decision made consciously and actively, not a default as a result of doing nothing or (worst of all!) of not even thinking about doing something.

The Hold Decision

The hold decision often results from an investor's bias toward a positive outlook on the future, justified by a standard of living that has been generally rising since the Great Depression. This subtle bias can persuade Americans to take enormous personal, career and financial risks in pursuit of reward.

Investing in the equity market certainly requires a degree of optimism, but that upward bias must be supported by the fundamentals of the situation, by thoughtful personal judgment and by the judgment of suitable advisors. It is appropriate for an investor to take some risks in search of the stock that doubles or in search of the next Apple Computer. But if that risk is too high relative to his personal tolerance, he should put his money into certificates of deposit (CDs) and accept a lower rate of return.

Unfortunately, however, an investment broker makes a living by catering to this investor optimism, which supports the buy bias described earlier. So investors lose billions of dollars every year because of the optimism they bring to daily living. Money is lost not only to fraudulent too-good-to-be-true, get-rich schemes, but also on the buying and holding sides of legitimate securities transactions.

To offset that tendency, proper buy timing and pricing can help reduce the pressure that inevitably surrounds the selling decision. There is a natural tendency to fall victim to excitement and buy a stock when it is already hot. Only the most disciplined of traders and investors consistently refuse to buy stocks on good news, on stories, or on excited rallies. Instead they demonstrate the self-control to stay with buy limits placed below the prices prevailing in the market at the time the buy decision is made.

So buying too high on a burst of optimism is the first source of optimism-induced losses for traders and investors. But even greater damage results from holding onto positions because of excessive or unjustified optimism. One major difficulty in overcoming this problem is that declining stocks occasionally do rally. But an occasional burst of countertrend strength in a weak stock does its die-hard owners more harm than good.

To illustrate, suppose an investor buys a stock (Exhibit 6-2) at $100 a share and then watches it decline by exactly ⅛ of a point every single day. In eight weeks, the stock eases to $95, and in 16 weeks it trails off to $90. The erosion is gradual but relentless. Every day he picks up the newspaper or calls his broker for a quote and the story is always the same: down again, down just ⅛.

Exhibit 6-2: Constant Decliner

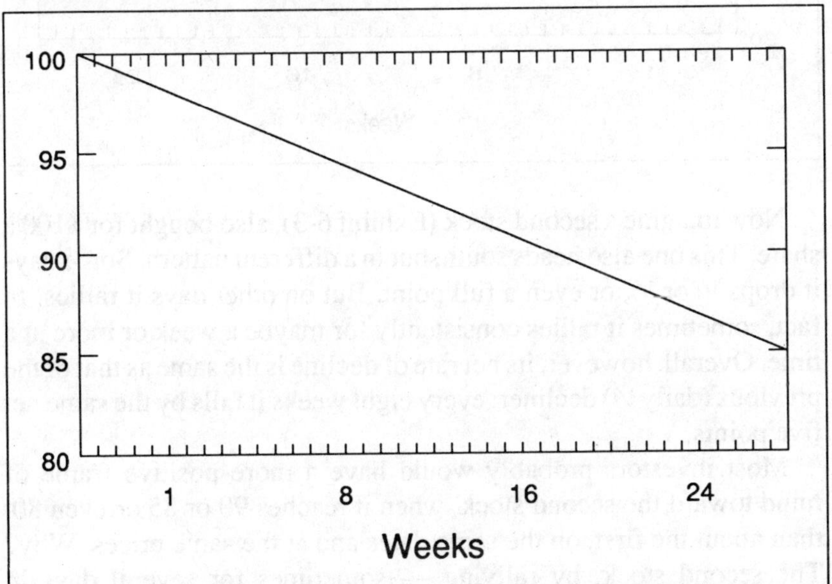

Exhibit 6-3: Jagged Mover

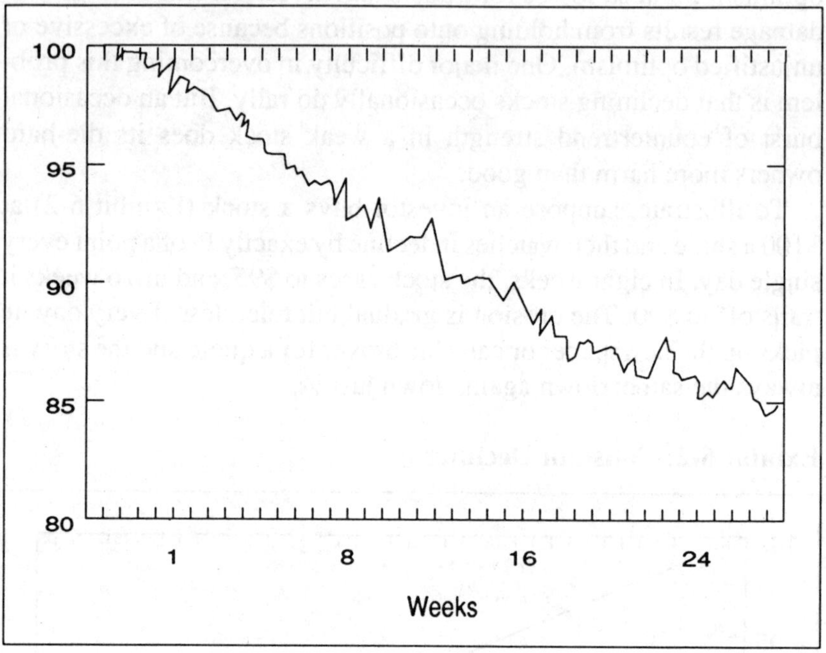

Now imagine a second stock (Exhibit 6-3), also bought for $100 a share. This one also heads south, but in a different pattern. Some days it drops ¼ or ½, or even a full point. But on other days it rallies. In fact, sometimes it rallies consistently for maybe a week or more at a time. Overall, however, its net rate of decline is the same as that of the previous (daily ⅛) decliner: every eight weeks it falls by the same net five points.

Most investors probably would have a more positive frame of mind toward the second stock, when it reaches 90 or 85 or even 80, than about the first, on the same dates and at the same prices. Why? The second stock, by rallying — sometimes for several days in succession and occasionally by a nice point or more — provides positive feedback more recently and certainly more often than the constant-⅛ decliner. Each time the stock turns up, a flicker of hope is kindled. The major problem here is that even bad (declining) stocks have their good days (or weeks).

Not only does the daily price action in the market sometimes renew hope, there can be positive fundamental news as well. A good quarterly earnings report or an optimistic brokerage recommendation can generate the renewal of optimism in the heart of an investor. So recognize that the holder of a specific common stock is not objective as a human being. Every plus wiggle in the stock price, every time the price holds steady against a 15-point drop in the Dow, and every good piece of news is a source of positive psychological feedback. Anything that goes right is a vindication of personal judgment.

Thus, if the dominant price path of the stock is downward, each and every cause for renewed optimism is actually a false signal. And in the cold light of reality, those false signals should be viewed as uninvited distractions from the truth rather than as rays of hope.

When hope springs eternal, the investor must separate the facts of the situation from the fiction. The separation process must include not only the real news background — what is actually true about the company and its industry versus what is rumor and hope — but also the psychological environment in which the investor has linked his state of mind with the company and its stock. Guard against being trapped by a personal, renewed sense of optimism when hope springs eternal.

Using Charts

The best way for an investor to calibrate his state of mind against the market is to rely on stock price charts. Aside from the great debate about the viability of technical analysis, a chart can be useful as an accurate road map of price movement history. The most accessible and useful charts for the big picture are those included on the front side of Standard & Poor's tearsheets. In a couple of inches, there is a 10-year motion picture of stock movements (although some analysts argue that a 10-year analysis is questionable because too much change occurs and the data may lose some relevancy).

Without any expertise in charting techniques, an investor can spot whether the stock is still in a downtrend or whether its price action has overcome negative momentum for the better. Only rarely will it be true to say, "I am not sure, it seems to be right at the point of reversing." If that is true, resolve to look again in a week and make a yes/no decision, refusing to take another time extension.

In order to make the process truly useful, impose the self-discipline of writing down some decision guidelines the first time — something like, "The stock seems to be right on the edge of the top of the down-channel with its present 39 price. If it moves up to at least 40, I will be convinced that it has really broken the downtrend and I will hold. But if it fails on this move by backing down to 37 ½, that will be a sign that this latest rally was a false hope. In that case I will sell."

The investor who needs a nudge should mail his broker a copy of this rule with a note asking to be called in 10 or 14 days to do the follow-up chart reading jointly. Note that what is written should be confined entirely to the action of the stock and not include anything about feelings, cost, target, gains or losses. Focus entirely on the factual reality of the stock and give up hopeful desire.

Above all, do not back into a non-decision by default through the insidious process that consultants call "analysis-paralysis." The market keeps moving with or without an investor. So do not wait open-endedly for just a little more news or technical confirmation. There is never going to be a final answer or a point of total closure. So exercise discipline: make an evaluation and take action accordingly.

If a stock declines and then rallies, take note of a change in personal optimism level. (See Exhibit 6-4.) Keep a daily notebook in which to write down the stock's price and the feelings that arise about

Exhibit 6-4: How Do You Feel?

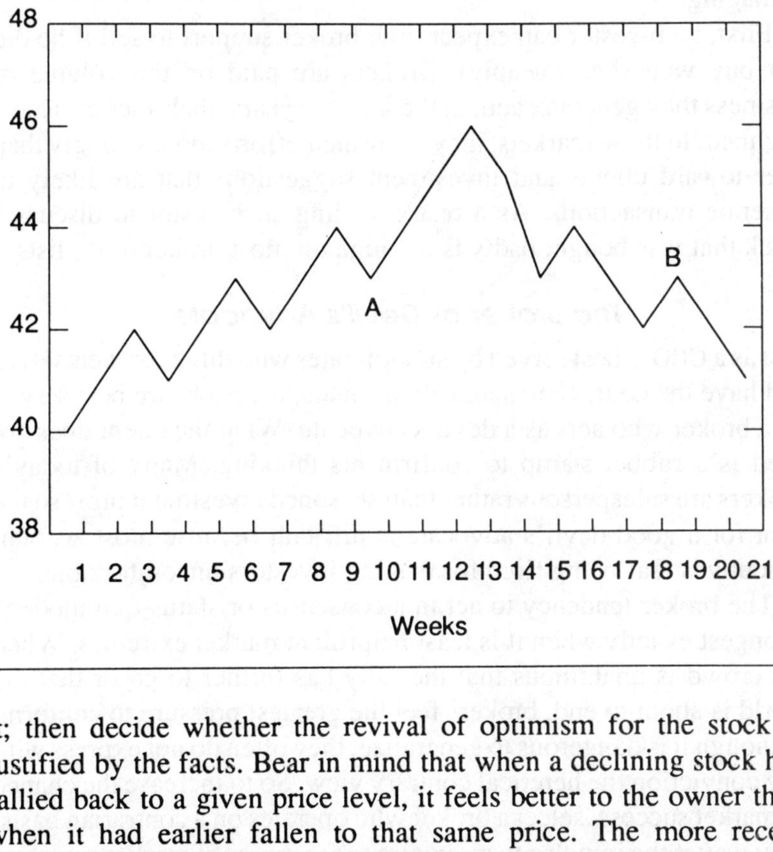

it; then decide whether the revival of optimism for the stock is justified by the facts. Bear in mind that when a declining stock has rallied back to a given price level, it feels better to the owner than when it had earlier fallen to that same price. The more recent feedback creates hope while the earlier move produced fear. Watch the emotional difference, even at the same price.

The price an investor pays for a stock can get in the way of prudent selling because it influences the willingness to sell in terms of both timing and price. So buying well is important but only half of the transaction. The investor also must exit skillfully. Failure to buy well not only puts all the burden of possible net success on the exit execution, but it also colors the holder's thinking in ways that are damaging.

First, an investor can expect little broker support to sell if he did not buy well (i.e., cheaply). Brokers are paid on the volume of business they generate, and, in the last few years, their incomes have declined. In these markets, they skew their efforts more strongly than ever toward clients and investment suggestions that are likely to generate transactions. As a result, calling an investor to discuss a stock that was bought badly is not high on most broker to-do lists.

The Broker as Devil's Advocate

Just as a CEO is best served by subordinates who think for themselves and have the courage to speak their minds, investors are best served by a broker who acts as a devil's advocate. What the client does not need is a rubber-stamp to confirm his thinking. Many of today's brokers are salespersons rather than seasoned investment pros, so the hunt for a good devil's advocate is difficult because most account executives fear being fired for making investors uncomfortable.

The broker tendency to act in a consensus or status-quo mode is strongest exactly when it is least helpful: at market extremes. When the crowd is unanimous that the rally has further to go or that the world is about to end, brokers feel the greatest pressure to conform. Although it is dangerous to generalize, they often do not express with any conviction the heretical contrary view. So to increase the chance of market success, select a broker who operates on a contrarian basis. That way if the impulse to act contra to the crowd at market extremes does not arise in the client, the broker can save the day if selected on his ability to be contrarian.

There are two aspects of brokers' reluctance about selling stocks that have not been well bought: time and price. Suppose a broker's research department has advised the purchase of XYZ Widget. It is possible that an investor got on board late because his broker paid little attention when the stock was still near its lows, the broker did not develop confidence in the recommendation until after a good rally already had taken place, or the investor did not become convinced until the broker had pushed it and it was already clearly going up.

The stock has risen from 30 to 40, and client is in at 38. Now what happens if (1) the research analyst turns bearish, (2) the company's fundamentals deteriorate or (3) the overall market signals it is time to move to the sidelines?

The broker is embarrassed to report the analyst's about-face just after the investor got on board; and he well may worry that the investor suspects account churning. The broker also may believe that the market is consolidating before a further rise, as many would in this case. In any event, the broker is subject to the optimistic buy bias, so phoning the investor about selling is not attractive to him.

Finally, the broker knows that since he just got in at 38, the investor is less prone to selling quickly at 40 than a luckier or more decisive client who entered at 32 several months ago. Deep in his gut, the broker hopes that the stock will rally further, allowing the lower-priced (early) buyers out here and getting his late-entry client a few more points' profit and more time from his entry point so he can call with better news later (higher).

The client should not expect a quick call when the rating drops from "buy" to "hold" or (rarely!) "sell." So one aspect of buying badly is short timing between entry and the new, less bullish recommendation. Of course if the buy was the investor's idea, the barrier is even higher: the broker will expect indignant "price" resistance (actually driven by ego) if he calls with a suggestion to sell.

The second problem is a price-driven sell, which occurs on a loss. Suppose that the investor gets in an 38 on the way to 40, and the analyst is right in thinking that things have gone sour. The price is now 37. Not only does the *broker* feel squeamish about calling now (an easy criticism is to say he should have called when it was at 40), more bad tendencies result from the *client's* own mind-set.

A typical client does not sell readily at a one-point loss, especially having first tasted a quick, two-point paper profit. So the investor compounds the broker's weakness: if one of them is inclined to sell, the other probably is not; the phone call may not be made by either party. So both the timing aspect of having bought late (recently) and the price aspect of having suffered a loss are dangers to the investor's financial health. A change of mind soon after a buy is an ego embarrassment because it is an admission of error. Taking a loss is a second ego blow. So it is evident how the time and price of a badly-made buy render the selling decision more painful and difficult than it is on a big gainer.

The truth is that when it is time to sell before the price goes down, it is time for everyone to sell, no matter what the timing is or what the cost at entry. But human nature seemingly demands that investors factor into the sell decision the stock's initial price. And the less time the stock has been held, the less the investor is willing to switch mental gears and say "sell."

What should determine the decision is whether the stock seems likely to go down from here and now; if it does, it should be sold as soon as possible. The central question that should decide the hold/sell dilemma is "Would I buy this stock today?" Many investors fail to ask that question at all.

There is no denying that buying better helps most investors cash in more effectively when the right time comes. Most buying mistakes (aside from acquiring inflated "hot" new issues and penny stocks) occur not in buying bad stocks but in buying mediocre stocks too late — again, because investors tend to be crowd followers. They wait for confirmation because they need courage. They are most ready to jump in when the market has already become overbought.

There are three places in the book that help investors contain and overcome the tendency to buy too late (too high): chapter 9 on contrarian thinking, chapter 11 on emotional red flags, and the checklist on common investing mistakes provided in Appendix I.

If a stock is held only because of perceived positive potentials for the whole market, it should be sold. Throughout the book, the acid-test questions appears, "Would I buy today?" A similarly revealing question is whether an investor would sell it here if he had bought better. If there is even a hint of an affirmative answer, he must recognize that cashing in is the right thing to do.

CHAPTER

7

Forget Your Cost Price

KEYS TO INVESTMENT SUCCESS

- The Irrelevance of the Personal Cost Price
- When Is Cost Price Relevant?
- Misusing Cost Price

Traders and investors unknowingly attach enormous subjective importance to their price in a stock. When this personal history takes on its a life of its own, it colors future thinking. Awareness of this historical cost-price point is a subtle, powerful and dangerous influence on a selling decision. Therefore, some exploration of its ramifications is required here.

The Irrelevance of the *Personal* Cost Price

The first reality that must be established regarding history is the total insignificance of an investor's purchase event. In the markets of the late 1980s and early 1900s, over 150,000,000 shares have changed hands daily on the New York Stock Exchange alone. A 100- or 1,000-share purchase, which may be a financial event of note and an emotionally-charged decision for the investor, is lost in the avalanche of daily Wall Street activity. Even so, the historic accident of the buy price becomes psychological baggage of great personal magnitude to the investor. And almost always, its effect is detrimental to the eventual execution of a successful sale. (It should be noted that a successful sale does not necessarily mean a profit. It can, under some circumstances, equally mean a deftly timed exit that prevents a loss or a greater loss from developing.)

A good sale point is a time/price combination on the stock's historical chart which, when viewed in hindsight, evokes the reaction, "Wow, that sure was a good exit point right there!" The successful sale point is, therefore, defined only in terms of what occurs *after* it in time — not at all in terms of the historical fact of the owner's related purchase price.

If a stock is to collapse from 50 to 30 in the next week, a sale at or around 50 now is a good sale for anyone regardless of whether the stock was bought at 52, 48, 65, 30 or 50.

This is a key point, so it bears re-emphasis: a good price or time at which to sell a stock is defined by what happens to the stock *after* the sale occurs, and has nothing to do with the prior event (investor purchase). A good sale is a good sale, whether it gives a small or large gain, breaks even or nets a loss. It is a good sale if it sidesteps a subsequent decline or if it avoids a loss of money's time value (a prolonged sideways market or a period of serious relative underperformance.)

All too often, however, the irrelevance of an investor's cost price is not reflected in the way he views his holdings. He has in mind that he owns 200 Chrysler at 25 ¼; in fact, he simply owns 200 Chrysler. But his cost price per share, unfortunately, has become a figurative line in the sand and, therefore, a historic hook. When the stock is above his cost price, he feels smart (and increasingly good as the distance between cost and current market widens). When the stock trades below his cost, he feels insulted, cheated, determined or deprived.

And when the stock's price is once again at his cost point at a date subsequent to his entry, that coincidence can trigger any of three conditions:

1. If the stock has recovered from an interim decline, he feels relief and ego vindication. Relief because the pain of having suffered a reverse has been alleviated (ignoring the time value of his money, of course). Vindication because once again he can look in the mirror and know he was right.
2. When the stock rallies back up to his buying level, he experiences excitement: now the action is really going to get started. If the stock happens to hang around his personal cost-price level for quite some time, each return to that level is likely to trigger some degree of boredom or frustration. But at the same time, prolonged trading at his cost level is likely to reinforce in his mind the concept that such a price is reasonable, represents

solid and attainable value, and is deserved by the stock (or, more dangerously, by the holder personally). But such firmness of feelings about a price (created by frequent reinforcement) is likely to intensify his difficulty in selling later if the stock moves lower. Conditioned to expecting a given price level and holding out for its re-attainment, the investor is fixed by his own perception.

3. The opposite emotional reaction occurs when a stock he buys has risen and then subsequently falls back to his cost-price level. The greater the price distance of the now retraced move, the more intense is the investor's emotional reaction. There is a very empty feeling of having given it all back — a sense of sadness that anyone who has gambled away a temporary profit will remember all too well. The primary reaction is one of disappointment with his indecisiveness or lack of discipline. But a stubbornness also takes hold. He recalls the previously reached high levels, and believes that the company's stock deserved to sell at those quotes and therefore should return to them. He resolves to hold on for that rally. Or he may plant the subconscious seeds of resignation to loss. He has done so badly by failing to sell at a profit, maybe he is doomed to a bad experience with this stock anyway. Of course depending on the size and tenderness of his ego, he may cover up the tendency to criticize his own failure in not taking the elusive profit. He can blame it all on bad luck or on the overall market, or even on "they."

So be very wary of the psychological trap that the memory of cost can represent. The greatest single problem it creates is that mental line in the sand — the dividing line between gain and loss, between wisdom and foolishness. Remember that an individual trade is an insignificant grain of sand on the beach.

There are only four cases in which the cost price paid actually may have some significance in the market at a later date. But even in these instances, the importance of the price is totally coincidental, and is not caused by or related to a personal purchase action. What these four circumstances have in common is that they each create price levels to which large numbers of *other* investors attach meaning. It is those large numbers that cause the importance of the price.

When Is Cost Price Relevant?

The first significant price level at which an investor coincidentally or accidentally may establish a cost is when a primary or secondary offering takes place. That level, by definition, involves a large number of shares and a large number of other investors. If a new issue comes to market at $10, that level becomes the mental mark in the sand for thousands of individuals — a win/loss inflection point.

That later may be viewed as the level to "get out and get even," or as a trigger point for a stop-loss order or as a point where an investor doubles up. But whatever the reaction of the mass, the historical pricing level of a primary or secondary offering has a significant effect on future price action.

An investor may buy into that offering, or just coincidentally buy at another time but at the same price. While the price at which he buys actually does have some significance in the market, in this case it has nothing to do with his few hundred shares. It is the distribution at that price of tens of thousands or perhaps several millions of shares to many investors that matters.

The second event that can make any price important is the so-called price gap. Much has been written by market technicians about the theory and importance of chart gaps in the history of a stock's price action. The point here to not to arbitrate that debate, however.

Briefly summarized, the market lore of price gaps is that all gaps tend to be closed. Actually, it is probably more accurate to say that upside gaps (except in cases of successful takeovers) tend to be retraced and filled. Some downside gaps are caused by such powerful negative fundamental news that they literally may never be filled. The company may never recover and, in some cases, it may eventually disappear following a devastating chain of events triggered by the news that causes the downside gap. So do not be gulled into a false sense of optimism about all gaps being filled.

The point about gaps is this: whether or not an investor is a technician or believes that price gaps are important technical phenomena, there are large numbers of other traders and investors in the market who *do* hold that viewpoint. Their collective actions or inactions, based on that belief, have an effect on market-price action. So the gap price itself becomes important in later market behavior.

Say an investor buys right at the moment the gap developed. While the market, in this case, does attach significance to his price, it is for reasons unconnected to him. It is like having a December 25th birthday.

Round numbers also may be significant price points for reasons that usually bear little objective relation to rational investment theory. In the same way a primary offering or a gap price level creates a memory in the minds of investors, a round number can become a trigger for action. Many recall saying, "If IBM ever gets back to 100, I am definitely going to buy some" Or, "If stock 'x' hits 25, I will take my profit there." In the case of lower-priced issues, it is the round dollar that becomes a target. When large numbers of people act on these targets, such price levels actually do become significant because of the action that takes place at or very near them. Again, however, it is not because of the investor's 200 shares acquired there.

Finally, any of several technical chart-price patterns may render a particular price level significant. Tops and bottoms of channels, tops of rising triangles, the apex or "breakout point" of a triangle, the neckline of a head-and-shoulders formation or the price at which multiple tops or bottoms have occurred — these can become significant price points.

And it is randomly possible that an investor's purchase price level may coincide, whether it is established before or after those events. Subsequent market action may call renewed attention to this particular price level, fixing it even more firmly in mind as important. But the reason is the larger technical importance of the price level, created by many other participants (some of whom *do* believe in charts) who attach meaning to that level.

So avoid building a strategy on the imaginary foundation that a personal price is important to the market for the same reason it is important to the investor. In addition to defining the very real (at least, pre-commissions) dividing line between profit and loss, an investor's cost price sets up several other constructs in his mind that do not have any operative importance in the marketplace.

Misusing Cost Price

What these constructs all have in common is that they are based on investor cost price as a starting point — the accidental moment that became subjective history. His cost forms the baseline for a calculation. For example, he may set as a goal making five points, 15 percent before commissions, or an ambitious goal such as a 50 percent gain or even a double. Or he may set either a mental or actual stop-loss point designed to limit a loss to a predetermined percentage amount. All these formulae share the commonality of the personal entry level. But the market is not conscious of any such formula!

If technical analysis has any meaning, the chart pattern itself defines reasonable resistance and support levels that relate to the stock's overall recent or long-term past history but do not in any way have cause-effect ties to an individual's accidental entry point.

For example, suppose that an investor's stock is locked in a lengthy and well-defined price channel between 39 and 45. (See

Exhibit 7-1: Locked in a Price Channel

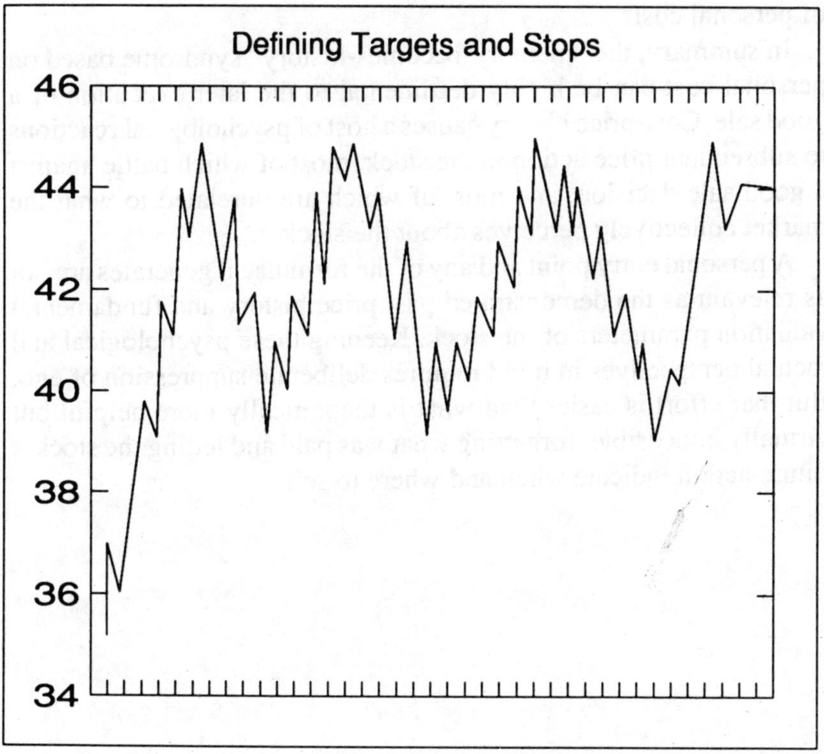

exhibit 7-1.) Assume that he is lucky or smart enough to buy at 40. If he sets an arbitrary upside goal of 15 percent above cost (before or after commissions), he will be frustrated by repeated retreats from the 45 level, just about a point short of his personal target of 46. If, on the other hand, he sets a 5 percent stop-loss error margin, his trigger will be 38 — a full point below the obvious breakdown level of 39 on a decline.

So setting any formula based on entry price is self-defeating in this case. Triggers should be based on the chart's evidence or on reasonable fundamental valuation measures, not in relation to the accident of personal cost.

In summary, the "memory-becomes-history" syndrome based on personal cost can be highly detrimental to the later execution of a good sale. Cost-price history causes a host of psychological reactions to subsequent price action in the stock, most of which battle against a good sale decision, and most of which are unrelated to what the market collectively perceives about the stock.

A personal entry point and any of the formulae it generates are not as relevant as the demonstrated past price history and fundamental valuation parameters of the stock. Keeping these psychological and factual perspectives in mind requires deliberate suppression of ego. But that effort is easier than what is theoretically more helpful but virtually impossible: forgetting what was paid and letting the stock's future action indicate when and where to sell.

CHAPTER 8

Understand That You Sell the Stock, Not the Company

KEYS TO INVESTMENT SUCCESS

- Separating the Stock and the Company
- Price Equals the Changing Level of Esteem

To become a logical long-term holder, an investor must find a comfort zone; there is none better than fundamentals, he says. When price behavior is unexpected, he rationalizes a flip from the technical to the fundamental orientation. "It is a really good company so it will come back." In fact, the more he knows about a company and the greater tie he feels to it, the more danger there is of switching from a trader/selling mode to an investor/holding mode. A switch in investment objective is a warning signal, and the alert investor takes pains to guard against any such switch.

Separating the Stock and the Company

The invention of a new reason to hold rather than sell is confused thinking. In the same way that weak decision-making causes a trader to become an investor ("collector") by default, another confusion can creep in which just as easily prompts holding: the mistaken idea that the stock is the company. Although a stock certificate is a fractional share in the corporation, the company and the stock itself should never be considered identical.

Often when a holder's position begins to erode, he changes tactical identity by default from trader to long-term holder. All he has done is mistakenly associate the stock with the virtues and strengths of the underlying company. This is a subtle but critical mistake that must be strenuously guarded against. Another danger arises when he does not perceive that a confusion of identities has taken place, and that this lack of perception further reduces his chances of correcting the situation.

No stock goes up forever, no matter how strong its issuing company. Even during a raging bull market, not every stock price advances. And even among those which do score an increase over a year or more, none progress in price at a steady rate without interim fluctuation and setbacks. Sometimes even the greatest growth stocks experience meaningful interim declines. While a given company may prosper consistently over time—like American Home Products with its lengthy record of consecutive quarterly earnings advances—its stock acts independently in the short to medium term. The reasons are usually completely unrelated to company fundamentals and can include an adverse trend in the general market, temporary factors such as group leadership rotations and simply a short-term correction of an exuberant earlier advance.

So a stock and its issuing company often do not move in harmony: there are times when the firm's business prospers but its shares decline in price; at other times the stock's price can even be advancing, seemingly against all logic, when fundamentals are on the decline.

Traders most often equate the stock and the company when the share price has fallen since purchase. The trader becomes an investor through the back door as he falls back on fundamentals or generalized faith in the company when the shares decline. Seeking justification for the decision to hold rather than sell, he waxes enthusiastic about the virtues of the company rather than focusing on the prospects for what is most important to making a profit: stock price performance.

Usually the symptoms of this misguided switch in investment status are rear-view-mirror in nature. Examples are, "They have reported 47 consecutive quarters of rising sales and earnings." Or, "You know, they are ranked number so-and-so in the Fortune 500 now." But something clearly has gone wrong because reputation and Fortune ranking have not helped the stock to rise since purchase.

An even more dangerous influence is a relationship between the stockholder and the corporation. Emotional ties (such as employment, or the enjoyment of company products) are difficult to keep in perspective. Exactly when the time is most critical, they usually stand in the way of a tactical sale of the stock.

And the difficulty of separating the stock and company is compounded when the shareholder has made his ownership position known to others. If people around him know that he owns stock in his employer or a relative's employer, he feels constrained when it is time to sell the stock. This psychological complication is avoidable with effort. It is at the same time a persuasive reason not only for mentally separating the company from the stock but also for not divulging personal investment positions.

Price—The Changing Level of Esteem

Another critical factor in the decision to sell or hold — or to separate the company and its stock in this context — is awareness of some common terminology used when buying. A broker or investor casually may say, "I think we ought to own some General Motors." Buying with this attitude subconsciously encourages the investor to identify with the company as an emotional owner.

But if he cannot distinguish his personal identity from his identity as a shareholder, the investment is virtually destined to become a long-term collector's item. So it is critical to realize that he has purchased the stock because of the rising or falling esteem in which other investors hold the company — he has not really purchased a share of ownership in the sense of buying into a law partnership.

The reality is that the company may reach new heights of prosperity while he owns it, but he still can lose money. Why? He has bought merely the right to cash in on the changing level of perception that people hold about that company. They may like it less tomorrow because he bought too late, because interest rates are rising (making all equities less attractive relative to T-bills), because of adverse public opinion about its products, because reputation deteriorates or because investment tastes shift in favor of other industries.

Other investors collectively may be right or wrong about the company. And the individual may prove correct while the majority are incorrect about fundamentals. However, the actions of the crowd determine share price in the short to medium term. And that is the most important factor because that determines whether he has a gain or a loss, and when. So buy and sell not on personal judgment of the companies behind the stock, but on personal assessment of what other investors think of the company and how that thinking will change.

In the same way, making investment decisions involves mentally and emotionally separating the facts — or the facts as they are perceived or expected to be — from what the market (i.e., the collective opinion of investors) believes and will come to believe. The company may, indeed, continue to be profitable and to grow. But if it falls out of investor favor, no matter how valid or invalid the reasons, its stock price will suffer.

To determine whether now is the time to hold or to sell, focus on changes in perception rather than on fundamentals. An investor can be dead-on right about fundamentals; but if the market collectively decides that it no longer is willing to pay as much for the company's reputation or earnings, the share price heads south. Over the long term, his logic may prevail again as value reasserts itself. But in the interim he is going to suffer a loss if he fights the tape.

The tape reflects market reactions and perceptions translated into buying and selling actions; it does not reflect the truth about a company's fundamentals. So keep in mind that the company and its stock are separate. The stock was bought out of a willingness to bet that others will pay a higher price. Purchase is a bet based on market perception, company reputation and personal emotion — it should not be perceived as the acquisition of a piece of the company.

SECTION

III

Mastering the Contrarian Approach

CHAPTER 9

Be a Contrarian

KEY TO INVESTMENT SUCCESS

- Mastering the Contrarian Approach

Nearly everyone who invests looks to the professionals for advice. The hope, of course, is that the alleged "secret" of professional successes can be learned. But it is not evident that investing success can be learned by anyone who aspires to it; some people have reasonable investing potential and some do not because investing is an art and not entirely a science. As in sports and the creative arts, a certain amount of innate aptitude is required.

For those who have some aptitude, there is no better guru than the man who was reported to be the richest man in the world. Three-billionaire J. Paul Getty once said:

> *"Buy when everyone else is selling and hold until everyone else is buying. This is not merely a catchy slogan. It is the very essence of successful investment."*

Because this is a book on *selling* investments, Getty's advice should be amended: "hold until..." means "sell when..." The essence of the message is the gospel of contrary opinion. Like any other prescription for investment success, the contrarian approach is never quite as simple to apply as its truth is obvious. This is because there are no exact yardsticks that indicate unfailingly when a trend is overdone.

But an attempt to apply contrary thinking to the investment process should not be abandoned. To ignore its wisdom because of a personal inability to catch the absolute tops and bottoms by using it is like refusing to eat healthy foods because death is inevitable anyway.

This chapter explains why it is necessary to maintain a contrarian mind-set in both buying and selling stocks. Statistically, it is known that the majority of investors lose money. Only a minority get richer. But it is also well documented that an investor can be successful despite losing more often than winning, provided that his losses are cut short and his profits are allowed to run. To become more successful at investing, then, it is necessary to act less like the majority and more like the minority, more of the time.

Although the zero-sum-game hypothesis in economics is mostly rejected, secondary investment markets taken in isolation and as a closed system are a zero-sum game. Assume that a company is going to sell a certain number of widgets this year, achieve certain margins, pay a given tax rate and deliver some specific earnings per share regardless of its stock price. The fundamentals help determine price action, as does industry-related and general market psychology.

Given that a stock is going to move from one price to another, retrace some or all of that change, arrive at a third price or just back at the starting one, and only a certain amount of trading volume will occur in the process, then some people make money; others lose or forego equal amounts. The entire net price move, in dollars per share, multiplied by the number of shares outstanding, equals the increased or decreased combined wealth that all shareholders experience collectively (before commission).

Those who buy at the top lose. Those who sell to them win. Those who scalp three points on the way up take potential profits from those who sold to them. Those who hold on and ride the entire price merry-go-round end up back where they started. They have lost the time value of their money and have failed to accept profits while prices were up. (They also have failed to learn the contrarian's skill of selling high.)

Others who did cash in at higher prices have taken profits and can now buy in again at lower prices. Those to whom they sold are now holding higher-cost securities. So it is basically a zero-sum game. Therefore to be successful, learn to play it better and/or more nimbly than the other players: do *not* follow the crowd.

There is so much emphasis on the buying end of the investment equation that there is plenty of available evidence to monitor how over-heated a market is becoming. Bullish pressure can be palpable if an investor looks and listens, and that is useful and valuable input. Because if he can sense when the clamor to buy is getting out of hand

and out of touch with reality, then he recognizes a classic contrarian signal.

Mastering the Contrarian Approach

To succeed as a contrarian, always look for these signals. They can be detected in the world around the market:

- Is the market front-page news in the media?
- Do television programs use stock-market jokes or plots?
- Are people talking stocks over lunch more than usual?
- Are brokers making more calls offering "exciting opportunities"?
- Is prosperity widespread and are expectations of continued expansion the norm?
- Are many more investment advisors and letter-writers bullish than bearish?
- Is the percentage of mutual-fund cash in equity funds low or fast declining?

These signs tend to accumulate gradually and, therefore, are subtle rather than sudden and shocking. No one rings the bell and declares the bull market over. It happens, literally, when people least expect it. So the investor's job is to out-smart and out-think the other players. It is hard to hit the exact top, so do not worry about that. The losers have absolutely no idea that they are helping to create a top by their classic overenthusiastic behavior. They miss selling at the top by a mile, just as they miss the bottom as buyers.

Savvy investors catch the greatest percentage of the move by cashing in near the top and are entirely content to sell to a potential greater fool who tries to hold for the top.

But make no mistake: it is not easy to lean against the tide. It is unfashionable to be a worrier near the top; and if an investor starts selling early (the best time), he is written off by others because he looks wrong for a long time. He may have regrets (seller's remorse) and second thoughts against selling stocks as they get increasingly overvalued.

In the short run, he is tempted to reverse field and jump back in to chase "just one more hot one" while it looks inviting. That impulse should be resisted above all: it is a classic final signal to cash in rather than buy more. In the long run, however, he proves right with a contrarian attitude.

The key to success is to do what is not easy. Almost invariably when a buy looks compelling and obvious, the investor actually is getting in too late. The best bargains are purchased when the investor has to struggle and debate, afraid even to tell his broker. When he loves the stock because it has treated him so well and wants to stay on board longer, he has overstayed the market.

Remember that the majority always feels it is right, even when it is not. When the feeling of bullish rightness becomes universal and powerful, a top is immediately at hand. Being successful in trading means leaning against that powerful tide. But that creates psychological requirements and strains not everyone can handle.

If by nature an investor is passive, a follower, he may lack the courage to do what is required for trading success. But if he can stick to contrarian principles despite the early suboptimization of profits, he gains a bucketful of cash near the top (plus some interest) for use when the next bottom arrives.

Perhaps the most forceful statement on the need to act in the contrary mode appears in *Confessions of a Wall Street Insider* by the self-named C.C. Hazard:

> *"(T)he stock market is built on a necessary foundation of error. You make money on the market mainly by living off the errors of other players. You become a predator, in fact, a carnivore, a beast of prey. Others must die that you might live...(T)he stock market requires an endless supply of losers."*

By not acting like the crowd, an investor raises his chance of not being part of that pool of losers.

C H A P T E R

10

Focus on the Time Value of Money

KEYS TO INVESTMENT SUCCESS

- Rule of 72
- The 9.2 Percent Long-Term Rate
- Avoiding Losses

Throughout this book there is a bias toward selling out positions instead of holding. The inertia behind holding is powerful and, combined with other psychological factors, often prevents investors from feeling comfortable about selling. So there is a deliberate effort here to make a strong a case for selling, in as many ways as are relevant to retail investing. The best, and perhaps most relevant, is the unstoppable march of time.

Although time works against an investor in many ways, it can be a very powerful ally when money is put to work in ways that generate high, compounded returns over a long period. But precisely because of the magic of compound interest, the value of time is great and so the cost of lost time can be staggering. Understanding the natural inertia that disguises itself as patience should have great enough impact that investors learn to become less patient with underperforming investments.

Probably the most widely cited study of long-term market performance was conducted by Roger Ibbotson and Rex Sinquefield[1], which examined returns on financial instruments over a half century. As brokers who know about equities are fond of pointing out to hesitant clients, the conclusion of this monumental study was that over a very long period of time common stocks provide higher average returns than the other investments covered. They yielded on average 9.2 percent per annum, including both capital appreciation and dividends.

This is not high compared to inflation since the late 1960s, or compared to the rapid increase in the Dow-Jones Industrial Average from 1982 the 1987 or 1990 highs. But in the longer-term perspective, it is reasonable to expect that recent equity return rates will prove extraordinarily strong in the year 2027, for example.

In the meantime, the 9.2 percent rule of thumb is a useful starting point for evaluating reasonable long-term returns. Investors and

---

[1]Roger Ibbotson and Rex Sinquefield, *Stocks, Bonds, Bills, and Inflation: the Past (1926–1976) and the Future (1977–2000).* Charlottesville, VA: Financial Analyst Research Foundation, 1977.

traders who take greater risks should aim for higher returns, in the 15 percent range or more per year, as compensation for the intellectual work and emotional energy expended to own stocks.

The Rule of 72

Most investors are familiar with the "Rule of 72," which is an easy way to determine how long it takes to double a sum of money at annual compounded rates. (It is not 100 percent precise, but it is operationally realistic.) For example, 7.2 percent for 10 years, compounded annually, produces $2,004.22 from an original $1,000.00 investment. There are three formulations (see Table 10-1) of the "Rule of 72":

- Years times rate equals 72
- 72 divided by rate equals number of years required
- 72 divided by available years equals required rate of return to double a sum

Table 10-1: The Rule of 72

Years	Rule-Implied Rate in %	Multiple of Starting Sum	Actual Rate to Double
3	24	1.907	26%
4	18	1.939	18.9
5	14.4	1.959	14.9
6	12	1.974	12.25
7	10.3	1.986	10.4
8	9	1.993	9.05
9	8	1.999	8
10	7.2	2.006	7.2
11	6.5	1.999	6.5
12	6	2.012	5.95
13	5.5	2.006	5.5
14	5.1	2.006	5.1

The table is truncated at 14 years because the returns implied by the rule at that point decline to below the savings passbook rate, a level considered very unacceptable for investors assuming the risks of equity ownership.

The 9.2 Percent Long-Term Rate

The Ibbotson and Sinquefield study defined 9.2 percent as the long-term annual rate for equities. And 9.2 percent is close enough to the "9-percent/8-years" convention of the "Rule of 72" so eight years can be used as a reasonable investment horizon for doubling money in stocks. In fact, the 9.2 percent rate compounded annually for eight years produces $2021.99 for each $1,000 invested up front, implying accuracy within 1.1 percent over eight years.

Suppose an investor has conservative expectations and is willing to settle for the long-term norm of 9.2 percent per annum. Look back at the table and see what happens when a stock that has been held goes nowhere. If it is held for one year, the average annual compounded return that is now required to catch up to the schedule of doubling in eight years becomes 10.4 percent over the remaining seven years (moving up the first column to shorter time periods to locate the required returns in the fourth column).

This is not too dramatic. But if the stock goes nowhere for two years, the required catch-up return rate for the remaining six years jumps to 12.25 percent. And that is 35 percent more than the 9 percent required originally to double the investor's money; it is 33 percent better than the long-term mean rate discovered by Ibbotson and Sinquefield — a significant overperformance that must be achieved over the next six years. This is an indication of the performance required of a stock that is going nowhere when it is patiently — and erroneously — held by a stubborn, fearful or psychologically-paralyzed investor.

Now look at the big damage that occurs when the stock's performance falls below breakeven. Watch what happens when there is a loss of capital and when the investor dawdles before accepting that loss. Assuming for illustrative purposes a 9.2 percent long-term rate on equities to double capital over eight years, the required catch-up rates become greatly higher, obviously, with both the severity of the starting loss and the amount of time consumed.

Table 10-2: Loss of Capital

Percent Lost at Beginning	Years Until Loss Taken	Required Compound Return in Years Left, to Double in 8
10	1	12.1%/yr for 7 years
	2	14.2 for 6
	3	17.3 for 5
	4	22.1 for 4
20	1	14.0%/yr for 7 years
	2	16.5 for 6
	3	20.1 for 5
	4	25.7 for 4
25	1	15.0%/yr for 7 years
	2	17.8 for 6
	3	21.7 for 5
	4	27.8 for 4
33.33	1	17.0%/yr for 7 years
	2	20.1 for 6
	3	24.6 for 5
	4	31.7 for 4
50	1	21.9%/yr for 7 years
	2	26.0 for 6
	3	32.0 for 5
	4	41.4 for 4

As Table 10-2 shows, taking a loss in the beginning requires that highly optimistic returns be achieved to catch up to the doubling schedule in eight years. If a higher expectation such as a positive 15

Exhibit 10-1: Sample Catch-Up Pace

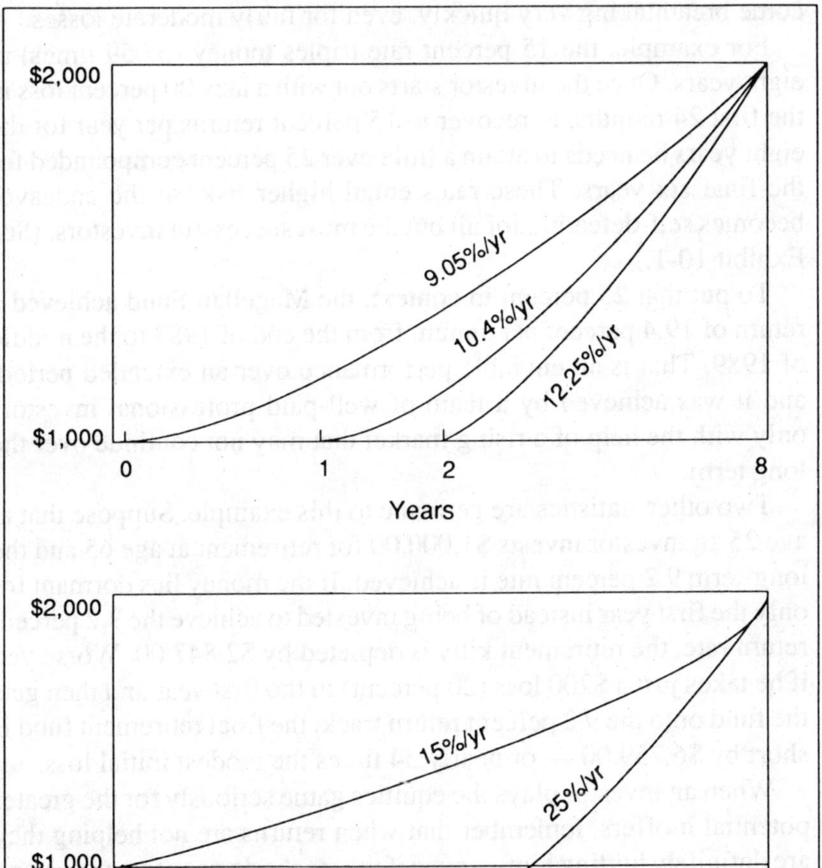

percent average return is imposed, the required catch-up paces become breathtaking very quickly, even for fairly moderate losses.

For example, the 15 percent rate triples money (3.059 times) in eight years. Once the investor starts out with a lazy 20 percent loss in the first 24 months, to recover to 15 percent returns per year for the eight years he needs to attain a little over 25 percent compounded for the final six years. These rates entail higher risk, so the endeavor becomes self-defeating for all but the most successful investors. (See Exhibit 10-1.)

To put that 25 percent in context, the Magellan Fund achieved a return of 19.4 percent per annum from the end of 1983 to the middle of 1989. That is an enviable performance over an extended period, and it was achieved by a team of well-paid professional investors only with the help of a rising market that may not continue over the long term.

Two other statistics are germane to this example. Suppose that at age 25 an investor invests $1,000.00 for retirement at age 65 and the long-term 9.2 percent rate is achieved. If the money lies dormant for only the first year instead of being invested to achieve the 9.2 percent return rate, the retirement kitty is depleted by $2,847.00. Worse yet, if he takes just a $200 loss (20 percent) in the first year and then gets the fund onto the 9.2 percent return track, the final retirement fund is short by $6,759.00 — or nearly 34 times the modest initial loss.

When an investor plays the equities game seriously for the greater potential it offers, remember that when returns are not helping they are definitely hurting him — even if the stocks do no worse than stand still. Therefore, unless the investor is actually allowing profits to run, investing patience is no virtue. Keep this in mind whenever hold/sell inertia sets in.

Avoiding Losses

A corollary of money's time value, and a sadly-neglected topic, is the importance of avoiding losses. The central objective of equity market participation is to keep making profits over time on balance, much like the effect of compound interest on a sum deposited in the bank. Expect ups and downs, but look for the main trend to go up. So the goal should be to increase capital more rapidly than is possible in risk-free investments such as the bank or T-bills. The key to making big money in the stock market lies not in making the big gain. The key is not losing money.

The overriding importance of not losing money is illustrated in the old saw about the two rules for successful investing:

Rule #1: *Never lose money.*
Rule #2: *Always follow rule #1.*

The closer and more constant attention an investor pays to not losing money, the more disciplined is his approach to selling. To make good returns in the stock market (or in other investment media, for that matter), an investor must both buy right and sell right. Once a stock is owned, the entire focus of attention and effort must shift to the only remaining relevant challenge: executing a close-out of the position with a successful sale.

A successful sale is not defined by the resulting gain or loss reported for tax purposes; the key is the subsequent action of the stock sold and subsequent action of other available investments. If the sold stock goes down or sideways in price, or even if it goes up less than the general market (adjusted for beta), the sale is a well-executed decision.

In order to succeed at not losing money, an investor must deal with objective realities as much as possible and must sort out and discard to whatever extent possible the emotional, the irrelevant and the misleading. If a stock is in a declining trend, rallies in price or good fundamental news items that do not reverse that trend serve only to create false hope. These developments encourage the owner to hold on because he believes prosperity is just around the corner.

But as indicated earlier, an optimistic mind-set rejuvenated by short-term, contra-trend positive feedback can be a serious impediment to achieving capital gains. The reason is that false hope tends to forestall the decision to sell at times when logic alone dictates a smart sell order. Simple and obvious as it may seem, the way to make maximum profits is to buy at the bottom of declines and to sell at the top of rallies. The losses to be avoided consist not only of actual sales below cost, but also of missed opportunities to capture the better price available on rallies in the interim.

There are several dimensions to the admonition in the first rule. The first, in an ideal and perfect world which does not exist, is to buy stocks that do not go down. Failing the ability to bat a thousand in that zero-defects game, an investor must do his best at the next-best alternatives. His capital at all times consists of the value of assets minus liabilities. In the stock market, some days capital goes up and other days it goes down. Each day — in fact, even from moment to moment — he experiences gains and losses as the prices of stocks rise and fall.

Anatomy of a Loss

If an investor buys a stock at 20, watches it go to 30 and then holds on while it falls back to 22, he has suffered just as great a dollar loss as if he had bought it at 20 and watched in horror as it shriveled to 12. The loss of eight points is every bit as real in the 20/30/22 case as in the 20/12 disaster scenario. He probably does not feel as bad about the retreat to 22 because he still has a profit, but he ought to. Even though it is impossible to catch the exact tops and bottoms and although he cannot expect a profit on every position, that loss from 30 to 22 is a very real loss in terms of opportunity. He missed out on the opportunity to cash in at 30 and do whatever he wanted with the money he would get at that price. Now he has only 22 left. So in addition to actual losses that get recorded on Form 1040 Schedule D, he wants to avoid these opportunity losses.

Then there is an even more subtle kind of opportunity loss related to the time value of money. The investor is stung when a stock goes from 20 to 12. He feels unlucky when it goes 20/30/22, but feels that is not quite as bad. But chances are that he does not feel bad at all when the stock just holds steady at 20 — or more realistically, when the price fluctuates around 20 for a prolonged period of time. Unless he is collecting a good current income in the form of solid dividend payments or is successfully writing out-of-the-money options against his flat-priced stock, he is losing money.

Again, this is not a loss he can deduct for taxes. And it is not a painful loss. It might get painful if the general market is zooming north and all his friends are gloating about their big winners. But among the three kinds of losses described here, it is, predictably, the least painful and therefore the most insidious.

A stock going nowhere, although not as damaging as a stock shrinking in price, is still a source of opportunity loss and, therefore, it is producing a real loss. First, the money could be in the bank, T-bills or short-term municipals, earning some interest and not at risk in the market.

Second, with the cost of living generally on the rise, the dollar tomorrow is worth less than the dollar today in purchasing power. Third, the holder is losing the one non-renewable resource he owns in life: time. While his stock meanders back and forth around the familiar 20 level, he is missing the chance to make money in other stocks.

And finally, he is suffering a psychic loss: he is becoming frustrated at the market and/or is losing confidence in his own market-playing abilities. And this negative thinking is doing damage, even if only subtly, to his ability to make other investment decisions coolly and smartly.

So setting aside the psychic cost, there are three kinds of money losses caused by underperformance in the market. There is the actual Schedule D loss, the loss in the form of profits not taken and then "given back" on paper, and the loss of time value when a stock sits at the same price.

In the real world, stock prices continue to fluctuate. The investor's job is to take advantage of the ebb and flow of prices. He sees a stock that is undervalued and he buys. But in order to cash in and realize the reward for buying cheap, he must also sell dear to capture the difference. He can always buy the same stock back later. Buying and selling does not make him a trader or a short-termer. Once he buys, he must sell or he becomes a collector with a full cupboard. Then he will be out of the game until he finds more money.

Suppose that for some combination of reasons an investor is relatively comfortable with the fundamental prospects of a company whose stock has an overall flat price over the long term. If he is extremely foresightful and a little lucky too, he could divine the annual tops and bottoms in the stock, and buy in and sell out a number of times over the years.

In that way, he would make much more money than by holding because, in the long term, the price seems to come back to its old level. In fact, that is the only way he will make money in such a stock (beyond dividends or option premiums). Buying it at 20 and never selling it, or many years later finally selling it at 20, is a tremendous opportunity loss compared with taking advantage of periodic fluctuations as they occur.

But investors should not be frustrated if they cannot capture *all* of the swing. Take what seems reasonable, what is in agreement with past patterns. If the stock that stuck around 20 periodically swings between 15 and 25, an investor certainly is doing a creditable job by buying around 17 and giving it to someone else at 23. So do not be afraid to pay a broker a little for the opportunity to nail down profits because moving out will prevent expensive opportunity losses, which are just as real as any other kind of loss.

CHAPTER

11

Calibrate Decision-Making to Personal Emotions

KEY TO INVESTMENT SUCCESS

- Know the Personal Warning Signs

The worry threshold can be avoided in most investments by limiting buying size and by selling when emotional concern rises. But most investors sell from worry when a market bottom occurs — not at market tops when their emotions *should* act as a signal to worry.

For example, the presence of gloating and smugness should signal concern about pending buy decisions that most likely are inappropriate. Gloating can consist of such behaviors as uncharacteristic celebrations, self-congratulations, bragging or an unscheduled counting of the chips — all of which propel an unwary investor into putting more cash into the market just when he should sell instead.

Remember that an investor must *lean into market emotions* as a contrarian. And the harder the winds are blowing, the more firmly he must lean into them. By definition, recall, a major bottom occurs in an atmosphere of fear and gloom, sometimes panic. Major tops form when investors are at their most euphoric; when all the newer buyers have come in and all the older players have exhausted their buying power, the balance literally must shift to the downside because there are no more buyers.

This point of overoptimism defines a top. When the euphoria gets to him, the investor must do exactly the opposite of what his emotions support: he must sell. Once that critical psychological signal that a top is at hand is received, he must not rationalize inaction, tell himself he can get one more eighth of a point or get swept away by the excitement of his peers.

Each investor has his own emotional reaction as a top arrives. Because this reaction is his most important personal indicator of the need for action, it is worthwhile to describe those reactions to each type of market move on paper in order to identify the most accurate personal signals. Some of those may include:

- Self-Congratulations: usually occurs gradually when an investor has a single major winner over time, and no offsetting losers or several large winners. These occurrences can signal taking profits because the market has performed well and is nearing a high.

- Smugness: can occur when there is a spectacular success in the portfolio or a run of several consecutive heady gains. If the investor starts to feel he has learned the secret formula for winning that cannot miss, it is a signal to sell.
- Strong Confidence: even the quiet, self-contained investor is not out of the woods emotionally when, secretly savoring his success, he notes that things have been going extremely well lately. The contained person usually does not recognize the feeling as a danger (sell) signal because it is so moderate — but it can be an important if subtle event.

Smugness and related emotions are danger signals because ultimately they produce two behavioral problems for the investor, and paradoxically they are opposites: one is hyperactive play and the other is inaction that results from complacency.

An example of excessive or hyperactive play is the investor who opens his first margin account, drains his savings for the big plunge, uses his new buying power to the maximum or speculates in situations that have an uncharacteristic high-risk/high-reward profile. Multiply this unnaturally aggressive behavior by just thousands of investors and there is a classic overheated market. Hindsight calls that market period a top.

Aggressive trading behavior like this is permitted only by a feeling of overconfidence, which is usually experienced only in the context of a highly successful recent history. Some investors increase the number of positions they hold, open new brokerage accounts, raise their level of activity, take on higher-than-typical risks, or become so satisfied and happy with their success that they hold their stocks stubbornly for imagined futher gains. In each of these instances, the investor is doing the wrong thing: he is either buying or holding when selling is the right course of action. Therefore at the first sign of any of these reactions, take it as a strong warning sign and sell.

For many investors, feelings or hunches alone are not a sufficient signal that the time to sell has come; for them, overt action is the key indicator to watch for. Investors who try to control and override their own feelings must examine past and current actions in relation to the stock market as a gauge to help them discover what works as a true signal.

It is unlikely that any investor exhibits all of the symptomatic behaviors of overconfidence; no one is by nature more right or wrong, or more valid a signal than another. The key is to identify which ones apply and then take selling action when they crop up.

This process of definition and discovery can lead to a second-level problem — an intensified need to become alert and ready to act (i.e., to sell stocks). This is because the investor becomes aware of what personal triggers signal trouble and he begins to block or suppress those actions when greed kicks in. When an investor reaches this stage of awareness, he must use a more sensitive screen; he should begin to interpret the mere impulse to act, even if it is overridden eventually.

Personal Warning Signs

Common actions that should act as danger signals range from cautious to bold; whatever his personally relevant signals, the investor should remain aware of them and not become judgmental or self-righteous in comparing self with others. Seven actions typically are key indicators:

- Quietly confiding investment successes to others
- Spending increased time on market study
- Openly bragging about winners or a hot streak
- Celebrating in unaccustomed ways
- Counting the chips

- Adding more money (including use of margin)
- Playing the new-issues game

These signals are listed in qualitative order of increasing severity. If these behaviors are absent from an investor's reaction repertoire, he should not necessarily take comfort in noting their absence; most people practice some variation on these themes.

In crossing the dividing line between feeling reactions and taking actions, probably the most restrained behavior is the quiet confession of successes. This is, of course, not a case of bursting into a colleague's office and announcing that XYZ stock just jumped six points for a 50 percent profit. It merely means letting others know "how it's going" in the market. It may be an unpretentious comment when someone else mentions his own success or frustration with a recent investment, or an opportunity missed in a roaring rally. It may be as innocent or intimate as mentioning how well it is going if that is not something the investor usually divulges. The point is, if an investor is not regularly in the habit of sharing personal financial affairs with others, the exception is noteworthy and should be considered a signal.

Spending an increased amount of time studying the market, devising systems, researching companies or reading advisory reports also can be a signal. Although serious study is good, excessive attention to trading can be a signal that the investor is excited; this occurs only when the market has run up quite a distance already. Collectively, advisory services reach subscription peaks at or just after market tops. So does trading volume. So does the number of people deciding on a career in brokerage.

An investor paying much more attention than usual should watch out. It may be time to direct that energy toward stocks that should be cashed in rather than toward new buys. But beware: a broker is very unlikely to comment disparagingly about new-found investor interest. More frequent calls to a broker can lead to more trading, usually in the form of buying.

More toward the overt end of the reaction scale is active bragging about trading successes. This usually means going out of the way to inform others about remarkable investment conquests or airing financial affairs in the presence of outsiders. When the investor behaves uncharacteristically in this way, it is a selling signal. Remember that bragging in any form occurs not after failure, loss or price decline, but after one or (usually) more successes. And contrarian opinion predicts a reversal after a series of rises. The fact that the investments have performed beyond normal expectation suggests that the bull market has been running for a while. Therefore, assume that the top is much closer than the bottom.

Bernard Baruch is reputed to have avoided the October 1929 bloodbath because he used the too-much-talking signal on the part of others as his indicator to sell in the summer and early autumn that year. Why? He noted that even cab drivers and newspaper vendors were talking about their market conquests and dispensing advice. He concluded that there was too much good feeling about the market for it to remain in an upward trend much longer. This was a classic contrarian observation and is akin to the tendency of tops to develop when the market is a frequent front-page story in the national media.

An even more overt behavior is celebrating market success uncharacteristically. Although most everyone goes out to dinner to celebrate a raise or a promotion, it is the *change* in typical celebratory behavior that should be considered significant enough to take action on. One example is taking the whole office out to lunch instead of a spouse or best friend. When the impulse to make a big gesture occurs, cash in some of the chips without further delay.

When the game has been so pleasant and profitable that an investor wants to total up his holdings, a top can be directly at hand. Naturally, the impulse to take an inventory is absent when the market and personal fortunes have declined, or when a listless period of sideways action has occurred. But let the market roar for an extended period or let an investor make several consecutive hot trades, and the desire to stroke the ego is stirred.

This is not to imply that investors should fail to track how they are doing. Take a regular inventory in the form of both historical tables and graphs. The easiest way to do this is to keep securities in street name so that the monthly brokerage statement includes a computerized valuation. Then be sure that all cash infusions and withdrawals are noted promptly so that the tally is kept on a fair basis.

The point is to heed excessive chip-counting because it is never done at bottoms. Valuation normally should occur every three to six months. In fact, some investors use as red flags even the conscious curiosity or semi-serious intention to count the chips too frequently.

Another even more dangerous indicator of a market top based on internal reactions is the decision or serious temptation to add capital to the equity account after a significant market rise. This takes place because the investor erroneously decides the bullish trend is well-established and, therefore, he should increase his exposure. Or he may decide he has an excess of attractive new ideas and — anticipating that price strength will continue — does not want to sell any existing holdings to fund new purchases. In effect, he is acting like the proverbial child in a candy store: he wants one of everything. He, too, will wind up with a bellyache when the feeding frenzy is over.

A variation of the adding-money warning is the substitute practice of selling in order to buy. This pattern occurs in cases where the market already has risen substantially, increasing the investor's excitement and storehouse of allegedly attractive ideas — especially when there are no funds to add to the account. Therefore in order to satisfy the urge to buy into the new ideas, he liquidates one or more existing positions not on their own merits, but as a source of funds to pay for greater excitement.

This substitute behavior is a good example of how the failure to exercise a specific red-flag behavior should not be excused. If the investor seriously *considers* adding to his stake after a long rise or if he sells in order to buy, the signal is just as validly in effect.

Ideally, each sale should be timed and made on its own merit. Over time as a market's cycle matures, a diversified portfolio gradually should be liquidated as an increasing number of stocks reach or exceed reasonable or targeted price levels. Unless the investor has identified truly counter-cyclical issues to buy at that time, the multiple sales he makes should act as a signal of topping out rather than as a ready source of funding for new buys.

A wary investor also should be suspicious if there is the urge to sell existing positions to move funds into new issues (initial public offerings). It is very likely he has become psychologically overheated by the market environment because he sees so many stocks doing well and hears so many friends bragging about their successes.

He also, typically, is getting no encouragement from brokers to sell at a time like this. They are enjoying the ride too, and are in a positive frame of mind. Their training, dependence on trading commissions and refusal to rain on client parades by suggesting that even bull markets come to an end all mean the investor will have to lean against the tide in order to sell in a timely manner. The investor will get a lot of unsolicited broker suggestions about new ideas to play, so the temptation to put in more chips will feel overwhelming.

Any or all of these phenomena should suggest an extended or overheated market that threatens to top out soon. So again, heed the signal and sell. Selling at the time can be a lonely exercise, but the reward is that the crowd is usually wrong and the contrarian usually correct. So when tempted to add money or when the list of "I oughtta buys" is getting long, sell instead.

There *are* some conscientious brokers who have the moral fortitude not to pander to a client's overexcitement when they personally believe it is time to sell. So get help from this kind of broker by asking one to give a loud warning as soon as an over-confident behavior arises. Incidentally, if a broker refuses to participate in this arrangement or says it is unnecessary because the market is in no danger, consider that a strong, probably urgent, signal to sell.

C H A P T E R

12

Adjusting Sale Targets Rationally

KEYS TO INVESTMENT SUCCESS

- The Price Objective
- Modifications

Most investors inevitably wonder if the market plays fair; this chapter demonstrates that stocks go where they want to despite what investors think is justified and despite what they wish would happen. For example, price objectives that seem valid to an investor when first established, i.e., the price he wants, tend to be generated by what he concludes initially is attainable. But what any investor *wants* is irrelevant, so it is important to avoid developing a concrete mind-set about price objectives.

Be prepared as well to let go of original price opinions, if or when events warrant a change. Remain flexible and realistic, rather than unreasonably optimistic and/or obstinate. An investor who is unable or unwilling to change — to become right — is doomed to lose.

There are two primary ways to stray off the track when setting price objectives:

- The initial idea, including the selling-price objective, may have been wrong from the start.
- Although right at first, the original idea can become outdated and, therefore, inaccurate as subsequent events transpire.

In both cases, original thinking can be either overly-optimistic or unnecessarily pessimistic. It is important to re-examine the market environment constantly in search of inputs that warrant adjusting the scenario on proper valuation. When analyzing the environment, do not be selective — noting only those factors that support the starting thesis. An approach that merely seeks to validate original thinking is worse than valueless because it misleads the stockholder and neglects to prompt valid cautions.

The Price Objective

While reconsidering the price objective, be careful not to become greedy and not to turn into a cheerleader for the stock. Only new and positive information that previously was unanticipated should prompt an upgrade of the price target. If good news — a new product, a contract won, strong EPS, a higher dividend or even a takeover proposal — is in line with earlier reasons for buying the stock, note merely that a part of the projected scenario is coming to pass and that the stock may begin to achieve the price objective. Do not double count such positives.

If good news does occur, it then becomes important to remain calm; excitement over the good news should not overwhelm judgment just because everything is going so well. The investor who counts positive factors twice is engaging in self-delusion. There are both positive and negative factors that legitimately prompt a reassessment of price objectives and they should be studied in light of two strong caveats: (1) price paid does not matter and, (2) while there may be reasons to cut the price objective while a stock is held, do not allow that decision to prompt lowering a stop-loss order.

It is generally not a good idea to use stop-loss orders. This heretical position is expounded in Chapter 19. But if entered, stops must not be pulled or lowered, or they become useless. They may actually become worse than useless because they provide false comfort if later allowed not to stick.

When examining a potential equity investment, an investor makes a number of assumptions, any of which can be unconscious or wrong. Some of those buying assumptions are:

- Information sources are accurate and disinterested.
- Something good will happen fundamentally.
- That event will be big enough to move price meaningfully.
- That event is not already anticipated in the price.
- Interest rates will be at a certain level, influencing the general level of future stock prices.
- The psychology of the market, irrespective of fundamentals such as earnings and interest rates, will be in a certain state.

- The projected price is not out of line with demonstrably reasonable valuation standards such as yield or P/E ratio.
- Major developments in the industry or in relevant sectors of the economy will create or allow the expected price climate.
- Political and/or geopolitical factors will be as expected.
- The projected scenario can happen in the time window used.
- The investor is not oblivious to important factors which, if known, would temper his enthusiasm or make him think the stock is not undervalued.
- He has not been misled deliberately.
- The world will go on as it is now.
- There will not be positive or negative wild cards in play.

Modifications

As indicated earlier, each of these factors may be in play when the buying decision is made, but they cannot all be expected to remain stable. So set a reasonable selling target for the stock at the outset, but understand that any target becomes subject to immediate and ongoing modification because the world does not stand still. Assume that change *will* occur.

Suppose, for example, that an investor is attracted to a certain drug company because it has a good record of increasing earnings and occupies a leading position in prescription preparations for diseases of the elderly, a growing population sector. The market in general has been soft lately, so as a contrarian, he senses the opportunity to buy a fundamentally attractive stock at a good price.

He checks several sources of earnings estimates and projects that at an historically realistic relative P/E ratio the stock could sell at $38 in 18 months, despite a current $28 quote. So he buys, setting $38 as the objective. (Actually, he should plan to sell out below his objective so that a 100 percent perfect analysis is not required to generate acceptable locked-in profits.)

Any of the factors in the list above is subject to change, so it is appropriate that the investor be ready to adjust the price objective for cashing in. Here are just some things that could go wrong:

- Product tampering on an over-the-counter medicine could hurt the company or cast a psychological pall over the whole group.
- Management could signal upcoming fluctuations in earnings due to product-testing and R&D costs, whereas smooth earnings had been the general expectation.
- The value of the dollar could fluctuate, changing translations of foreign costs or earnings.
- A strike may disrupt production or supplies of materials.
- The federal deficit could widen, putting pressure on medical reimbursements and/or raising interest rates.
- A competing firm could come out with an exciting new drug.
- Generic equivalents could gain market penetration faster than earlier expected.
- Tax or antitrust legislation could dampen takeover appeal across the board, causing drug stocks to lose attraction.
- The company could be sued by a competitor for patent infringement, or by the government for poor testing procedures or for antitrust violations by the industry.
- The market could become speculative, abandoning traditional growth stocks in favor of short-term concept plays.
- Tax laws could make dividends more attractive than growth.
- Margin regulations could be tightened.
- Fund managers could decide other industries are more interesting.
- On further reading, the investor could discover that some of the good things projected already were predicted by a major brokerage, implying that the remaining upside is smaller than he thought.
- Wild-card trouble of some sort could develop.

And here are some good things that could happen:

- Management could announce an unexpected but promising new drug.
- Major magazines could feature the stock as one of the top ten to buy for the next year, raising awareness and price.
- Tax laws more favorable to R&D could be proposed or enacted.
- Economic forecasts could shift toward the positive, implying that stocks are due for a more extended rise than earlier had been thought reasonable.
- Mild recession talk could develop, cutting interest rates and moving investors toward defensive industry groups such as drugs.
- A change in control of the White House or Congress could occur, implying more spending on health or reduced regulation.
- An existing company drug could be discovered to have positive side effects in the treatment of a second major disease.
- The company could have a breakthrough in research on a hot drug type for treating AIDS or cancer.
- The company could announce a restructuring designed to enhance shareholder value.
- A well-known corporate raider could take a position in this stock — or in another one within the industry.
- An actual take-over or share buy-back could be announced.
- Earnings could rise above estimates for sustainable reasons.
- Favorable foreign-exchange fluctuations could occur.
- Positive wild cards could develop.

Tactically, the introduction of dramatic new factors can serve to override previously established estimates of reasonable value. If such major new information arises, expectations must be adjusted up or down. Suppose in the example above, the initial judgment of fair value is $38 and the target for cashing in is $35. Suppose time has elapsed and other factors have not changed (unlikely), or there have been offsetting pluses and minuses that leave the target unchanged.

The investor has been lucky and the price is now at $33.50. Suddenly, a bid is made for another drug company by the Japanese. This opens a new round of potentials on the upside. The valuation numbers may get historically full, but the market senses that a phase of bidding up is just starting. The holder might suspend temporarily his resolve to sell at $35 because the sights for all drug stocks are going to be raised.

Suppose instead that a hostile bid comes in for the company. The bid is $40 and the stock goes to $41 in hopes that another shoe will drop. The investor thinks $40 is fundamentally excessive and he may be right. But if management, normally circumspect and credible, advises shareholders not to act hurriedly and to anticipate a possible company response that could raise prices further, he should suspend his standard of reasonableness by a few points and sell on the next concrete positive news. He must remain fluid but totally logical, and yet not get carried away with enthusiasm. The question, "Would I buy it now?" is always a revealing aid.

Now look at a few negative jolts. A major externality, as the economists call it, such as an oil embargo threatens to disrupt the economic expansion or to boost inflation sharply. Bonds and stocks will fall across the board, regardless of the attractiveness of specific companies or their present relative undervaluations.

P/E ratios, driven by rising yields, generally will fall, forcing the investor's relative-P/E-derived target lower. His stock remains undervalued, but at a lower price. And the timeframe for a possible realization of his scenario is considerably lengthened because inflation takes a long time to quiet down. He must lower his target, perhaps selling immediately regardless of the paper gain or loss. His old target literally has become an irrelevant relic of a past time.

Case Studies

Other major factors, not even related directly to the company, can force a lowering of targets. For example, companies in other high-technology or growth industries such as computers start reporting disappointing earnings. As a result, the bloom is off the rose for many growth stocks with traditionally high multiples even though their specific fundamentals may be unchanged.

So analysts cut EPS estimates. Investors trim their levels of tolerable risk. On seeing signs that a major shift is occurring among institutional investors, assume that — right or wrong — this new trend will take some time to play out; it will end with prices lower and attitudes less favorable toward the growth drug company than they are today.

In this scenario, the investor's earnings forecast may prove correct, but his relative P/E ratio proves too high for the timeframe originally established for cashing in. The psychological damage may take a long time to repair. On a multi-company scale, he is looking at the longer-term equivalent of a company announcing good news on a day when the market is down 40 points on heavy volume. The positive fundamentals are swept away by the negative psychological tide of the time. So he must adjust his expectations or he will be holding to a now-unrealistic goal.

Now look at a less dramatic case that also illustrates the need to modify targets. Say an investor in late 1989 purchased Long Island Lighting Company (LILCo). The company, under an agreement with the State of New York, has scrapped its costly Shoreham plant and will get needed rate hikes for several years. It is publicly-committed to dividend rates of $1.00, $1.50 and $2.00 by the years 1989, 1990 and 1991. The downside scenario for late 1991 is that even if no further small dividend increases are in prospect at that time, the stock should sell on an eight percent current-yield basis, or at $25. That implies a very attractive total return over 24 months from a buy price in the 17 range.

And downside risk appears limited because the regulatory climate has been resolved. Assume that in late 1991, the directors are to raise payments to $0.50 quarterly. What would cause an investor to modify the $25-minimum target? Suppose that inflation has gone higher, pushing interest rates up. Or suppose that rumblings of financial trouble in New York City require another bailout from Albany, with higher taxes and a generally negative climate toward New York stocks resulting. In either of these cases, LILCo would sell on a higher yield basis than projected. The investor should lower his price target accordingly rather than stubbornly holding out for $25.

Conversely if disinflation or a mild recession sets in, interest rates would work lower and defensive stocks would enjoy a period in the sun. In such circumstances, closing out the two-year position on LILCo early at the target of $25 would be too rigid a policy and would cut off realistic prospects for further gain. In either case (up or down), the buyer had originally assumed a constant interest-rate climate, but history provided plenty of reason to expect that some change, rather than none, should be experienced in two years. So the investor should remain flexible.

Sale-price targets must be set from the start or there is no focus and no discipline. But those targets must be written in pencil because circumstances will change. And the ego must be firmly under control so that changing the target is not a psychological problem. The mind should remain fluid, looking for important factors to add to the equation as plus or minus adjustments to the price objective.

It is critical, and by no means easy, to sort out in real time the truly important from the passing and trivial. It is crucial to resist emotional tides and take action only after the mood of the crowd has abated. The market moves to manic tops as well as to panic bottoms, so the investor must adjust targets and risk tolerances for such extremes. And at all times, he must be mindful of the need to remain dispassionate by resisting the temptation to become a holder turned loyalist or cheerleader. Again, the critical question should be asked: "If I did not own the stock already, would I buy it today at the current price?" If the honest answer is not affirmative, it is time to cash in and move on.

CHAPTER

13

A Suggested Exercise in Self-Discipline

KEY TO INVESTMENT SUCCESS

- A Tutorial for Options Novices

It is said that there is no substitute for experience. In the real world where decisions are required in an on-line, real-time mode, experience picks up and fills in where theory ends. In making decisions to hold or to sell stocks, reality is a great teacher. In fact, the decision to hold generally is not conscious; usually it is an action by default. The purpose of the non-decision to hold is to spare the investor the tension of making the decision to sell and of actually executing that decision. This chapter presents an exercise that helps investors learn the discipline necessary to make the selling decision conscious.

In this exercise, investors are asked to buy options; worse yet, short-term options. This experience, carefully chosen and timed as outlined here, has a great deal of educational and psychological value that does not exist in a paper exercise. An imaginary experiment with options cannot teach the lesson of urgency and discipline that is required for real market trading because there is no money involved in the fantasy. And no emotions are involved, including the pitfalls of and tactics to use against greed, fear, pain and elation. The profits are not real, so they are not exciting enough to cause mistakes.

In a similar way, there is no means to create true time urgency artificially. One of the aspects of selling that subtly leads investors to fail is the lack of closure point: the market opens up again tomorrow, so the game continues if an investor does not take action to stop it. It will continue until he takes such action. If he never takes the action, the game goes on in spite of him (and because of him); he has become a collector rather than an investor.

Options have a unique characteristic which makes them ideal for teaching discipline: they have a finite life. There is an absolute end to each option's life: the Friday afternoon before the third Saturday of the month. So there is no time-out. Option-holders must sell or exercise, or lose whatever value remains. (Some brokerage firms exercise *for* the option-holder if he fails to respond to expiration notices and if there is enough value to cover round-turn commissions.)

Although this exercise entails probable cost (there is a way to minimize the cost), consider that cost worth the opportunity to learn how to make a decision to sell in a real-world environment.

Assume that the options are calls because people usually think in bullish terms and because understanding value in these contracts is easier if the investor is an options novice.

To limit the possible net cost of the exercise, buy options that have a very short period of time remaining to expiration — about two weeks is a good period for this purpose. Further, choose a stock whose trading price is at, or slightly above or below, a multiple of $5.00, which is the multiple of striking prices on listed options.

Finally, select a stock that is relatively stable or nonvolatile and provides a good dividend yield. All three of the suggested criteria — short remaining life, proximity to strike price and underlying price stability — will contribute to a low exposure in terms of dollars.

A good example is a telephone or electric utility stock. Choose a company with a record of ongoing annual dividend increases in order to avoid falling into a snakepit by accident. Also, be sure that the stock does not go ex-dividend during the option-holding period. And do not purchase in the month the company reports quarterly earnings (i.e, the month after the quarter ends).

For illustration, assume that on or about September 1, 10 calls on XYZ Electric Service are bought with a strike price of $25 and expiration September 16. Suppose the stock is trading at $25.25 at the time and that ⅜ is paid on a limit order for the options, plus commission.

For 10 calls, which give the right to buy 1,000 shares, $375 plus commission is put on the line. Thus a game is created that must be played actively. The goal is to make money. The secondary goal, or fall-back position, is to minimize loss. Consider the clock an enemy, and a helpful goad as well.

A Tutorial for Options Novices

For options novices, following is a description of the purchase: A call option is a contract which allows its owner the right to buy 100 shares of the related underlying common stock at a specified price (strike price) up to and including a specific date or expiration.

In this case, each call entitles an investor to buy 100 shares of XYZ Electric at $25 per share up to market close on September 16. After that moment, the option will have expired with zero value if it is not exercised. It can be sold at any time before it expires, thereby transferring the right to a new buyer. With the stock trading above the strike price, namely at 25 ¼ per share, the option has intrinsic value: it can be exercised now and the stock would be worth above the 25 paid on exercise. The option is inherently worth the difference, or ¼. But the option trades above that intrinsic value due to its remaining life. It has a time value, although in this example there is only minimal speculative value to that time. So ⅜ as a total price is realistic.

Sometime between purchase date and expiration date, the time-value premium of ⅛ essentially disappears and the option trades at intrinsic value alone. But this disappearance of premium for time happens late in the game — so late that the slight premium should be paid in order to buy a remaining game that will take enough time to be a useful teacher.

The object is to come out of this trading experience with as much money as possible and with a new-found sense of urgency and decisiveness about the choice to hold or to sell. As noted earlier, nothing forces an equity investor to make a decision about selling. If he holds today, he can think about it again tomorrow. And if he holds tomorrow, there always is another trading day after that. With a stock, there is no imperative closure deadline.

But option rules are different. There is no escaping the expiration date; a decision must be made. Playing this option trading game intensifies on a daily basis all the feelings normally experienced

Exhibit 13-1: Option Market Value

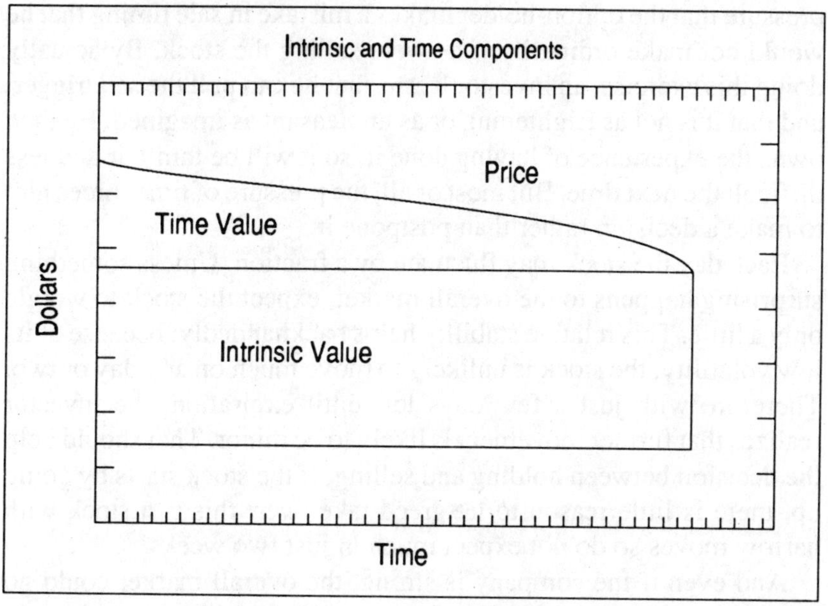

when a stock is owned. But a sense of urgency is overlaid because of the approach of expiration. (See Exhibit 13-1.)

If an investor buys a two-week contract, 10 percent of his profit window disappears the first day. With four days left, 25 percent of the time horizon evaporates the next day. With two days left, it is 50 percent. He must decide to act today or accept tomorrow's verdict.

Normally when an investor owns a stock, he feels good when it rises; he wants more and fears giving back the paper gains. When it goes down, he resents the loss and fears the price may evaporate further, causing more loss. But because it is a stock, he can stretch out the time horizon, and let the stock and the general market do what they will. He is under no requirement to sell at any time.

The option, by contrast, dies at a known time. So choices are defined within a very specific time window.

This tension is unpleasant. Often, passing time generates such pressure that the option-holder makes a mistake in sale timing that he would not make ordinarily if he were selling the stock. By actually doing this exercise, an investor learns that he can pull the sell trigger, and that it is not as frightening or as unpleasant as imagined. He then owns the experience of having done it, so it will be familiar and less difficult the next time. But most of all, the pressure of time forces him to make a decision rather than postpone it.

Each day the stock may fluctuate by a fraction. Unless something surprising happens to the overall market, expect the stock to wiggle only a little. This relative stability helps backhandedly; because of its low volatility, the stock is unlikely to move much on any day or two. Therefore with just a few days left until expiration, the investor realizes that further movement is likely to be minor. That should help the decision between holding and selling. If the stock starts by going up, there is little reason to let greed take over: this is a stock with narrow moves so do not expect much in just two weeks.

And even if the company is strong, the overall market could go down tomorrow or the next day for some reason, taking away the gain swiftly with only a brief opportunity for possible recovery before expiration. If the stock instead begins by going down, the investor does not have the luxury of being a trader-turned-collector: the game will end on the appointed expiration date, and his job is to salvage what he can.

The point is to try to get the best execution in the remaining days. Early in the game, there is a time premium that can be sold to someone else. But later on, the value of that premium is consumed as a price for having stayed in the game.

Note that the emotional effect of each fluctuation is intensified. For example, a mere ¼-point rise in the stock's price virtually doubles the option price. The investor starts thinking that if it would go up just a dollar he could make several hundred percent. But the press of time should curb such wild imaginings.

What if the rally reverses and he starts giving back what he earned? He will be tighter on the trigger than if he owned the stock, which he could keep holding for months in hope or in stubbornness. If he owned the stock, a ¼-point rise would cheer him little if at all because he would know the stock is typically stable and might give it back in a week just in normal fluctuation. And by owning the stock rather than the option, he is signalling a possible long-term relationship that he does not intend to terminate for just a quarter-point.

But with the option, he is in a damage-control mode in which he must pay a second commission to get the best price in two weeks' time. Should he hold and take another eighth's risk — or cash in now? What if he cashes in to end the risk and tension, and the stock runs to 26 but corrects back to 25 ¼ a week later?

No matter whether the stock rises, falls or holds steady in the first week or so, if he is still holding the options, he will have completely forgotten the meaning of the phrase "Thank goodness it's Friday." The Friday deadline will be a sword of Damocles hanging over his head, forcing him to make a decision. If he holds, each day of no change or fractional loss leaves him less time for potential gain or for recouping losses. He starts looking at each eighth or quarter of fluctuation as a big percentage against his stake — and it is. But the time constraint allows him no chance to relax because all could be lost with one wrong decision to hold too long. The option could go to 1⁄16. Or it could be 1⁄16 offered, no bid. So he will decide not to allow himself to forfeit everything he has put on the table.

Expect that the decision will not be perfect. Unless it is sold very late into the two weeks, the stock and the option will probably have time to tick up above the exit level at some point before the final bell tolls. So learn to accept that result as virtually inevitable. Do not expect to beat the market for all the profit it offers. Then learn to live with the choice and move on to the next situation. This exerise in decisiveness may cost a few hundred dollars. Consider it tuition well spent.

CHAPTER

14

Separate Selling From New Buying

KEYS TO INVESTMENT SUCCESS

- Rotational Group Leadership
- Beware of the Simultaneous Switch

There are several reasons why investors should not sell stock to raise funds in order to buy stock. It is frequently true that a stock sale transacted solely to fund a new purchase is a double mistake: the sale can be badly timed and the purchase can be badly-chosen or poorly-timed. Based on a matrix of relative post-switch performance, the odds (unweighted by frequency of occurrence) are 5:2 against a successful transaction. (See Exhibit 14-1.)

Exhibit 14-1: Relative Post-Switch Performance

		Action of Replacement Bought				
		Up More	Equal Move	Down More or Up Less	Flat	Down
Action of Old Stock Sold	Up	Good	Out Comm's Cost	Bad	Bad	Bad
	Flat	Good	Out Comm's Cost	N.M.	Out Comm's Cost	Bad
	Down	Good	Out Comm's Cost	Bad	Good	Out Comm's Cost

In general, the odds are more favorable if an investor is buying but not selling, or selling but not buying, at any given time — rather than doing both at the same time. The exceptions to this guideline involve pinpoint accuracy in detecting rotational group leadership in the general market, or just plain blind luck. Smart investors dismiss blind luck. It is something to accept when it happens, but not something to count on. That leaves rotational group leadership.

Rotational Group Leadership

Significant stock market movements tend to carry the majority of stocks with them in one overall direction — either up or down. In fact, market historians and technicians use a tool called a "diffusion index" (see in Chapter 15) as an indicator to detect the end of an advance. By definition, a top occurs when a majority of stocks is no longer moving up within the timeframe studied.

Because the majority of stocks move in the same direction most of the time, mathematically the odds do not favor the investor or trader who buys one stock and sells another at the same time. If the market is in a period of broad advance, the odds indicate that both the stock currently held as well as the proposed buy candidate are advancing. Conversely if a declining period is to follow the switching action, the odds favor both the stock currently held and its proposed replacement moving lower at the same time.

Naturally there are exceptions, as in any case in which mathematical probabilities are operating. But the odds exist as described above and, over time, an investor fares better by playing on the side of the odds rather than against them. Most expert advice steers investors away from situations in which the odds are heavily negative and toward seizing those opportunities in which the probability of winning is higher.

As described above, the single exception to not selling and buying at the same time involves successful timing of group rotation. During a period of market advance, not all stocks rally at the same pace. While the overall bias for the majority of issues generally is to the upside in a bull market, some individual stocks or entire industry groups push ahead for a while even as others seem to lag behind and rest. Then a rotation of leadership takes place; prior laggards come to the front of the pack while the old leaders rest.

At the bottom of a major market cycle, those investors who have the courage to buy at all tend to concentrate in blue-chip stocks. At the top when optimism reigns supreme for weeks or months, speculative fever takes hold and lower-quality issues provide most of the action and the leadership for the rally. This is a very broad, or macro, example of rotational leadership. Industry-oriented rotations take place as well. The industry that leads at any given time depends to some extent on what industry has been lagging lately and, so, becomes more attractive. This has become even more apparent in recent years as money managers use computers to monitor market movements more closely and comprehensively, and more in real time than was the case during the 1970s.

Another factor that affects rotational leadership is the national (or even world) news environment. Depending on what news dominates the media at a given time, certain industry groups lead and others lag. For example if inflation is quiet, the expectation of lower interest rates is likely to develop. Then interest-sensitive industry groups get a play to the upside, including banks, savings & loans, insurance firms and utilities. Housing and automobile-manufacturing stocks may move up in this phase in the expectation that lower interest rates will encourage consumer purchases.

Or if the dollar is low or falling in international value, the idea of a boom in basic industry stocks, supported by favorable changes in export/import trends, can take hold. Steel, machinery and chemicals issues do well in this phase. The point is that in a sustained advance, one group leads for weeks or months only to be supplanted by another.

In this scenario, simultaneously buying one stock and selling another makes statistical sense only if the investor presumes to identify the rotational leadership changes and to act on the timing accurately. This is very difficult to do; and unless he can do that successfully, the statistical odds of his winning in a simultaneous buy and sale are low. The likeliest probability is that both stocks will move up or both will move down.

So except for the possibility of a much greater percentage move in one stock versus the other, there usually is insufficient justification for a sale-purchase switch. To recap, if the preponderance of issues is about to decline, sell and postpone reinvesting the proceeds. When stocks are about to rise, it is better not to sell at the time. Buying is more profitably accomplished with added funds or even through the use of margin. But such choices should come only in a contrarian mode.

Beware of the Simulataneous Switch

There is a dangerous psychology in the purchase and sale in a simultaneous switch. If an investor is buying a stock and is already fully invested, it is probable that he has begun to indulge a prevailing bullish frame of mind to overrule logic. Presumably if he is already so fully invested that a sale is required before he can make a purchase (to generate funds), the market itself might be well into an advance. He is probably not invested fully at the bottom.

As the market moves higher, particularly for a stretch of a few years or at least many months, he begins to see more success stories and to feel some performing stocks are passing him by. The game seems to be easier, the odds more in his favor.

When this scenario develops, it seems a time for the investor to retain what he already owns. Although he also wants to grab for a little more gusto and ride the bull full tilt, he should consider it a warning signal if he feels himself getting into this frame of mind because he is falling prey to prevailing psychology instead of leaning against the trend.

Elsewhere in this book is the suggestion to keep a notebook in which to record market movements, stock actions, personal emotions about the market, personal gain/loss performance and where the focus of personal attention is drawn. If these notations are correlated with past market action over a period of time, this notebook can serve as a useful way to calibrate personal habits against the emotions of the marketplace. The object, of course, is to discern when a good feeling is too good and when a down feeling signals that a bottom is close. The easy way to track market phases is to write in red ink on down days and green for up; blue or black for sideways.

It is a natural human tendency to study the market and individual stock opportunities more intensly as an advance becomes broad and mature. That spreading of enthusiasm is why bull markets occur on rising trading volume over time. So if an investor is caught up in the predominant optimism of the cycle, he is studying possible purchases.

If he is still at this intense study when already fully invested, it is very probable that he is neglecting the selling side of his investment strategy. Remember that the crowd is usually wrong even though it always feels right. So develop an innate sense of contrarianism to serve as a warning signal against the natural, easy thing to do.

In the mid-to-late stages of an advance, the investor should ideally be examining each of his positions to identify which stocks should be retained and which need to be sold. If he is fully invested and has not identified sale candidates, he has been devoting insufficient attention to the selling side of the equation. If he is fully invested and is still spending mental energy looking for new stocks to buy, that is also neglecting sale discipline. Fully committed investors who think about additional buys literally are working on the wrong problem!

So the exercise of selling a stock as a forced activity driven by the need to raise funds for a new purchase reflects an ill-timed or over-optimistic purchase. A surefire way to detect this investment pothole is to note frame of mind and very recent short-term trend action. Is there real excitement about the new buying idea? Does it look more like a sure thing than any other that has come around in a while? Is there fear of missing a major chance by not getting on board right now?

If the answer to any two of these questions is yes, then back off and postpone the buying because it is too late in the current game. In this kind of environment, the buy side of the simultaneous buy and sell is poorly-timed. It is time to sell, but too early to reuse the funds. The time to redeploy funds will come later; a good buying time occurs in the *absence* of excitement — when there are doubts about the market's ability to pick up and rally again. So lean against the tide. Do what feels uncomfortable.

Turning to the mechanics and psychology of the sell side of this proposed sale/purchase combination, how or why is the sell side likely to be a mistake? As stated above if an investor is focused on the buy side, sale questions are getting short shrift so he needs to refocus on selling. If a sale is forced, the sale probably is not well chosen because it is likely to be done in haste. Each sale should be done on its own independent merit and timing.

Visualize here the random-walker's favorite cartoon caricature: a blindfolded investor throwing a dart at the quotation tables and buying the stock he hits. In a similar way, a sale forced by a proposed purchase is equally foolish. In effect, the investor is throwing a dart — not at the price page, but at the calendar. He sets up the sale-timing randomly, without due consideration for the reasons behind sale. He is forcing himself to sell not to benefit from the performance or revised prospects of an owned stock but for a completely unrelated factor: the need for capital driven by a proposed purchase. It is possible, even probable, that a sale made to raise cash on an emergency basis for funding a purchase is a sale poorly chosen among the available alternatives.

Whether a stock is trending upward, downward or sideways in a channel, the best time for its sale is when the price reaches one of its periodic high points along the continuum of fluctuation. If an investor chooses a stock to sell from frustration or boredom, it is likely that the stock has not been acting in a positive way lately. Therefore, it probably is nearer the bottom than the top of its price channel. So it follows that a frustration sale may turn out to be a disadvantageous transaction.

If an investor needs to sell to fund a buy, he should acknowledge that he has a serious problem and should step back to impose self-discipline (some analysts will disagree with this assessment, unless the investor already has a large portfolio). The easiest way is to complete a thorough and logical inventory of all stocks currently held; for each stock, write down the answers to such questions as:

- What is a realistic price target and over what time period (and what is the implied return per annum from today if projections are correct)?
- Is the stock now undervalued, fairly valued or getting full?
- How does the stock match today's market tastes and group leadership patterns?
- Is this a volatile or a stable stock, and what does that imply if the market should correct and move lower?
- If stocks cannot be reviewed for three months, how high on the comfort order for continued "blind" holding would this one be?
- Is this a stock that over-represents in the portfolio one sector of the economy or one industry?
- Would this stock be purchased again today? If yes, why?

CHAPTER

15

Use the Personal Diffusion Index

KEYS TO INVESTMENT SUCCESS

- Advance/Decline Indicators
- The Market Diffusion Indicator

This chapter presents quantitative indicators to use as actual selling signals. It introduces as a useful indicator a "personal diffusion index," which falls under the broad category of technical indicators and, specifically, overbought/oversold timing oscillators. The first few pages describe indicators generally; the later material reveals how to personalize the analysis.

Advance/Decline Indicators

The simplest overbought/oversold indicator is the easy, 10-day total of net advances less declines. This market statistic is tracked by subtracting daily declines from advances (usually on one exchange such as the New York Stock Exchange) to arrive at a net figure for the day. Then the last ten days' daily figures are added, resulting in a number that generally ranges from a few thousand positive to several thousand negative. While precise buy-and-sell signal ranges vary over time depending on the emotion level of the market, following this indicator over a period of months is a useful way to time short-term swings within about two days. One can readily see where the high and low ranges are.

The overbought/oversold indicator is a short-term measurement and is useful only for limited purposes. So is the weekly net advance-decline measurement used by some market analysts. In contrast, many market technicians consider a measurement called the "cumulative advance/decline line" to be one of the more powerful indicators of changing intermediate-term direction in the market. This line is calculated in very much the same way as the 10-day line, except that there is a cumulative total kept from the time the investor starts the project. The current plot of anyone's indicator has exactly the same shape, no matter when the data-collecting start date occurs; but the net total of each differs (by the same net amount) ad infinitum into the future.

Exhibit 15-1: More Stocks Join the Party

This year's advance-decline line — cumulative total of advancing stocks minus decliners for the year-to-date — has turned up since April. It has regained about half the territory lost in the first four months of the year.

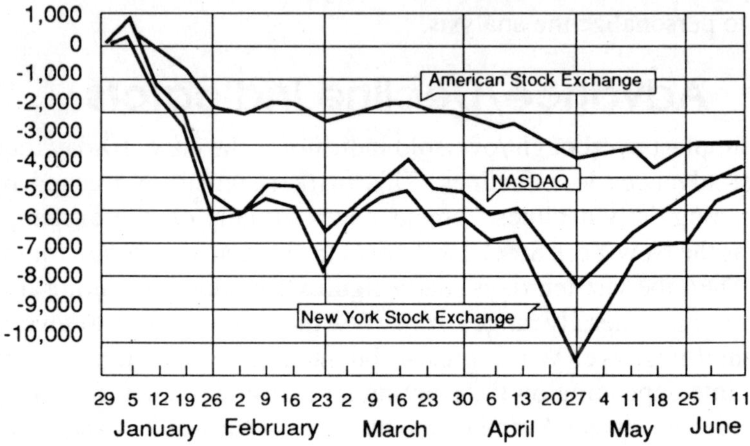

Source: Reprinted by permission of *The Wall Street Journal* © 1989 Dow Jones & Company, Inc. All Rights Reserved World Wide.

Technicians use the cumulative advance/decline indicator to detect divergences in market behavior. They plot this indicator graphically against a popular market measure such as the Dow Jones Industrial Average and look for differences in the shapes of the lines. Because the cumulative advance/decline total is much broader (encompassing all stocks on the exchange(s) studied), it is considered a more valid signal of market direction than is a narrower index such as a 30-stock average.

So what technicians look for are points in time when the two lines move in different directions. As a selling signal, they watch for the cumulative advance/decline line to move sideways or even downward while the market "average" is still moving up — or for the advance/

Exhibit 15-2: Fewer Gainers

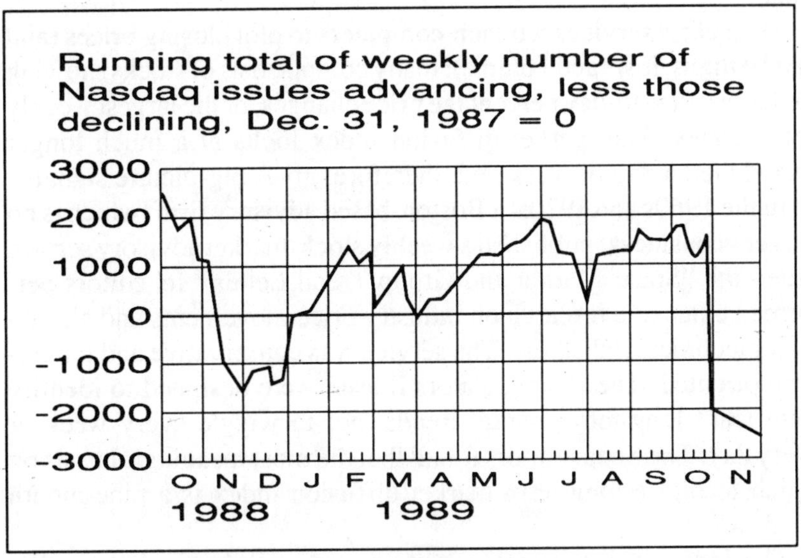

Source: Reprinted by permission of *The Wall Street Journal* © 1989 Dow Jones & Company, Inc. All Rights Reserved World Wide.

decline indicator to move down while the Dow moves sideways, as occurred in late 1989. The theory behind the divergence reading is that the larger list of stocks tells more truth than the mathematical average of a few, which can be skewed by only one or two individual performances among its components.

The Market Diffusion Indicator

Another useful indicator based on advance and decline data, which has even longer-term implications, is the market diffusion indicator. This is constructed somewhat differently and because of its difference, tends to reflect more profound changes. Surprisingly, it seems not to be tracked by major charting services these days, probably because of the methods by which computers have been programmed to store data.

Most chart services tell their computers to plot closing prices (and maybe highs, lows and volume); many compile lists of stocks showing the largest day-to-day percentage price changes, or the largest weekly net changes. The market diffusion index looks at a much longer period than a day or week and, therefore, gives big-picture signals.

In the 1960s and 1970s, a Boston-based advisory firm (which is no longer in business) published a weekly stock-market advisory service called the "Spear Market and Group Trend Letter." Its editors performed extensive research on industry price movements and also on major technical indicators. The service was conservative and longer-term oriented. The few indicators it used were designed to identify significant long-term market trends, not to wiggle every week or every day. The Spear editors found that the most meaningful basis on which to plot a long-term market diffusion index is a nine-month window.

The index took time to compile, but the work was less mathematically intense than the research supporting advance/decline indicators as described above. The analyst simply compared each stock within the defined universe to itself as of a fixed earlier time (adjustments were made for stock splits). October 10 was compared to January 10: October 17 to January 17; and so on. The number of stocks up in price, net, over that period was plotted as a percentage with no adding or accumulation. Each period's calculation was a snapshot.

Market diffusion indices, when plotted, tend to be shaped somewhat like the first derivative of a mathematical plot of overall market level. Well before the market makes its top in a major cycle, the diffusion index tops out and heads down. The diffusion index falls through the all-important 50-percent level at the time when the overall market makes its top as recorded in the major "averages." (A fall to near the 0-percent level indicates exhaustion on the downside and signals that selling is too late because a bottom is near.)

What the long-term diffusion index records is the tendency of the market's leadership to narrow as a bull market matures. Fewer stocks continue to make new highs over a period of months. More seem to be consolidating (but hindsight shows they are actually forming distribution tops). (See Table 15-1.)

If the percentage of net advancing stocks is dropping in the later stages of a bull-market advance, it follows that the odds of making profits on the long side, or even of achieving increased profits on positions already held, decline before the overall market averages hit their final cyclical peaks.

This is a very important observation to understand when the investor is considering holding versus selling. The urgency of diffusion data and the importance of heeding the warnings it provides are all the more critical for another reason: it is precisely during the late stages of a major advance that excitement builds and the temptation to jump in (or to commit more cash or to use margin) is greatest. That is exactly when the odds are starting to swing against holding and toward cashing in because, while some issues make spectacular advances, statistically fewer stocks still are going up. The diffusion index tells that tale.

Unfortunately, it appears that none of the current popular chart services track this indicator at present. But an investor can do it relatively easily if he is willing to invest the time. Use a chart service such as Daily Graphs by William O'Neil (see the reference list at the end of the book) or use the *Monthly Stock Guide* handbook by Standard & Poor's in the local library (or, a broker may be willing to supply a used copy). Or follow the prices in *Barron's* or *The Wall Street Journal* and post them in a tracking ledger.

The chart-inspection method is the fastest way because it requires only quick visual comparisons. Only a few stocks trade so close to nine-month-ago levels that an investor needs to look closely. Select a

Table 15-1: Diffusion Index for 1987 Using DJIA 1990 Components

Diffusion Index for 1987 Using DJIA 1990 Components

(prices monthend or nearest Friday)

	Mar86	Apr	May	Jun	Jul	Aug	Sep	Oct	Nov	Dec86	Jan87	Feb	Mar	Apr	May	Jun	Jul	Aug	Sep	Oct	Nov	Dec87
ALD	46.0	45.3	45.2	44.6	39.6	41.1	40.0	41.4	41.4	40.0	47.2	45.7	45.7	45.7	40.3	44.2	44.2	45.0	45.2	36.1	29.6	28.2
		example: up/even/down vs. 9 months earlier								–	+	+	+	+	–	+	+	+	+	–	–	–
AA	42.3	40.1	41.0	38.1	33.5	37.0	37.0	37.2	36.6	36.0	39.6	41.0	42.6	47.6	47.6	53.1	63.3	55.0	61.4	48.0	46.2	46.6
		example: up/even/down vs. 9 months earlier								–	–	O	+	+	+	+	+	+	+	+	+	+
AXP	34.3	29.1	31.2	31.2	29.1	32.8	27.8	29.5	28.7	28.3	34.0	37.0	37.2	33.7	33.6	34.1	36.7	36.4	35.7	24.1	23.4	22.7
T	22.1	24.7	25.1	25.3	23.5	24.5	22.4	24.7	27.1	25.0	24.6	22.4	23.5	24.1	25.6	27.4	31.5	33.1	33.5	29.7	28.0	27.0
BS	19.5	16.4	16.3	14.6	7.0	8.5	7.4	7.0	5.2	6.3	7.7	8.7	9.3	13.2	14.4	15.0	18.6	17.7	17.6	12.0	14.4	16.6
BA	57.0	55.3	58.2	63.0	58.7	60.1	13.2	52.6	51.0	51.1	50.2	54.1	52.6	45.3	45.4	47.0	53.1	52.1	51.0	38.5	35.4	37.0
CHV	36.4	39.2	40.1	38.4	36.5	44.2	44.0	43.3	47.2	45.4	53.0	49.0	56.1	56.2	58.6	62.0	60.5	58.0	54.0	44.3	38.4	39.5
KO	35.1	37.4	38.5	42.0	38.2	37.7	34.5	37.1	36.4	37.6	42.6	45.0	45.7	42.0	43.0	44.3	47.5	50.2	54.0	44.3	38.4	39.5
DD	76.4	75.4	84.6	83.0	75.4	82.2	79.0	86.2	89.2	84.0	97.6	99.6	112.0	110.0	111.2	100.0	124.4	123.4	119.0	90.2	81.4	87.3
EK	41.6	37.4	40.2	39.1	37.7	37.8	36.7	42.6	45.2	45.6	51.7	51.4	51.2	50.4	53.0	57.0	62.6	66.0	67.7	55.6	47.2	49.0
XON	27.8	29.0	29.7	30.3	30.2	35.2	33.7	34.6	34.5	35.0	41.3	39.2	42.7	42.7	43.4	46.5	48.7	49.0	48.4	42.5	39.1	38.1
GE	39.2	77.0	39.7	40.4	36.0	38.3	35.5	38.6	41.4	43.1	50.1	51.6	52.4	51.2	52.0	54.4	59.2	62.5	61.2	47.1	43.7	44.1
GM	86.2	78.6	79.6	77.4	67.2	72.0	68.3	72.4	73.0	66.0	75.2	74.4	78.0	91.4	85.2	82.6	89.0	89.7	83.2	58.4	35.2	38.4
GT	35.3	30.7	31.0	33.0	30.4	34.5	34.7	48.2	43.2	42.0	47.6	52.6	54.6	68.2	67.0	67.6	76.0	71.4	71.6	47.7	51.1	60.0
IBM	151.4	154.1	152.2	146.4	131.4	138.6	134.4	126.4	127.4	120.0	128.6	139.6	150.0	160.4	160.0	162.4	161.0	166.2	150.6	122.4	115.0	115.4
IP	30.7	28.2	31.3	31.5	31.5	34.0	34.5	37.0	39.2	38.7	46.1	45.6	53.1	49.0	45.4	48.4	48.6	53.4	51.7	37.2	38.4	42.2
MCD	42.8	43.7	45.5	48.8	42.1	45.3	38.4	42.0	42.2	40.6	46.4	45.6	53.1	49.0	45.4	48.4	48.6	53.4	51.7	37.2	38.4	42.2
MRK	87.2	86.0	96.2	104.0	107.6	115.4	99.0	110.0	110.0	123.0	137.0	153.0	154.0	147.0	158.0	170.0	189.0	202.0	206.0	181.4	175.0	158.4
MMM	52.5	51.0	53.2	106.7	54.7	56.1	50.6	54.4	56.0	58.4	65.0	63.4	64.4	63.2	64.0	71.0	73.4	78.4	81.4	59.6	60.6	64.3
NAV	10.6	10.6	9.6	9.1	6.7	7.7	7.1	6.0	5.5	4.6	6.7	7.3	6.7	7.0	8.1	7.4	7.3	7.8	7.2	4.6	4.1	4.2
MO	58.6	63.0	69.6	74.4	70.6	74.0	66.4	73.4	74.2	72.0	88.0	84.4	85.4	82.2	85.4	90.0	99.4	116.0	119.0	92.7	86.0	85.3
PA	38.0	35.7	36.6	38.0	40.5	44.1	40.6	44.4	42.6	42.2	47.4	51.4	48.4	42.4	40.0	40.6	45.6	47.0	45.1	28.7	27.2	24.1
PG	73.4	73.0	78.0	80.2	77.2	80.0	67.6	77.0	78.0	76.4	88.6	85.4	92.0	83.2	91.2	98.0	93.0	100.0	101.0	88.2	84.6	85.2
S	49.4	43.1	47.5	48.4	43.2	45.6	40.0	43.6	44.0	39.6	45.4	51.2	50.6	52.2	51.0	50.3	53.0	55.6	51.6	36.1	33.3	37.2
TX	30.0	31.7	32.7	31.4	29.0	34.2	34.4	35.0	34.2	35.6	37.4	33.7	37.3	34.3	37.5	40.4	46.2	42.3	40.4	32.5	33.4	37.2
X	22.2	19.7	21.7	20.6	15.5	18.6	23.5	25.3	21.2	21.4	23.2	23.3	28.2	28.4	30.1	31.4	38.3	37.2	37.2	27.4	29.2	29.6
UK	22.0	24.3	23.5	21.1	22.0	22.4	20.5	22.0	23.3	22.5	25.6	28.0	28.5	30.0	28.6	29.5	28.3	29.4	28.2	21.4	20.0	21.6
UTX	53.5	50.4	50.4	49.4	40.2	46.0	42.2	43.0	44.6	46.0	49.2	54.5	51.0	46.2	45.4	52.2	57.6	57.2	58.0	35.2	34.1	33.7
WX	54.7	53.3	53.6	53.3	54.2	58.0	52.4	58.0	59.6	55.6	63.0	64.4	64.4	61.6	59.6	63.4	69.1	69.2	73.0	47.1	44.6	49.7
Z	38.0	37.4	45.4	48.0	43.0	43.1	39.1	44.4	44.0	38.6	42.6	47.0	50.1	49.0	47.4	53.3	57.1	55.6	49.5	33.6	34.2	34.4
Changes vs 9 months earlier: UP										18	22	23.5	26	29	27	28.5	30	30	29	10	6	6
DOWN (even counts as 1/2 each)										12	8	6.5	4	1	3	1.5	0	0	1	20	24	24
UPS as percent of 30:										60	73.3	78.3	86.7	96.7	90	95	100	100	96.7	33.3	20	20

Note: prices are shown in dollars and eighths.

universe (of perhaps 100 major companies covering a full sample of industries, for example) and track them each month, comparing the latest price against the nine-month-earlier price (adjusted for splits). Plot the percentage of total issues up. Purists might want to take unchanged issues at a "½" value and include these, if any, in the total; whatever method is used, be consistent so that the graph is meaningful over time.

Some market students reduce the workload required to use a diffusion indicator by narrowing the universe further. To do that, follow the 30 Dow-Jones Industrials. This list changes only rarely, so it is consistent over time. Tally the total of "up" components and divide by 30. Plot the result.

Because the difference created by one Dow Jones stock equals 3.33 percent in the result, be sure to score unchanged stocks as ½ each to refine the reading a bit. Once the tally reaches extremely high percentages, the process of a rounding top will begin, with progressively fewer stocks moving ahead. The key change in momentum and the all-out sell indicator occurs when the index reading declines below 50 percent from a high of 90 percent or more.

Another way to do the same exercise without subscribing to charts is to keep a list of chosen stocks (it should be consistent over time, with changes due only to acquisitions or leveraged buyouts, for example). Tally these once a month in a vertical column. Compare the price at the latest date with the price nine months earlier and score one for each up stock. Divide the total "ups" by the size of the universe and plot the percentage result on graph paper.

Another source for this exercise is a local Sunday newspaper. If a weekly source is used, go back approximately 39 weeks or take the Friday prices closest to the end of the calendar month. The manual posting and comparison method takes longer than chart inspection, so be careful to adjust for stock splits when there are major drops in price from month to month.

The signals that a market diffusion index provides are:

- Over 90 percent, early selling warning: Do no more buying and start to weed out stocks to build cash.
- Decline from over 90 percent to 50 percent: Immediate final sell signal: this is the market top. Act without delay or excuses.
- Under 10 percent: Do no selling because it is already too late. A major panic-type bottom is forming.

Note that the market diffusion method is a much better selling indicator than buying tool. This is because tops in the overall market form gradually even though individual stocks may display exhaustion peaks; bottoms are violent. At bottoms, an oscillator-type index such as an advance/decline or diffusion index can appear numerically oversold; but the most violent decline can take a few days or a couple more weeks and still result in severely lower prices. Therefore, as a buying indicator a diffusion index is an imprecise tool — as are most other technical indicators when severe panic psychology is running the market.

Creating a diffusion index can be a highly personalized exercise. Investors not only can choose a universe to follow to customize the diffusion indicator, but they can and should keep a tally of the stocks they own. As an indicator per se, this is cruder and subject to statistical imperfection because the sample size is small and the list itself is subject to revision over time as the portfolio changes. However, it is a useful exercise if done in the following manner. (See Table 15-2.)

Keep a loose-leaf sheet in a notebook on which to log the periodic closing price of each stock held. For personal diffusion-index purposes, use the last Friday of each month or the one closest to month-end rather than the actual last day of the month. This allows more time for real-time recording and for prompt weekend study of the data. Record the current quotation and compare it with a past period's price.

Table 15-2: Example of Personal Diffusion Index (12/31/86–12/31/87)

Stock (Cost)	86 DEC	JAN	FEB	MAR	APR	MAY	JUN	JUL	AUG	SEP	OCT	NOV	87 DEC
Boeing (50)	51.1	50.2	54.1	52.0	45.3	45.4	47.0	53.1	52.1	51.0	38.5	35.4	37.0
up/dn	+	+	+	+	–	–	–	+	+	+	–	–	–
G.M. (60)	66.0	75.2	74.4	78.0	91.4	85.2	82.6	89.0	89.7	83.0	58.4	35.2	38.4
up/dn	+	+	+	+	+	+	+	+	+	+	–	–	–
IBM (145)	120	128	140	150	161	167	163	161	166	151	123	115	116
up/dn	–	–	–	+	+	+	+	+	+	+	–	–	–
McDonald's (45)	40.6	46.4	50.6	52.4	54.4	52.4	53.0	55.2	57.4	54.0	45.4	43.6	44.0
up/dn	–	+	+	+	+	+	+	+	+	+	+	–	–
Sears (40)	39.6	45.4	51.2	50.6	52.2	51.0	50.3	53.0	55.6	51.6	36.1	33.3	33.4
up/dn	–	+	+	+	+	+	+	+	+	+	–	–	–
Texaco (40)	35.6	37.4	33.7	37.3	34.3	37.5	40.4	46.2	42.3	40.4	32.5	33.4	37.2
up/dn	–	–	–	–	–	–	+	+	+	+	–	–	–
Total Up	2	4	4	5	4	4	5	6	6	6	1	0	0
Percent of 6	33	67	67	83	67	67	83	100	100	100	17	0	0

Personal sell signal came in July @ 100%

Note: Prices of stock expressed in points and eighths (e.g. 36.4 = 36 ½)

With a personal portfolio list, use a three-month rather than a nine-month window. There are two reasons: portfolio turnover, overlaid on a nine-month window, reduces the number of stocks in the sample at any time quite significantly. Second, the shorter window is more sensitive. The indicator should say something soon, when a significant market move has occurred.

Also consider this guideline: when a personal list shows all winners over a three-month period, do some selling. Such a reading means that the market has been strong, and/or the investor has been hot (probably aided by the overall trend); and this probably will not last for long. Because the market makes just a few meaningful wavelike swings per year on average, a three-month window is likely to help catch roughly a full wave.

Note also the need to make mental adjustments about one or two stocks in the list. For example, one stock in a list of 10 took a bad tumble several months ago, but the investor held it. If there are problems with this company and the investor remains stubborn, he effectively must forgive the index for including the stock because realistically he cannot hope for a 100 percent reading while this laggard remains on the short list.

One final caveat: be sure to look at price performance over a fixed time interval for all current stocks, not net price performance since the dates they were bought. It is obvious that a hugely successful, long-term growth holding always gives a plus reading on the latter basis, providing no guidance. So track changing intermediate-term momentum and use the three-month comparison window.

Again, not only should some stocks be sold when there are all winners (because momentum cannot get stronger); also use a fall through the 50-percent level as the trigger for serious selling. This means that either the market itself has rolled over and lost momentum, or judgments about stock performance and prospects have deteriorated. And consider contrariness as a virtue in investing. When an investor feels the most confident, that is exactly the time to lean the other way deliberately and sell. The diffusion index is a powerful mathematical guide to use when contrary selling should be transacted. The personal diffusion index tailors the signal to personal holdings and provides an excellent disciplinary tool for portfolio reviews in the process.

CHAPTER

16

Overcome Greed: Stop Chasing the "Last Eighth"

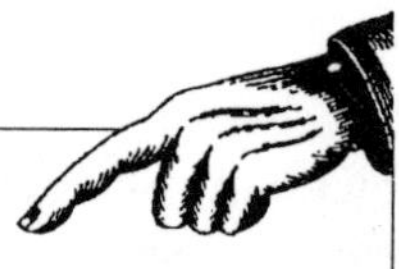

KEYS TO INVESTMENT SUCCESS
- Learn to Walk Away
- Beware of Rush Sales
- Hurried Thinking; Hurried Sales

Investors, and particularly traders, all too often succumb to the temptation to seek what is virtually impossible: the legendary "extra eighth" of a price point, both as a literal (micro) and as figurative (big-picture) market issue.

In the literal sense, logical investors realize that the odds against selling a stock at the highest price — on a short-term swing or in a major bull market move — are overwhelming. For example, a reasonably seasoned blue-chip, exchange-traded, low-beta common stock might trade in a range between, say, 40 and 50 over a 12-month period. Examples of these stocks are General Motors, Sears and Exxon.

Elementary mathematics indicates that a 10-point price range includes 81 eighths (with the extra eighth), so the random odds are 80:1 against selling at the top price. From the technician's viewpoint, volume peaks before prices in a bull market; therefore on a volume basis, the odds are that fewer shares will trade at the top eighth than at prices several points lower. So the 80:1 odds against are actually too low. (It also can be argued that if volume has begun to subside at the price top, there is a greater chance for a fill because there is less competition.)

Even if an investor watches a quotation machine all day long with an uncanny, intuitive sense of technical action, he still needs terrific luck to catch the top eighth. What kinds of things can go wrong even if he is that smart?

His timing, indeed, may be perfect; but his broker may be on the other line and cannot get back to him until 15 minutes later. Or, with the stock trading at its absolute high for the day and the year, he enters a sell order and it is executed down an eighth at the bid, while someone else's buy order at market is transacted at the offer, coming in 30 seconds later.

Contrast the two traders' feelings: one buys at the exact top and the other's worst failing is to sell one eighth lower! Or say a seller somehow catches the top of the day. But overnight the dollar is up against the yen and the president makes a speech that Wall Street likes. Program trading opens the market ahead 20 points, so yesterday's high eighth is now eclipsed. Clearly, by any objective standard, the chance of getting out at the high is slim.

Despite these odds, a surprising number of investors and traders get trapped into trying for the last eighth by ego, fantasies of wealth and the need to "win". These people literally want to go for it all. But going for the last eighth can be very costly. Or, it can be an excuse not to act at all.

Learn to Walk Away

The expression "the last eighth" is misleading and too literal. In the industry it means the attempt to squeeze out just a little bit more or it can mean staying around too long. Either way, the meaning is reduced to the notion of getting greedy when reason, logic or the predetermined target price say it is time to sell.

When the time to sell arrives, it takes tough mental and emotional discipline to pick up the telephone and call a broker with the instruction to sell (do not wait for the broker to call unless the relationship is unique with an excellent, old-line stockbroker). But even with the discipline and good sense to call the broker, an investor can confound his own sell decision with poor tactical execution. Any number of factual inputs, hunches or emotional reactions can induce him to enter a limit order above the market. Those limits should have been entered long ago, not when he is feeling giddy and greedy.

He may muse that, after all, the stock has been strong enough to land on the 52-week high list, so why not let nature take its course and let the momentum give him a couple of extra points just for being patient? Surely sometime today or tomorrow the stock's current strength and natural fluctuation volatility will net just a little more.

Such thinking is deluded; selling a stock near its top is a difficult exercise that requires tremendous discipline, a contrarian's mentality, an updated feel of the tone in the particular stock and the overall market and a strong dash of luck as well.

When the stock has exceeded the investor's objective or when new market/industry/company developments prompt him to reduce his stock-specific price objective, the most prudent course is to enter a market order. An even more judicious action, which would avert the entire situation, is to enter a GTC order at the target price when the stock is originally purchased.

Knowing that he is out on a market order, he can move on to the next selling or buying idea without the distraction of waiting or worrying. He can feel less exposed to a possible drop in the overall market because he will have lightened up his position.

When a stock is peaking, an investor runs the serious risk of missing the top area altogether if he tries to stretch winnings too far. Once a stock stops rising and starts declining, the difficulty of selling it becomes even greater. Giving up points that have already melted away is more painful than imagining giving up points of paper profit that have not yet been created.

Usually, an investor's tendency is to remember each high in a successful stock rally. Then each further advance to a new price peak establishes a new psychological high ground from which he operates. He begins to view that level as an entitlement and believes that height is attainable again.

If, in fact, the real lasting high already has been reached (a fact the investor will not know for some time, and then only with useless hindsight), his efforts and hopes for just a little more already are doomed from the beginning. His mental state heads south with the stock's price, weakening his decision-making abilities. Keep in mind that when the price objective is reached, the best policy is to sell at market and walk away.

When an investor makes the decision to walk away, he should just keep walking: unless there is a specific reason to continue watching the sold stock, don't look at the quotes once the stock is sold. Count on not getting that final eighth, or point, or two points. Move on without regrets and without looking back. If the stock reached its sale target, anyone who bought it higher — even if he now has a small profit — is one of the greater fools and just does not realize it yet. Do not worry about him getting the extra point because it was not obvious in real time that the stock would go any higher; this type of hindsight is not only useless, but self-defeating.

Beware of Rush Sales

Ironically, the flip side of the error in holding on for the proverbial extra eighth of a point is overstaying when it is smartest to cash in. The exit is needlessly hurried once the sale decision has been made. This is not the macro-level problem of failing to let profits run; it is the micro-tactical tendency of many investors simply to throw in a market sale order and depart in haste.

When a trade is to be closed, bypassing a market order and making other reasonable efforts over the short term might net a better execution without unnecessarily exposing the holder to a nasty downside erosion. The objective here is, at the margin, to increase the profit (through good micro tactics) from many positions as they are sold out. The way to do this, in defined circumstances, is to slow down and take what the market allows instead of insisting on the immediate gratification and relief brought on by a hasty sale.

This advice applies best when the sale is made in response to the achievement of a fundamental target rather than as a technically-driven action designed to avoid danger. It should be emphasized, however, that if the stock's sale is being made for technical reasons, say to avoid declining prices caused by bad news or a failing general market, slowing down is not the right action.

But if an investor is selling a stock because it has reached his objective on a fundamental basis, why should he be in a hurry? Suppose his studies indicate that a stock is likely to be fully priced when it reaches 120 percent of the market's P/E multiple, 140 percent of book value, eight times cash flow per share or a dividend yield of two percent.

Those specific targets are not likely to be shared universally by other holders. So there probably will not be a sudden huge rush of sell orders entered (or even a large cluster on the specialist's book) when the stock hits his particular fundamental target.

Nor is he a market guru like Gabelli, Zweig or Granville, whose publicized targets and known actions create headlines and move stocks. Bear in mind that just as the market does not pause to note an individual's purchase, it takes no notice of an individual's fundamental target prices.

If the sale is made on the basis of fundamental measures, barring sudden bad news or a slumping overall market, be in no special hurry to get out. Do not let ego cloud the exit maneuver. Take a little more if the market will allow it, but never expect perfection. Always recall that the odds of selling at the very top price (for the year, for the move or even just for the near-term future) are very low. A perfect exit is nearly impossible to execute.

Hurried Thinking; Hurried Sales

There are several reasons for the emotional baggage carried by investors who jump quickly and get bad executions of what should be no-rush sales. Not all past sales closed out profits, and some closing trades later were regretted (whereas all buying decisions are made in an upbeat frame of mind).

The tendency to "get it over with" when selling is supported by one or more of the following six excuses to hurry:

- Selling to raise funds for a new purchase,
- Wanting to end an unsatisfactory experience,
- Selling out of frustration or boredom,
- Being accustomed to instant gratification,

- Wanting relief from uncertainty,
- False urgency over shifting expectations.

When an investor decides it is time to sell, earlier patterns and experiences pop up from the conscious or unconscious; they define the way he feels about present sales and contribute to current actions unless they are recognized and controlled. This is important to remember for fundamentally-driven, non-urgent sales, especially if sale proceeds are not being recommitted the same day.

On the other hand, some fundamentally-driven stock sales — even though they are not urgent — are caused by reassessing prospects and lowering expectations:

- The company has not accomplished the accelerated sales projected.
- Interest rates have risen sooner or higher than expected.
- The general market looks like it is topping, which implies a need to prune in the near term.
- Group rotation seems to be moving away from the stock, indicating that the anticipated P/E is not to be achieved.

Often, a revision of expectations, although not a sudden disaster, is a disappointment when compared with original hopes for the stock position. So the investor rushes to sell a mildly-disappointing investment when there is no solid reason for hurrying.

Selling a stock out of frustration or boredom has similar results. For example, an investor may hang in with Dullsville, Inc. stock when it has not lived up to expectations instead of riding Whiz-Bang Spiffycorp. Then he wakens to the fact that he has wasted the time value of his money and that the stock is going nowhere fast.

But this does not mean that the smartest way out is an immediate market-sell order. If there is no reason to suspect the stock will crack over the short term, at least he can try to do better on the exit than he did on the enter. The best action is to control the desire to move impulsively away from the frustration and proceed more slowly.

A subtle reason for making foolish sales when it is unnecessary is the nature of America in the 20th century. This is the age of instant gratification and computer speed. In just the past 15 years, the concept of speed has changed radically. Computers churned on big problems for minutes in the mid-1970s; now if spreadsheets take more than seconds to recompute, Americans are annoyed and impatient. With this mind-set shaped by so many experiences in daily life, Americans are subconsciously programmed to reach for the instant sale confirmation when it is time to sell. But if there is no real rush, they pay in lost dollars for irrational, habit-driven impatience.

When an investor finally decides to sell a stock, the conditioning created by uncomfortable past experiences with uncertainty comes into play. He feels that he can at least take control in one aspect of trading by selling immediately. He may jump instinctively for the market order when there is no good reason. If he becomes aware of this unconscious, ingrained tendency, he can take conscious steps to control it and usually get more profitable results.

All an investor has to do in these circumstances is slow down. Stocks have a natural tendency to fluctuate — over a week, day-to-day and intra-day. If there is no immediate deterioration in the fundamentals or in the overall market, on average a seller can presume to do moderately better than the last sale or the current bid if he exercises patience and enters a smart order on a limit instead of a market-sell order.

Note that over the market's long history, it averages a small net gain per day — not a small loss. So, on average, waiting can gain a fraction if there is no bad news in immediate prospect. Learn to take advantage of natural random fluctuations instead of ignoring them. Be satisfied with a quarter, half or point gain improvement over the past. In many instances, improved exit tactics can pay the commission cost.

C H A P T E R

17

Sell When It Feels So Good

KEYS TO INVESTMENT SUCCESS

- How Fast Can the Stock Rise, for How Long?
- What Other Good Can Happen to the Stock?
- What If Good News Does Not Move the Stock?

All stocks have peculiar behavior patterns triggered by news, by actual conditions in the general market and by the movements of owned investments. The ways in which stocks behave often are signals to exit.

This chapter focuses on how fast a stock can reasonably rise and for how long. Such information should discipline investor-thinking regarding successful positions that are so good he falls in love with the stock and marries it for the long haul.

Because nearly all good things do come to an end — or at least simmer down — the successful investor steps off before it becomes obvious to the majority that the direction of the market is overdone and due for change.

How Fast can the Stock Rise, for How Long?

When a stock starts acting heroically, that in itself is a sell signal. Acquire a set of charts, either daily basis or long-term format charts. Again, technical analysis is not the purpose; simply study wavelike movements in broad terms.

Take, for example, a growth stock like PepsiCo or McDonald's. Over the very long term, these companies achieve growth in revenue and earnings of perhaps 15 percent per year. And over the long term, a stock price tends to move in proportion to earnings and dividend growth. To ask for more requires a secular increase in P/E ratios, and such changes tend to reverse when interest rates rebound or during a recession. All an investor reasonably can hope for is price growth in line with long-term earnings trends.

Stocks do not climb a steady, slight incline from day to day or from month to month. Prices gyrate up and down at percentage rates well in excess of the fundamental growth rate of the underlying company. In the process, the stock swings from being "ahead of itself" or overpriced, to being oversold. With perfect foresight, an investor

Exhibit 17-1: McDonald's Price Chart

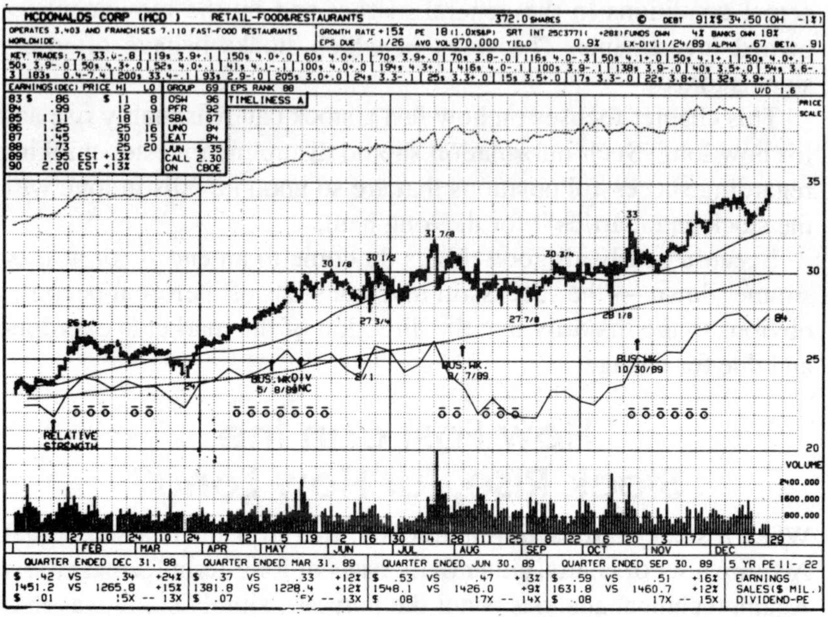

Courtesy of *Daily Graphs and Long Term Values*; P.O. Box 24933; Los Angeles, California 90024.

theoretically could catch each top and bottom to become wealthy rapidly.

But reality demands that an investor not attempt to catch the top and bottom of each swing because he will fail and create self-defeating frustration. What *is* possible to track are the multiple wavelike movements that prices exhibit while swinging around their long-term growth slopes. In these movements lie the opportunities for above-trend returns as well as for investment education.

Look at a McDonald's price chart, for instance. While the earnings momentum is fairly steady at about 15 percent per year, and the stock tends to mirror that over the long term, there are both large and small wavelike up-movements of much more rapid pace (interspersed with corrections). Even in a year when the stock rises a theoretical average of 15 percent from January to December, there are three or four moves of 10 to 15 percent each. Those moves were unsustainable over the longer term, due to underlying fundamentals, but they provide very profitable opportunities for the nimble investor. The trader tries to catch most of the move over the short term. But the investor should see the move as unsustainable and use it as a timing opportunity to cash in; he can always reenter later. (See Exhibit 17-1.)

Because this is not a study on technical analysis, there is no attempt to quantify the number of moves per year or the average percentage slope that can be achieved. Such parameters differ for each stock and they will change over time for any one stock. But the phenomenon of unsustainable upward movement is described here because it offers an opportunity for well-timed sales. In fact, some of the best selling opportunities occur when it cannot get much better. (See Exhibit 17-2.)

The investor may still like the company fundamentally for the long term. But suppose an analyst's recommendation envisions a 25 percent increase in stock price over a 12-month period, driven by good fundamentals and rising appreciation of the company's strengths. If the broker calls after the stock has just risen 15 percent in less than a month, he shouldn't chase strength. He should be advised to place a below-market limit and buy the stock better on the next reaction. This requires patience and guts for both broker and investor, but it pays handsomely in the longer run.

The same principle applies when his stock is running ahead sharply while he owns it. Omitting the occasional spectacular move on rumored takeover offers, when a stock moves several percent in a week, exciting but unrealistic annualized capital growth rates are imagined. Just three percent per week is 156 percent per year! But each stock and its moves are unique. And the tone of the general market affects each stock differently on each movement. So there is

Exhibit 17-2: AMEX Charts

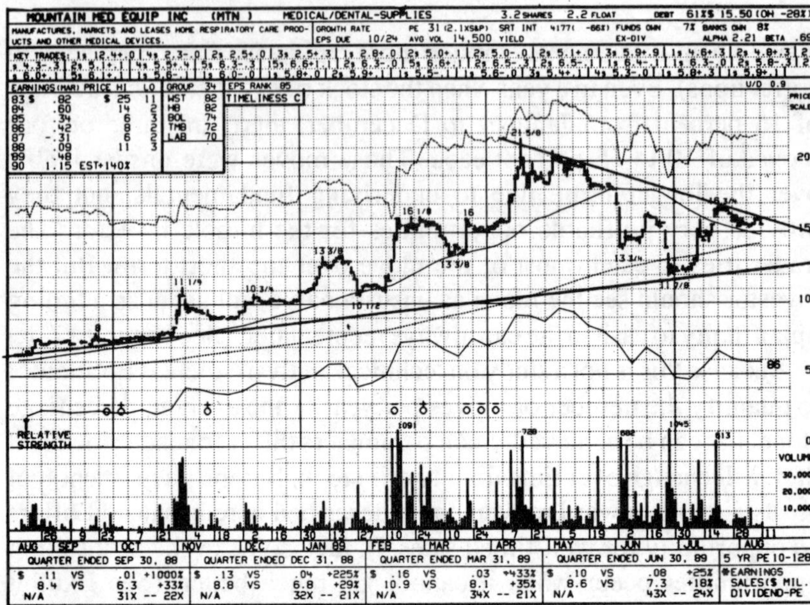

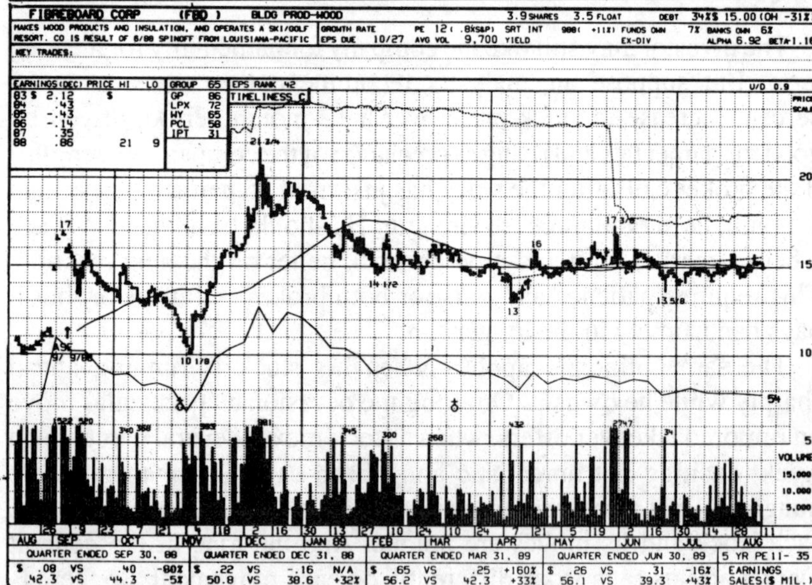

Courtesy of *Daily Graphs and Long Term Values*

Exhibit 17-2: AMEX Charts (continued)

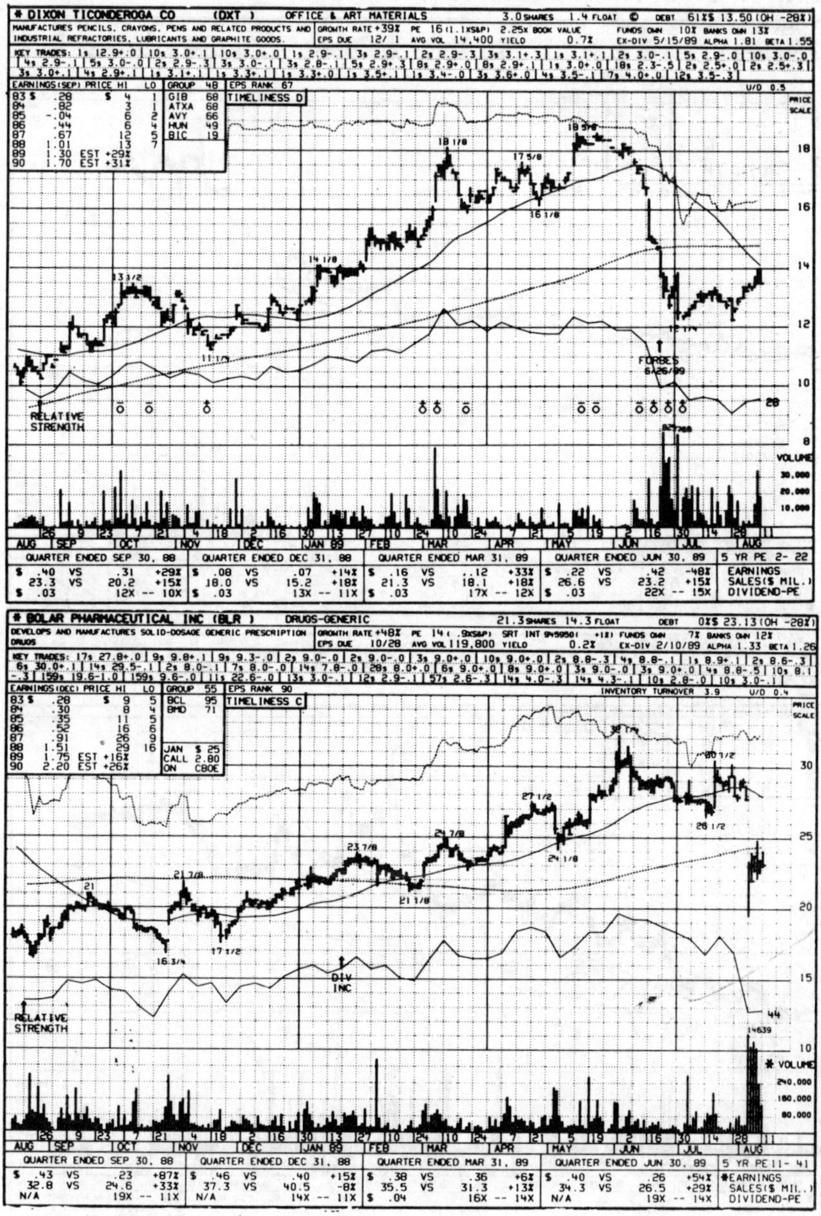

Courtesy of *Daily Graphs and Long Term Values*

Exhibit 17-2: AMEX Charts (continued)

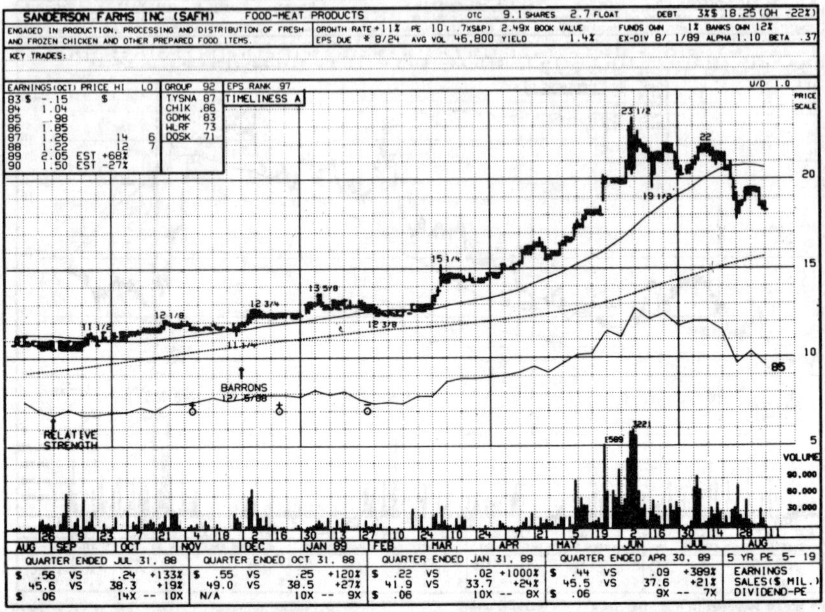

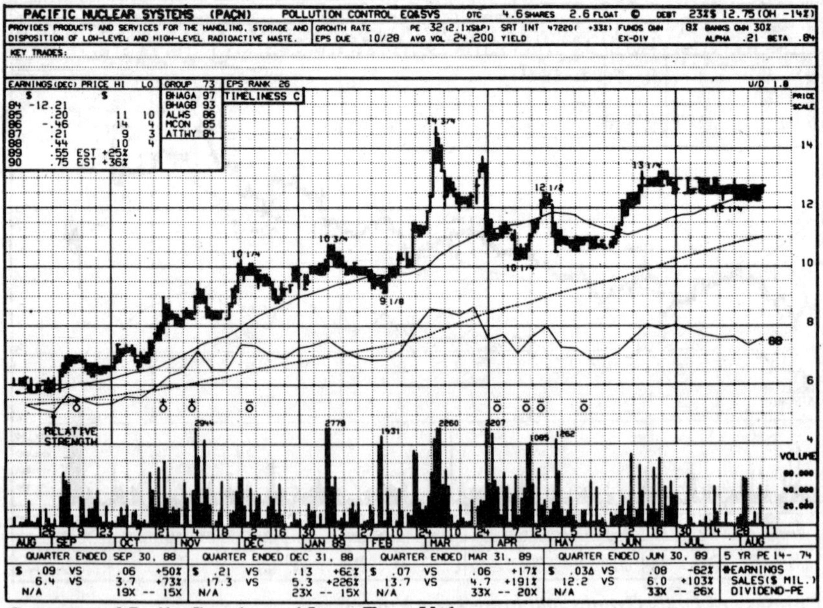

Courtesy of *Daily Graphs and Long Term Values*

Exhibit 17-2: AMEX Charts (continued)

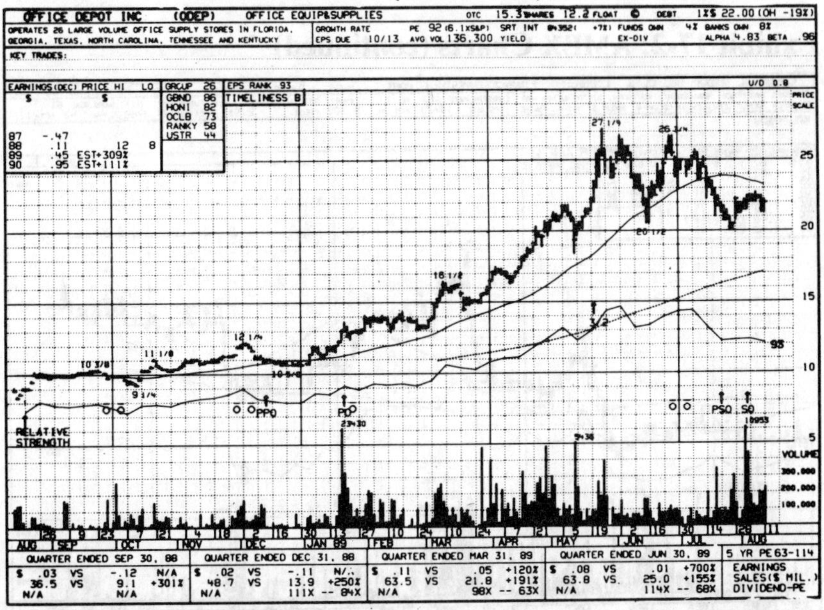

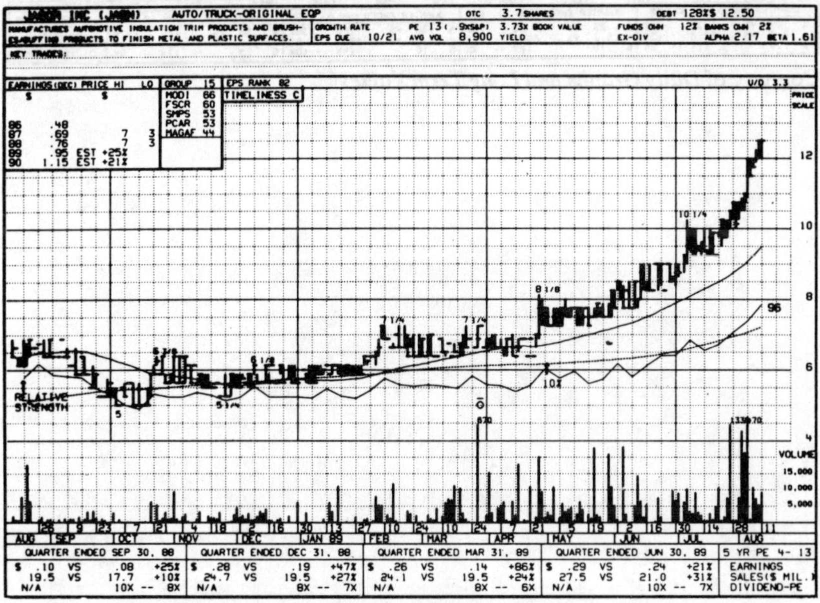

Courtesy of *Daily Graphs and Long Term Values*

Exhibit 17-2: AMEX Charts (continued)

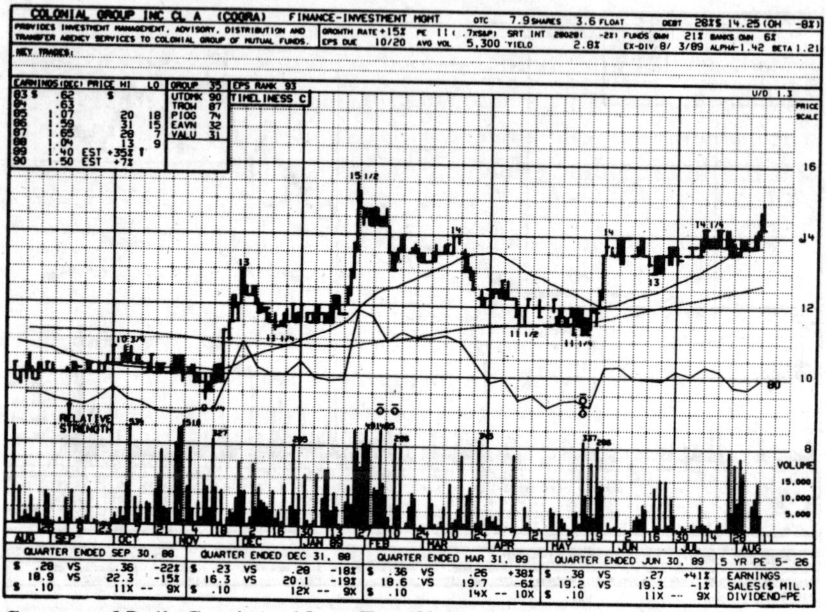

Courtesy of *Daily Graphs and Long Term Values*

no universal formula or meaningful average measure that can be applied.

In an orderly market, each stock — particularly a stock that is traded heavily by institutions — tends to form its own patterns. Some technical traders notice these patterns and assume they will repeat. Their buying and selling tends to make such expectations somewhat self-fulfilling, but the exact percentage or point moves are unequal each time.

So look at each individual stock chart and see what the stock's past moves were. For example, use rules of thumb such as these: in McDonald's, be a seller rather than a buyer after a rapid (two-week or less) 10 percent price move. On General Electric, five percent to seven percent in a week is a major move that should be sold into. Discover the typical patterns in each stock owned and lean against the happy tide when these fast moves occur. The charts on the past few pages illustrate sharp but unsustainable rallies.

What Other Good Can Happen to the Stock?

When a stock stops rising it almost never levels off calmly at the new higher level. Get out of the way rather than risk exposure to the emotions and imaginings that take hold once the pullback gets underway.

Another important cue for assessing how much better it can get lies in fundamental developments. In the same way that a stock can get so technically strong that there is no encore possible, company news can line up at the ceiling. When that happens, it is a signal at least to become extremely cautious; at most, it acts as a direct signal to cash in. This observation is more than an extension of the old admonition to buy on rumor and sell on news. At issue is fundamental exhaustion on the upside. Sometimes there simply is nothing left that has not already gone right. At some point, investors collectively expect everything to continue positively, so there is no longer any price impact from good news.

Once again, this measurement is more an art than a science. Point values cannot be assigned to dividend increases, stock splits, contracts awarded, earnings gains, important new technology or patents. Simply observe a number of situations and from them develop a sense of how good it gets. From that rough measure, project approximately when the party will wind down.

It is extremely dangerous to try to sell at the very top during an emotionally-charged market period; be resigned beforehand to the certainty of missing tops in a spike-shaped move by quite a bit. Be content to come out a decent winner and to learn a little each time from the micro experience of making an exit.

Following is the story of one stock that illustrates the boundaries of the possible on the upside, and what good news can and cannot do for a stock. A small electronics company in the southwestern United States — followed in 1987-88 through the post-crash period — had good products and a smart management team that kept overhead expense low. Sales fluctuated as big orders came and went, so the stock moved in a wide range.

In 1989, it became apparent that big developments were afoot: the company developed highly significant new markets for its product line and started hooking some very impressive prospective customers. The selling cycle was predictably long on these deals because they involved major corporate decisions by the buyers. But the array of pending deals, across a number of new customer industries, was exciting.

The stock was bought from below $2.00 per share. When management hinted in brief quarterly reports about important orders, the stock perked up to over $3.00 per share. The pending deals involved a first-echelon bank, two major international oil companies, a major foreign government agency, a leading retail organization and a top-quality financial-services provider.

Two of the potential orders exceeded the company's highest previous total annual revenue. The prestige of capturing industry leaders as customers would have spill-over effects on sales. Predictably, brokers and investors started asking the analysts how high it was expected to go. The reply was that market conditions would dictate that at the time announcements were made. One analyst suspected that each of the two most important awards, if received, would be good for a point in the stock almost overnight.

The scenario was to wait for the majority of the anticipated contracts to be won and announced, and then exit with good profits. Some brokers, appropriately trained to think in terms of fundamentals, asked what the earnings stream would look like and what P/E would be appropriate.

The analyst's response, to their surprise, was that it did not matter. Once the company was actually delivering on the orders, the excitement peak would have passed. The hottest news would already be past. The critical task was to identify when the sizzle was so hot that it could not get much hotter. The prospect was for blockbuster contracts compared to the company's previous contract history. The earnings probably would follow, but there would be no way to top the near-term string of news announcements in the future. The revenues would be nonrecurring, as in the past. Therefore, the market would not assign a high P/E when the actual earnings would become known. It literally was a classic illustration of "just how good can this get?"

The seasoned analyst does not hold illusions about divining the peak of excitement in the stock in this scenario. But he does feel confident that with expectations for what can be announced, coupled with a string of actual news events, prices probably will reach a point when staying for more is greedy. So the analyst does not quote a price objective or a timeframe.

Without knowing what is really going on at a company, investors can create mental scenarios about what is realistic; they can make up a wish list. When a few of those wishes come true, especially over a short period in a generally uptrending market, investors then must ask themselves what more can go right. Because at that point, *any* of those playouts of the company's plot is a signal to sell. The psychology becomes incapable of further improvement.

Remember, too, that it takes rising volume to take stocks to higher price highs. That requires increasing doses of fundamental news, investor excitement and/or sponsorship. An investor may not know exactly what the upper limit will prove to be, but he can develop a good intuitive feel of when "enough is enough" if he observes a number of these situations carefully.

Once again, take written notes and record personal feelings in real time. Keep a chart of the stock and date the observations, keying them to price history on the chart. This helps develop a documented record that is useful as a model for parallel games. Also track major concept stories in unowned stocks that are in the news. See how long they take to play out.

What If Good News Does Not Move the Stock?

Now what happens if good news does not move the stock? This requires only brief treatment: the bottom-line answer is that it is time to sell without delay. One of the definitions of a bear market is a time when investors do not care about good news. Applying this logic to individual stocks, if good news fails to elicit positive stock-price action (in a reasonably hospitable market climate), there is no longer enough unsatisfied buying interest in the stock to push it higher.

The excitement has passed its peak; volume will be unable to build to new highs, and the price must erode. A sophisticated market observer can use this insight as a signal to cash in, while others less savvy use the latest good news as reason to buy the stock. Unfortunately, they fail to realize that they are buying into distribution and are starting too late to be able to win this game.

What causes a stock to fail to react on good news (relative to non-routine news such as big contracts, new technology or patents, or acquisition — not just positive quarterly earnings)? First, the general market tone may have turned so cautious that not enough investors to move the stock are willing to buy. Second, the news itself may have been anticipated, so the item that looks like news is actually already in the stock.

Or the news may be less exciting than previous news, implying that the best is no longer yet to come. The stock already could have been sponsored heavily by brokerage recommendations and pushed ahead by institutional buying, so there is little untapped buying available. In any of these cases, project lower prices for the stock. The game already has played out past its peak of excitement.

It is important to exit a stock promptly when expectations are wrong. Holding a stock, dead-sure the market is wrong not to be excited and after there has been a good upside move already, is a mistake. That means the investor has gotten too enamored of the stock, has gotten greedy or has misgauged how good it can get. It is imperative to close out the position to protect profits and to insulate oneself from second-guessing and regret.

C H A P T E R

18

Sell Into Strong Price/Volume Crescendos

KEY TO INVESTMENT SUCCESS

- Gauging the Momentum

One of the most essential facts underlying technical analysis of stock-price behavior is that it is based on the attempt to locate, measure and act on changing relationships of supply and demand. Whether the technical approach is point-and-figure charting, the study of trends and channels, the identification of resistance and support levels or the price-volume methods popularized by several authors, its core is supply and demand.

Most of the time, stock prices move in a primary direction — up or down — on heavier trading volume than they experience when making counter-trend or sideways movements.

Recall the record trading volume on October 19, 1987, when the Dow-Jones Industrial Average lost 508 points and made its bottom for the move on record volume. Even less-dramatic major bottoms typically are referred to as climaxes, because they consist of prices falling in a cascade or waterfall shape (if plotted on a graph against time), accompanied by a pick-up in trading volume as investor emotions take hold and outrun logic.

This is the profile of a typical bottom, that is, the end of a selling trend and the end of a downward movement in prices. Selling pressure gets so intense that it cannot be exceeded; it becomes exhausted. That is the bottom. On the way down, each temporary bottom is typically characterized by increases in fear and in trading volume, with panicky dumping to mark the new interim low.

This stage usually is followed on lower volume by timid bargain-hunting. When that process runs its course and the bulls run out of guts and/or ammunition, the basebuilding or rally falters. That failure to hold ground leads to renewed fear, which builds in a minor crescendo to a new, lower, cascade-shaped bottom on high volume.

Because most investors do not like to think about bottoms, this chapter is illustrated with examples of how stocks rise rather than how they fall. That emphasis helps identify and define high-volume tops as they occur. But the focus here is tops in a rising market because volume tends to build when prices move in their primary direction; it tends to fall during the counter-trend, during corrections or during pauses in a stock's move.

One of the major tenets underlying technical analysis of volume-price behavior is that a continuing price advance requires successively higher trading volume over time. Many technicians base their analysis and decision-making on this important relationship. When they see a stock continuing to rise to new highs without ongoing strong trading volume, they refer to the price move — even if it is to new highs — as a weak advance.

The term "weak advance" has nothing directly to do with the increment of rise (as in ⅛ being weak, ⅞ being stronger). It refers to the cause of the rise. If bulls who have been pushing the price higher continue to have strong bullish conviction and to remain unsatisfied buyers in large numbers, they still will be active buyers and the trading volume will remain heavy.

However, if interest shifts to other stocks in the same industry or if the market as a whole continues a strong advance but with other industry groups in the lead, the stock simply may rise in sympathy with the trend. Because it has done well, there are many happy holders and few sellers, so the stock can still rise briefly on low volume.

But this situation is inherently unstable and self-terminating. At some point in a price advance, more and more owners will view the stock as getting high in price or ahead of itself and will want to sell. If there is no longer any real heavy buying power left to be satisfied, the sellers will overwhelm the few buyers and the price will crack.

The speculative bulls, seeing that the excitement is at least temporarily at a halt, will pull back and wait for confirmation from other buyers that there is still some upside play left. But if volume is broken, price cannot be long behind. Because of these supply/demand, volume/price dynamics, tops in stock prices tend to occur on high trading volume. In timing sales, sell when they are hot, which is

Exhibit 18-1: Price Tops Coincide with Volume Crescendos

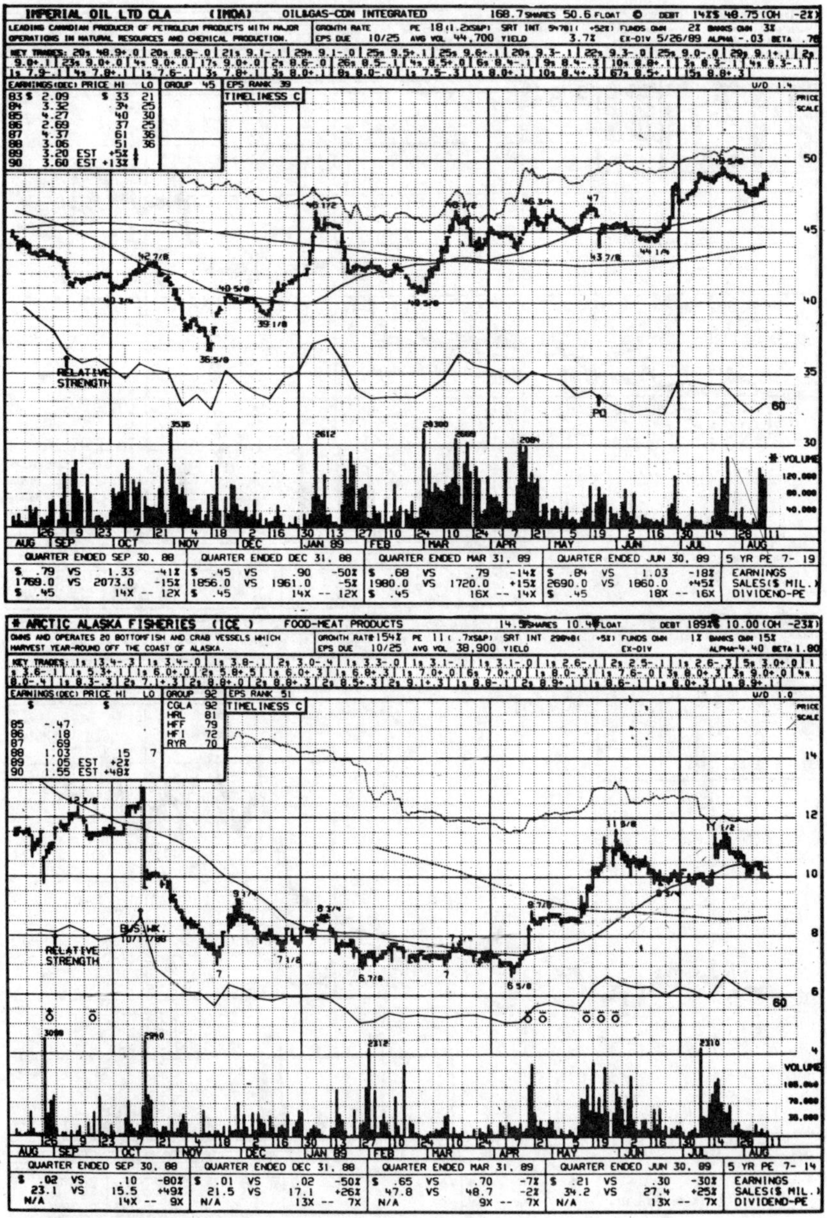

Courtesy of *Daily Graphs and Long Term Values*

Exhibit 18-1: (continued)

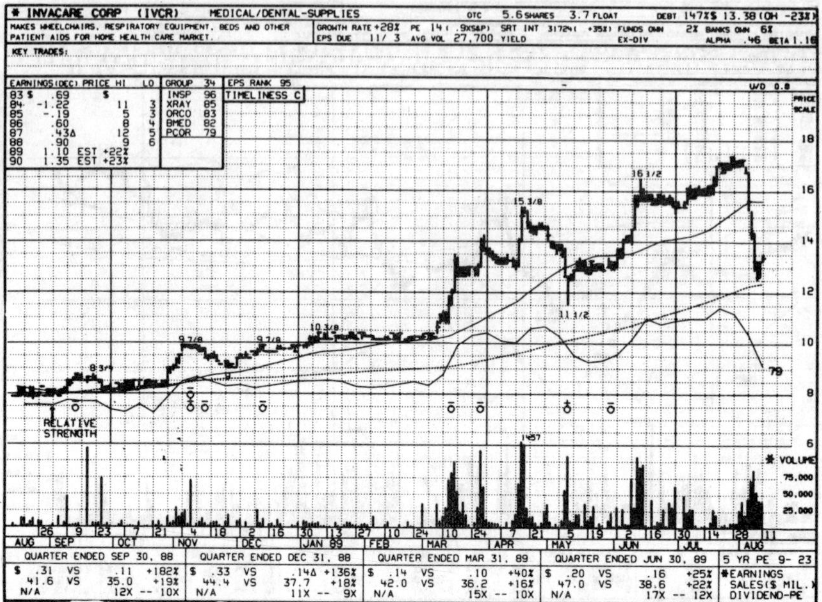

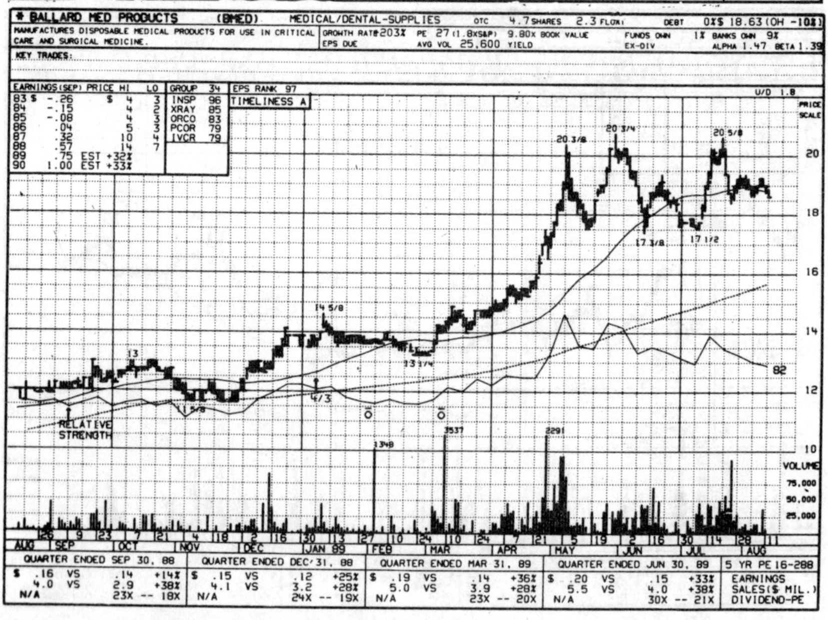

Courtesy of *Daily Graphs and Long Term Values*

Exhibit 18-1: (continued)

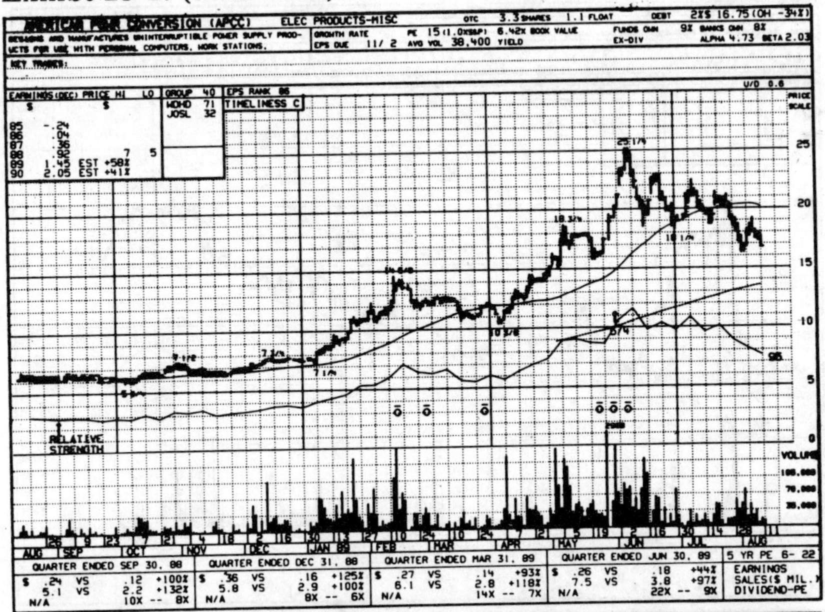

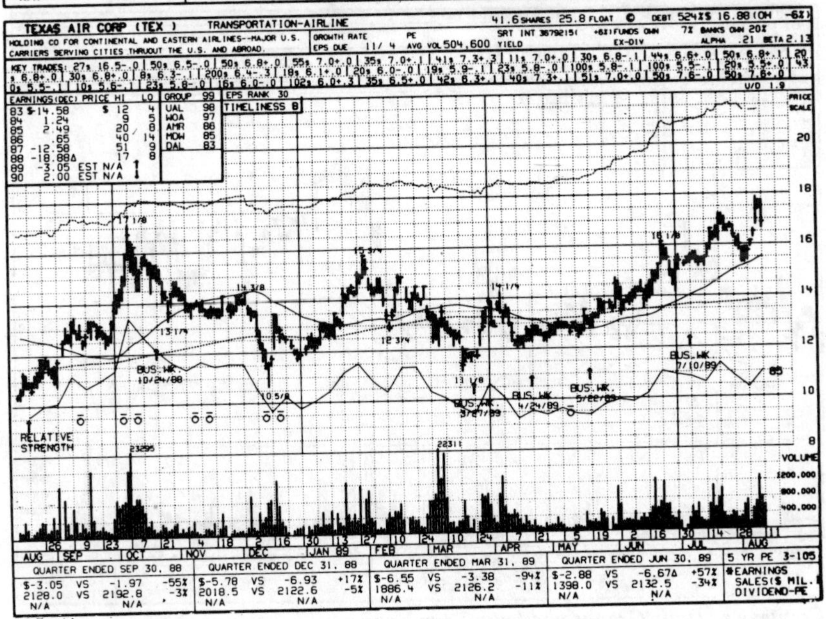

Courtesy of *Daily Graphs and Long Term Values*

Exhibit 18-1: (continued)

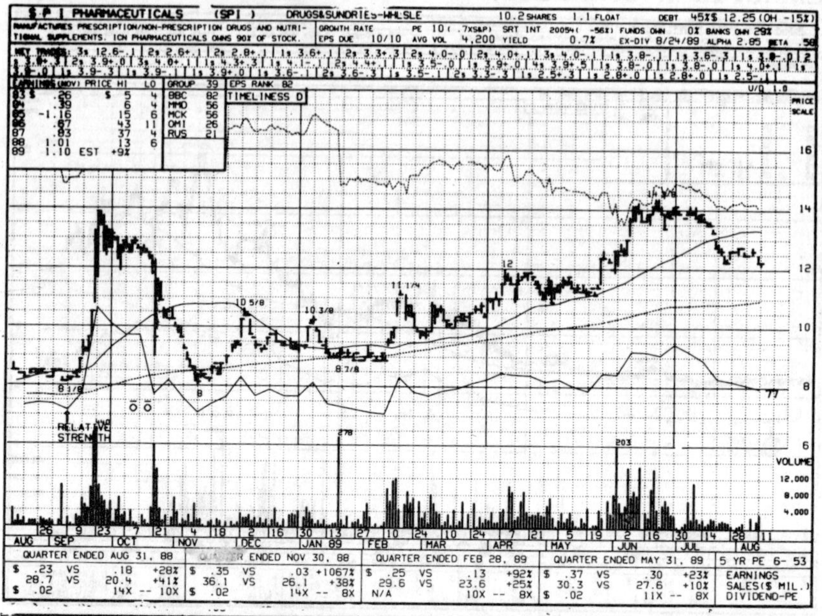

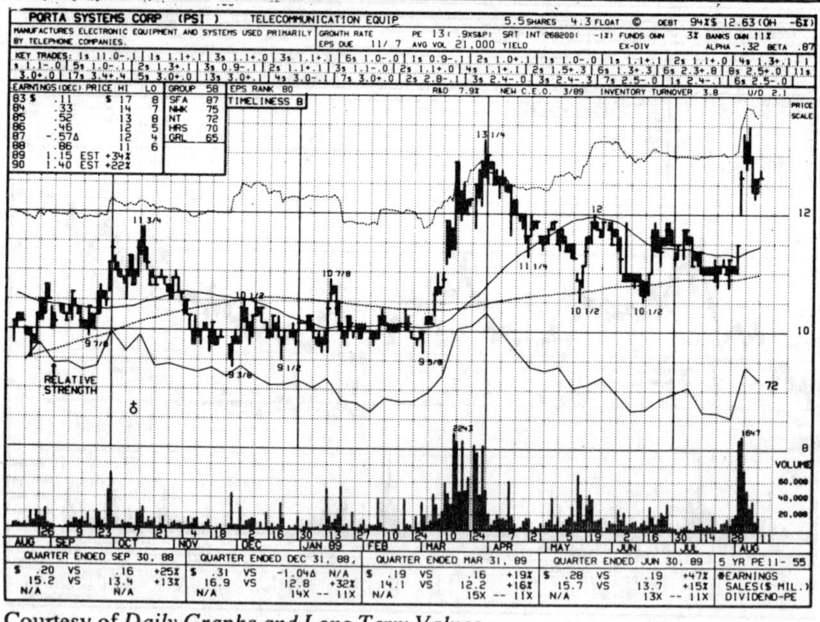

Courtesy of *Daily Graphs and Long Term Values*

Exhibit 18-1: (continued)

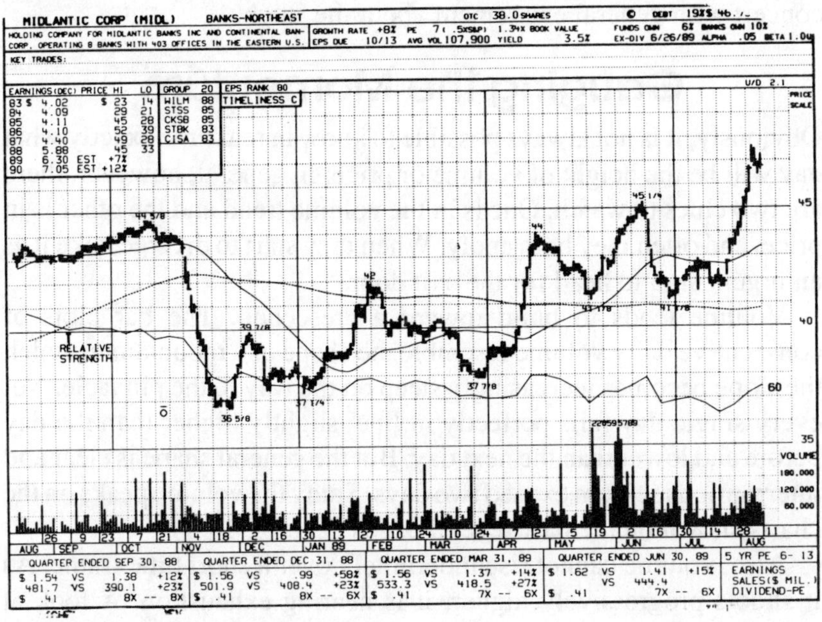

Courtesy of *Daily Graphs and Long Term Values*

exactly when the trading volume is peaking on rising prices and in concert with general excitement about the stock.

Gauging the Momentum

Obviously, it is not always possible to know in real time exactly what day will be the height of volume or price. In general, however, there are two clues to watch. One is in the volume trend and the other is in price, and often they both apply. When they start to diverge, take it as an urgent sign to head for the exit door.

Volume tends to build toward a crescendo. The bar plots of consecutive daily volume resemble the shape of a mountain in which the slope becomes increasingly steep on the way to the pinnacle. Not every single day falls perfectly in line, slightly higher than the day before and lower than the next day. But the general shape is clear and interruptions seldom exceed two days. Study the volume peaks on the charts shown on the past several pages (Exhibit 18-1).

Also, volume cannot rise indefinitely over a short time frame. As it shoots progressively higher, it is nearing exhaustion. A look at historical charts can be useful in identifying what the peak volume was when previous high points were reached. A look at a one-year daily chart, such as those supplied by the Daily Graphs service of William O'Neil and Co., Inc. (Los Angeles) quickly shows what the rough order of magnitude of the individual high-volume days was over the past 12 months, or about 250 trading days.

These can be used as serious warnings, but do not expect them to be exact or necessarily to be exceeded. When current volumes of daily trading reach into the *neighborhood* of old highs, be ready to sell without delay.

Price also provides a clue. While the broad market averages very seldom reach a high on a pattern of sharp acceleration called a "spike", many individual stocks do. This apparent anomaly is explained by the fact that averages are exactly that: they combine individual elements that sometimes diverge, but smooth the results. Not all stocks make their individual highs (or lows) on the same day or even in the same month. But viewed individually, many make highs on successive spike-like rallies accompanied by frenzied volume.

What is happening and what causes it to change? For a while, successive price rises generate interest in a stock. The price starts to accelerate, which means it starts to rise by larger increments each day or each week. But trends don't last indefinitely: at some point, traders begin to get cautious about owning, let alone still buying, the stock.

In effect, the acceleration begins to discourage new players and the most nimble players sell their shares, causing the price first to halt its rise and then to start falling. Remember, too, that each day's trading includes equal amounts of buying and selling, but the personality of the players shifts. As price has risen sharply, more holders become nervous or satisfied with the price action, so selling volume is building. (And more owners are recent short-term buyers, often referred to as hot money; these are unstable holders.)

When the buyers finally go away, sellers remain who have been waiting for one more good day or one more point. So when the price does stop rising, it falls sharply from its peak as those latest satisfied owners or nervous sellers fail to find enough interested buyers and volume falls off. Note again that stocks can fall of their own weight, but it takes buying pressure to boost them up.

It is true that it is usually not possible in real time to identify with certainty the exact high day in price or volume. But a careful study of past patterns can define an intertwined pair of yardsticks — price and volume — with which to assess when a stock is close enough to make a sell decision wise.

There is something in human nature that makes it difficult to execute this maneuver. One unscientific, but effective, approach is self-monitoring. To calibrate himself, an investor needs to be in a given stock and watch it closely on a daily basis. Record in a notebook how many consecutive days the stock has risen, and also whether a strong run in the major market averages is helping it. (Doing this exercise on paper while not owning the stock is sterile because emotions are not involved).

As the stock crescendos in price and volume, note personal daily reactions like the tug among fear and greed and excitement; then record them daily on a chart for future reference. When a sale is made during this flagpole run-up, take note afterward whether the sale was premature or late — and by how many days the peak was miscalculated.

Note also what the best hunch was at the time the sell order was given. In effect, that is calibrating a personal pressure gauge. Photocopy the daily price chart a week later and attach it to the notes. Then next time, incorporate the latest results into an operating plan. Naturally this is imprecise, and alternating (later/sooner) approaches may feel unscientific. But after a few experiences, a good feel develops. Again, this exercise works only in real trading in the presence of risk and tension. It is also most effective if several observations can be made in a fairly concentrated period of time, at most a couple of months. Otherwise even with written notes, recall is not accurate because of lack of intensity.

One of the key points to remember in a rapid price run-up is not to aim for a perfect exit. The stock's action will be very volatile from hour to hour and if an investor is typically busy, he probably has only one decision time per day with a broker, two at most.

So do not expect to get the highest eighth. If an investor can hit the best day, he is partly clever and partly lucky. If he hits within one day on either side, he is quite accurate. So keep a cool perspective: if a stock makes three high-volume price peaks a year, being within a day of the top when selling means picking one of the nine best trading days out of 250 in a year. That is besting odds of over 25:1. Congratulations.

As a general rule, remember to trade successfully in up markets by selling into strong price and volume crescendos. That is selling when the buying crowd reaches fever pitch rather than becoming one of the crowd. Do not worry about catching the top perfectly, and enter sell instructions in this circumstance at market rather than getting greedy. Even if there is more frequent (than once-daily) contact, decide to make only one choice (selling or holding) per day. That construct imposes a degree of structure on sell decisions. Resist wanting to think more about it. Come to closure.

Be content to look again at the stock no sooner than a week or two later: if it was sold at the height of a mountain of trading volume, it is more than likely that its price has fallen back and that the sale was a good one.

In summary, there are two aspects of selling on high volume to remember:

- Realize that volume will crescendo only so high, and use stock-specific past history as a guide to the reasonably likely upper limits.
- If volume starts to trail off after a build-up and price keeps going up, it is the weak, later portion of the price rise and time is running out. The charts of Inracare and Midlantic presented on prior pages illustrate the failure of volume build-ups to support further price advances.

SECTION

IV

Selling Tactics

CHAPTER

19

Analyze "Market Stock" and "Loner Stock" Characteristics

KEYS TO INVESTMENT SUCCESS

- Know the portrait of a Market Stock
- Know the portrait of a Loner Stock

When considering whether to hold or sell, one of the determining factors is whether the stock is what is termed a "market stock." This is an important consideration because it can tilt investor judgment at the margin: if there is a forceful trend in the overall market (either up or down), this can affect the stock's performance in the short term; or it may not, depending on its nature. The opposite issue is characterized here as a "loner stock."

The following lists differentiate characteristics for these two stock categories. Note that a stock need not fit all of the descriptors in either list:

Market Stocks are:

- Held primarily by institutions,
- Consistently heavily-traded and liquid,
- Big-capitalization issues,
- Stocks with high betas or betas near 1.00,
- Among the Dow-Jones Industrials, or especially the S&P 100,
- Sometimes in the trend-carrying industry group,
- Stocks in which options volume is heavy,
- Nonfinancial and nonutility companies,
- Household names with average individual investors,
- Outstanding fundamental achievers in their industries,
- Not noticeably out of favor,
- Familiar and acceptable to non-U.S. investors.

Loner stocks are:

- Not widely-held by institutions,
- Small-capitalization companies,
- Medium-capitalization but not heavily-traded,
- Often listed on the Amex or over-the-counter, with few market-makers,
- In interest-rate-sensitive groups,
- Concept or story stocks,
- High-technology, unseasoned companies,

- Low-priced issues,
- Stocks with betas below 0.50 or negative,
- High-yield situations,
- Not widely followed, if at all, by analysts,
- New issues,
- Held primarily by insiders or parent companies,
- Countercyclical,
- Stocks that fall outside conventional industry descriptions,
- Regional or local companies not widely-known,
- Regarded as fundamental laggards in their industries.

Portrait of a Market Stock

What defines a market stock is a high coincidence of daily price moves parallel with the direction of the major market averages. Statistically that means perhaps seven days in ten, because on days of clear market direction, typically 60 percent of stocks move in the dominant direction. But such a high correlation of individual daily movement with the overall trend is not something that can be checked readily when the need for a real-time decision to hold or sell arises. The investor must know in advance.

A recent run of seven out of ten days could be just a coincidence, or it could be driven by unusual sweeping and emotional trends in the overall market. Therefore in testing whether an issue is a market stock, refer to the lists of traits above. The benefit of knowing these characteristics is that they can be reviewed at any time before the pressure of a sell/hold decision occurs. Make a mental or written note about which characteristics of the stock apply when it is bought, or even before.

Knowing whether the issue is a market stock or an independent stock is important when making the hold/sell decision, and also when it is time to cash in for a good sale in terms of micro tactics. With a market stock under these circumstances, look even more closely at the short-term trend or at likely action in the general market.

This review is important because, statistically, the stock is likely to perform in line with the overall list direction and may move by a meaningful percentage. In this case, the consideration should be the merit of selling at market versus an above-market limit (or conceivably a stop-loss order) in the context not only of the stock's action and chart position, but also in light of the overall market's dominant trend and probable daily action.

Take McDonald's, for example, which tends to move with the market on most days when there is a clear market trend. With the exception of being in a trend-carrying group (restaurants have not been trendy for most of the 1980s), McDonald's fits the list of typical market stocks. If there is a broad market rally or a sharp selloff in which major money moves the market, McDonald's is very likely to move in the dominant direction. This is because the stock is a leader in its group, a component of the major averages, subject to inclusion in program trading and a big-capitalization name that institutional and individual investors — domestic and overseas — readily trade when they expect a sharp market move.

Except shortly after one of its periodic splits, McDonald's is usually high-priced enough so that a change of a point or more is not unusual on a big-move day in the overall market. So if a McDonald's investor has decided to cash in, he should pay more than the usual amount of attention to the general market's near-term direction.

Suppose McDonald's has had a pretty good run to the upside lately and an investor, therefore, thinks it is getting overextended. If the general list is moving up or is likely to react sharply to some favorable overnight economic or geopolitical news, the seller ought to give McDonald's a little more running room right now because it is a market stock. Instead of selling at market, he puts in a limit above market (unless the stock is running into serious resistance, or unless some company-specific news is out).

Or if the stock on merit is not thought be an urgent sell but the dominant market trend seems sharply down and/or the current day's direction is a real "flusher," he should lean more heavily toward the immediate sale of McDonald's because of the market context. The seller assumes that the stock will move with the overall list because of its personality and because of the deep pockets who are likely to be trading in it.

In this case, the stock is unlikely to "fight the tape" of the general decline. Because of the nature of the stock and its holders, it probably will drop with the list despite its own merit. One is better served to sell at market rather than to reach for an above-market limit. It is better not to miss the market and give back a fast point or more of the gain.

Portrait of a Loner Stock

In contrast is the typical non-market-influenced, or loner, issue. By any one or several of the listed characteristics, this stock simply is not in daily rhythm with the general list. Probably the most common keys to identifying these loner stocks are low daily trading volume, nonstellar fundamental performance within their industry and regional rather than national or international stature.

These attributes make a stock somewhat unattractive to big players, which can cause holders disappointment on the upside; but there is a consolation: except in crashes and temporary panics, non-market stocks probably hold well against a market downdraft lasting a day or two. The reason is that there is no hot money in them and they are not vulnerable to profit-taking by active big players.

It is most important not to count on the strength and direction of the overall list when making a sell/hold tactical judgment about a loner stock that marches to its own separate drummer. That is because it is too easy to become overly-optimistic about the stock's short-term prospects in a strong market. Here, an investor often decides the overall market is so strong that the stock should get some benefit; he holds on in the belief that the rising tide will raise all boats.

If he is dealing with a stock that acts independently, his mistaken logic is likely to cause disappointment. He is probably allowing the market's action to provide a subtle rationalization for postponing the sale decision. So it is important to know the personality of market and independent stocks, and factor those traits into the hold/sell decision. On a short-term tactical basis, this added insight helps get better selling prices.

C H A P T E R

20

Use Above-Market Instead of Stop-Loss Orders

KEYS TO INVESTMENT SUCCESS

- Understanding the Weaknesses of Stop-Loss Orders
- Knowing the Advantages of Above-Market Sell Orders
- Summary of Contrasting Styles and Results

The few brokers and investment books that provide selling guidance to clients generally advocate the use of stop-loss orders as a selling strategy. This chapter advocates, instead, the use of above-market sell orders (except in very limited circumstances), which tend to be more profitable.

To illustrate, consider the old investment slogan: cut the losses and let the profits run. The theory is that investors and traders should be relatively intolerant of nonperforming or weak positions, and should resist the temptation to pocket a quick, small gain on successful buys, holding on instead for the big, long-term payoff.

This prescription *sounds* simple and obvious, but it is difficult to execute tactically. There is no quarrel with the objective of avoiding losses or with noting the time value of money, which can be a friend or a subtle enemy. Obviously there is no argument with letting big profits accumulate.

The trick is choosing between these orders in real time. When there is actual money on the line and when emotions are clouding the decision-making process, it is difficult to discern which current, small-loss stocks will hibernate at present quotes or go south even further, and which others will turn into glorious successes.

Weaknesses of Stop-Loss Orders

Stop-loss orders should be used in very limited circumstances because their success depends upon being handled with near-surgical skill. Their most common usage is often a cop-out on the part of the supporting writer, the broker and the investor who implements the tactic.

Cop-outs and Crutches

Brokers, as described in earlier chapters, are loathe to deal with money-losing positions. One convenient way for the broker to avoid the bind of discussing losses is to advise the client to limit exposure with a stop-loss order that is a moderate percentage away from the buy point (recall the critique of that tactic in Chapter 7). If an account shows a mixture of profits and losses, and the losses are never drastic, the broker and his firm are safe from charges of incompetence or inattention with this strategy.

While stop-loss orders routinely placed below the buy level do limit the size of individual losses, their main function is to relieve the broker and the investor of making a decision — in real time, when money is on the line — about selling, holding or doubling up on a losing position. The market does it automatically for the broker and the client, or it does nothing. The automatic pilot gets the credit or blame.

Bad Placement

In addition to this shortcoming, routine stop-loss orders have two other weaknesses: they are usually not placed at a logical price level and they necessarily cause a sale on weakness rather than on strength.

For example, many advocates of the routine stop-loss order advise its placement at a standard percentage below cost basis. The most common allowable losses are 10 percent, 5 percent and 15 percent. To all but the most timid market players, such losses are acceptable even though they fall short of the desired result. There are three objections to the use of arbitrary percentages:

- The entry point (purchase price) is irrelevant to defining a good exit point, as detailed in Chapter 7.
- Routine use of a fixed-percentage-width cushion ignores the inherently unique volatilities/liquidities of different stocks.
- The stop-loss point should be set on the basis of support levels or trendlines, which may be closer or farther away than the percentage method dictates.

The importance of the first point cannot be overemphasized: the level used for a cost price has no relevance to the question of where to cut losses (or take a profit). Without solving the longstanding debate about the merit of technical analysis, any participant who so wishes can look at a price-history chart and make some reasonable judgments about the prices at which a given stock will have proven something (on the upside) and at which it will have shown fatal weakness (on the downside).

If a chart analyst is told by a stock's owner, "But I should have told you that my cost price is 44," the only logical response is, "So what?" The point is, if a stock breaks major support by breaking 43 ½, that is a fact regardless of who the unlucky holders are and regardless of whether they paid 44, 21 or 65.

If this book described how to buy stocks, it would define how to buy to avoid the danger of being so close to the break-down point. But the selling perspective emphasizes that cost basis is irrelevant to a sale decision. Therefore, attaching any specific percentage limit below the cost point is an irrelevant formula. It is about as logical as basing salary on a fixed multiple of age or height.

Setting aside the problem of using cost price as a starting point, the use of any fixed tolerance measure (x percent, for example, or y points) is unrelated to the characteristics of the position. Stocks have inherent tendencies toward volatility, which may be defined roughly as percentage fluctuation within a day or week compared with the percentage fluctuation of a broad market index (students of market action and measurers of investment managerial performance refer to this as beta.)

There is no need to know whether the price volatility of a given stock is caused by price level, floating supply, player emotions or other factors. Just observe that stocks fluctuate with their own amplitudes that change over long time periods. For one stock at $20.00, a daily range of plus or minus $0.125 is normal (check many utility shares as examples); for another $20.00 stock, a $1.00 daily range is typical (look at biotech and computer-peripherals issues).

What is tolerable "in-the-noise" movement for one stock is a sign of significant change in the supply/demand balance for another because they have inherently different personalities. Because of these observable and very real differences, imposing a standard percentage of breathing room on all stocks is nonsensical.

So a well-placed stop-loss order at least ought to take into account the natural fluctuation tendency of the stock rather than assume all are alike. A staid utility is reacting to a massive change in interest rates or major risk to its dividend by falling 15 percent, so a 15 percent stop is too loose. A wide-swinging growth stock might gyrate 20 percent around its moving average, so a 10 percent or 15 percent stop-loss range is self-defeating at the start.

Finally, a stop-loss should be at the level dictated by trend lines or support levels rather than a percentage subtraction from a level such as entry. Take a stock which has an established trading channel for several months between the prices of 40 and 44, for example. If it is clear that 39 ⅞ is a breakdown in support, then the proper stop-loss point is 39 ⅞. That means that if an investor buys the stock at 41, the 5, 10 or 15 percent-down tolerances are too wide. And, if he buys at 43 — near the top of the range, in the hope of a breakout — the 10 and 15 percent allowances are still naive in light of what the chart says. The 5 percent level would probably whipsaw the investor, getting him out below 41 just before the stock tests support in the lower end of the channel — from which it might rally again.

The point is that the stop-loss order, if used at all, should be placed based on the market condition of the stock and not on a percentage formula. Also, it should be placed where its violation signals a significant negative move for the stock: not higher and not lower. This involves a precise analysis of the chart and should not be related to the investor's entry point.

This chapter takes the position that stop-loss orders should be used sparingly, if at all. Their placement should occur after taking a close look at a stock and deciding — on merit and on the basis of the chart pattern — what price says bail out and what price indicates that the market is saying something unknown is going wrong. If the reader developes the mental discipline this book teaches, the psychological crutch of a stop will be unnecessary.

If an investor is in contact frequently with his broker (daily or more), he does not need an order on the specialist's book. If he has noted the critical level in advance and is disciplined, he will prefer to sell at market when it happens. However, if an investor travels or is inaccessible, then a stop-loss order should be used.

Harmful Market Influences

There are common times when a technically well-placed stop-loss order is an error. For example when general market weakness takes place on rumors, or in response to massive program trading, price levels in individual stocks become meaningless as their usual liquidity disappears and as all buyers run for cover.

But here again when the problem passes, the stop order will have proven too tight even if placed with logic beforehand. In 20-20 hindsight, it is easy to see that the investor was stopped out for market-driven rather than stock-specific reasons, and he will have cash rather than a full portfolio after the temporary panic bottom has passed.

Finally, it is important for an investor to fine tune the use of stops within the broker relationship. If he uses a discount broker, he will need to lean more toward stops for any given situation. If he uses a full-service firm, he may get a warning call from the broker when something starts to break down or the news goes bad. In this way, he can get out at a higher price than if he waits for the stop to be exercised.

In essence then, it is better to rely on broker assistance than to use the mechanical stop-loss order. Some brokers occasionally accept discretion in placing an order if they cannot reach a client. If a broker agrees to operate on this basis, here is yet another good reason for not using stop-losses.

Advantages of Above-Market Sell Orders

Rather than using a stop below the market, which means that the sale, if any, will occur at a price below the available level at the time the order is first entered, it is preferable to use targeted sell stops above the market. When targeted sell stops above the market are executed, they give a better price than the price prevailing when the order was entered.

Like stop-loss orders, these orders also carry caveats and qualifiers. An above-market stop-sell order is not appropriate in all situations; sometimes a market sale is better. And the above-market stop-sell order must also be placed with precision and care.

To place a stop-sell accurately, first visualize what kind of overall market climate prevails and is likely to exist over the time period of the projected above-market stop-sell. A stop-loss below market is there to provide protection against further loss, while an above-market stop-sell order should be used to exit a stock when the investor believes reasonable patience and the market's normal fluctuation working together can get a better price. But a reasonable expectation for upside potential is determined to some degree by the overall market trend and by the stock's own price pattern.

Going back to the stock with a lengthy channel between 40 and 44, assume that a sale seems in order but is not extremely urgent. In a market moving sideways or moderately higher, an investor would set an above-market sell-stop order at 43 ¼ in this situation.

If the overall market is quite strong but the stock remains frustratingly trapped in its channel, he might have more aggressive expectations and put the order at 43 ⅝ or 43 ¾. He certainly would not put in a sell at 44 ¼ or higher because it would be triggered exactly and only when the stock surprises him with an upside breakout. That level would give exactly the wrong sale timing by being at the wrong price.

On the other hand in a moderately weak market, the owner might be happy with anything at all in the upper half of the channel; so he might set the stop-sell at 42 ½ or 43, at most.

In a violent bear move, there would be no sense in setting an above-market sell level: if the investor is not willing to hold this stock through the coming carnage, he should assume the damage will continue and should, therefore, sell now rather than wait for a rally.

On a short-term basis, also observe the trend of the stock and the general market in recent days: lean against it in direction and degree. If the stock and/or the major averages have been up several days running, any further upside attempt with a stop-sell above current levels should be quite limited. On the other hand if the stock or the market has fallen several days running but has not destroyed important uptrend lines or support levels, look for some rebound and place the order a bit farther away (higher).

Another strategy for placing the stop-sell is to measure actual recent daily fluctuation. Calculate the actual daily price ranges for the last two to four weeks, from daily newspapers or from a good, detailed daily-basis chart service. Suppose that an investor learns that a stock has an average daily range (high minus low) of 1 ¼ points. And he also learns that on most of the days in the study window the issue moved by at least ⅝ of a point during the day (measuring total daily range here, not net change from close to close).

In this example, the investor might place a stop-sell about ¾ to ⅞ above the current close, assuming that the close was roughly in the middle of its daily range. On average — assuming that the whole market does not collapse and that the company does not suddenly issue bad news — a few days or a week's patience should get a better price.

Summary of Contrasting Styles and Results

Again, the degree of aggressiveness in placing the order compared with the actual fluctuation pattern is influenced by the direction of the stock and of the overall market. It bears repeating that if the reason for sale is bad fundamental or technical news for the company or if an exit is considered because the overall market is creating tension, an above-market sell-stop is a bet against self.

The major message of this chapter is that above-market sell-stops give a reasonable chance of better sale proceeds if there is more to be had; below-market stop-loss orders guarantee a worse price than is available right now. Do not use arbitrary percentage stops, and do not use stop-losses as a mental crutch. Instead, face those selling decisions head on and do what is necessary in real time. This discipline serves well in current dollars as well as in greater wisdom about the market in future situations.

CHAPTER

21

Use Special Rules for Selling Low-Priced Stocks

KEYS TO INVESTMENT SUCCESS

- Consider Brokerage Firms' Policies
- Maintenance Margins

There are three key dollar levels to keep in mind when buying or selling stocks in the low-priced category: $2.00, $3.00 and $5.00. (See Exhibit 21-1.) Their effects are different, depending on whether the low-priced stock is rising or falling through these price levels. The extent of their effects is more pronounced on the downside, so it is important to pay close attention to selling tactics in this price category.

First consider the $2.00 price level, which is often thought of as the badge of respectability by most brokerage houses. If an investor wants to buy a stock that is trading below $2.00 per share, most brokerage firms require him to sign what is called in the trade an "unsolicited letter." This is a pre-written form letter from the client to the firm saying the stock was picked by the client, who realizes that trading in low-priced stocks is a risky business and that he will not blame the firm if this stock loses money.

Because of the nature of the letter, there is no requirement to sign it to *sell* a low-priced issue. Theoretically, the firm is supposed to have the letter signed and filed before purchase, unless the client is known and trusted. The terms of this letter requirement should serve as a mild deterrent to buying stocks under $2.00 a share. But this has only a moderate effect in bull markets, when people are optimistic rather than fearful.

By contrast, in bear markets the letter requirement has a chilling effect. If media headlines concern layoffs, recession, bankruptcies and similar news, many investors hesitate when their broker tells them about the requirement. And that means the chances are low that the buy order will get placed, for several reasons.

The hesitant investor muses about the bear market, the fact that his broker seems not to want a commission and may be erecting legal defenses in advance if he does accept the trade. So the effect of the unsolicited-letter rule can be a depressant on price in a bear-market climate as stocks slip below that $2.00 level. The converse, however, is not true: when a stock goes above $2.00 per share, additional buying is not likely to be generated by the fact that brokers are silent, not needing to exercise the unsolicited-letter routine.

Know also that many brokerage firms waive the rule if the stock in question is traded on a major stock exchange, so ask in advance. Ironically, an investor who buys stock in a profitable, dynamic company trading over-the-counter at $1.75 is required to sign an unsolicited letter. But if he buys the most shaky, debt-ridden, exchange-listed company whose sales are shrinking, whose equity is negative and whose prospects of turning around are slim and none, selling at $0.25 per share, no letter is required.

Exhibit 21-1: Price Drops Through $5, $3 and $2

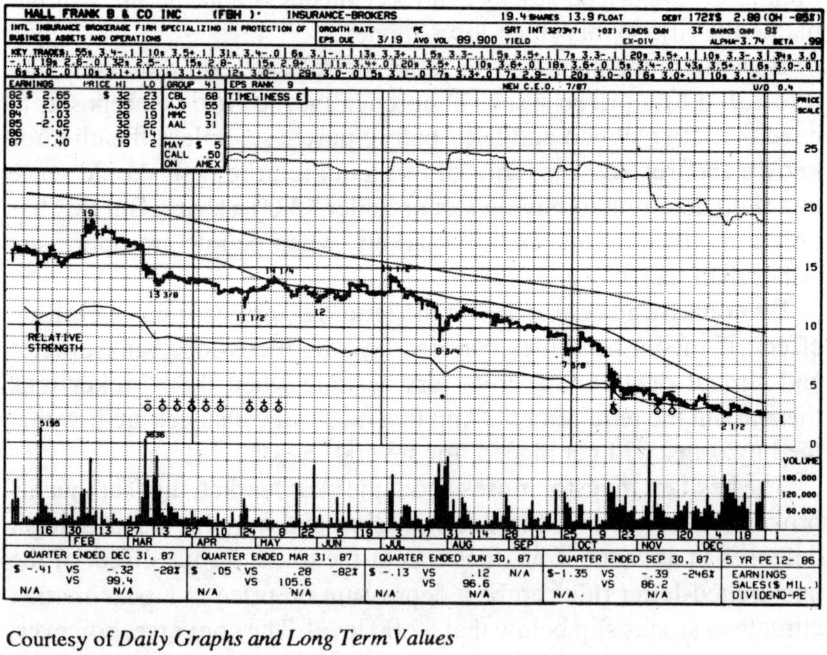

Courtesy of *Daily Graphs and Long Term Values*

Exhibit 21-1: Price Drops Through $5, $3 and $2 (continued)

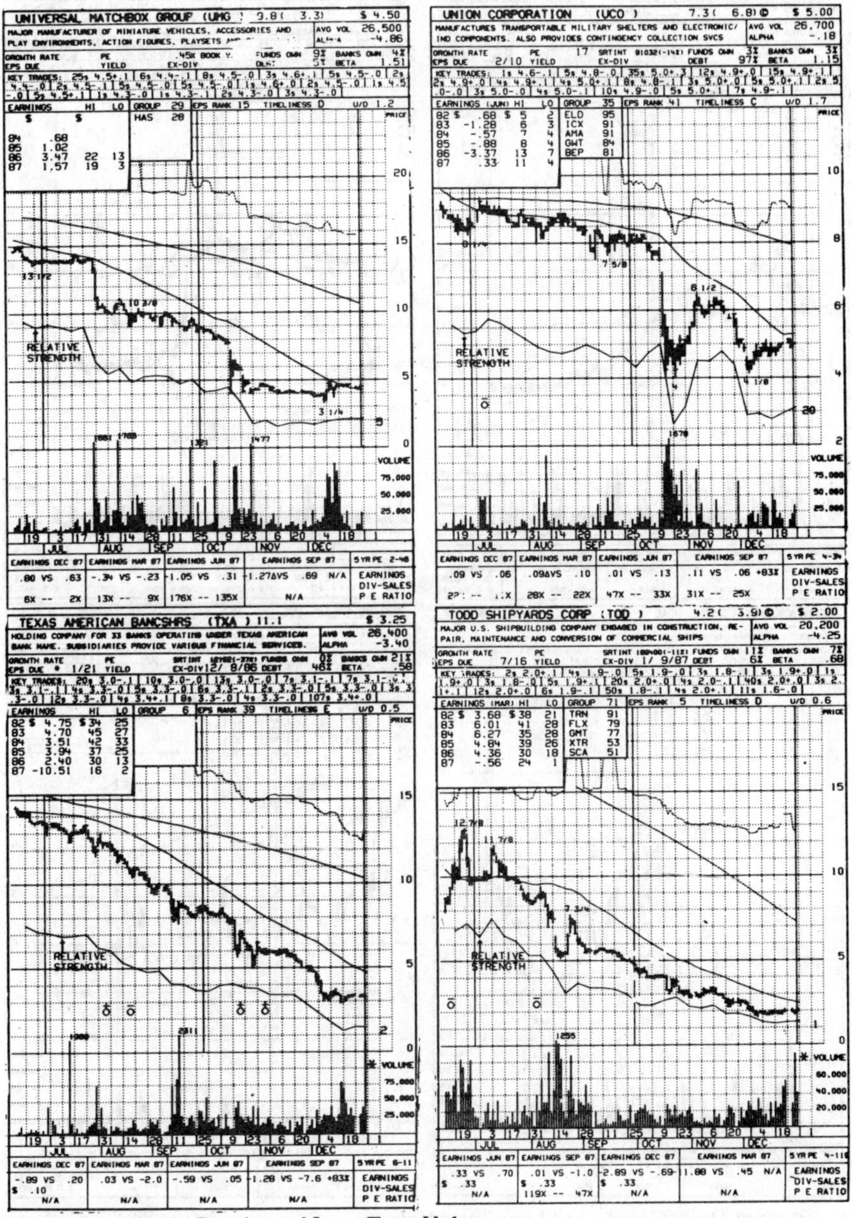

Courtesy of *Daily Graphs and Long Term Values*

Exhibit 21-1: Price Drops Through $5, $3 and $2 (continued)

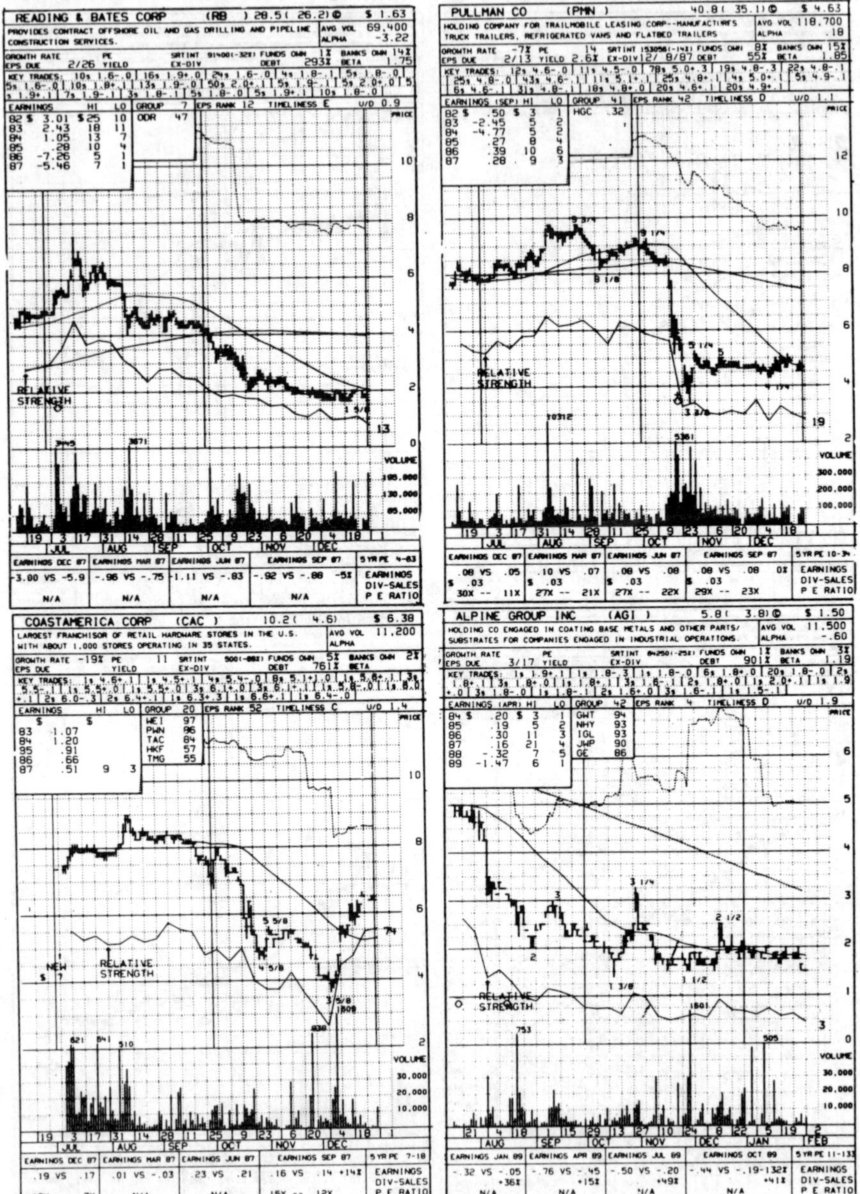

Courtesy of *Daily Graphs and Long Term Values*

Exhibit 21-1: Price Drops Through $5, $3 and $2 (continued)

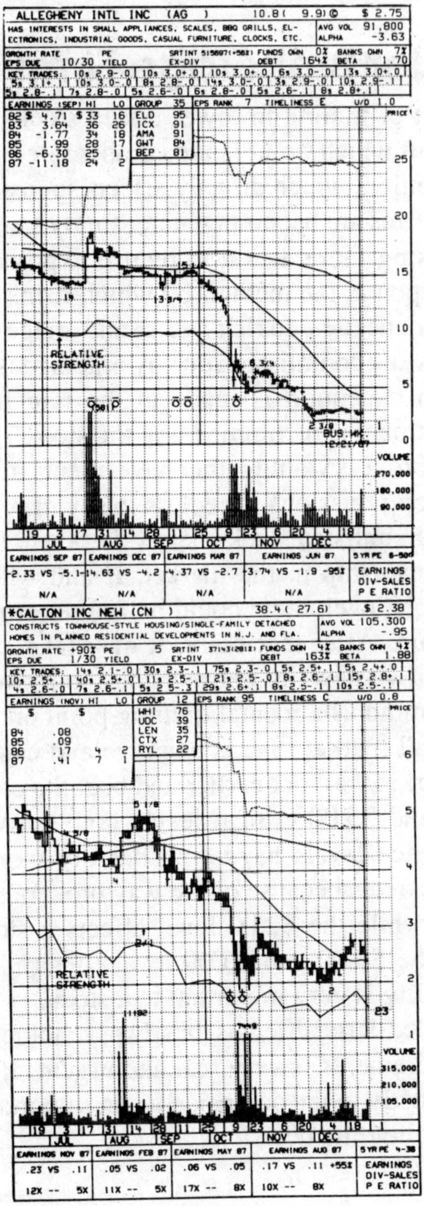

Courtesy of *Daily Graphs and Long Term Values*

Consider Brokerage Firms' Policies

Another aspect of trading in lower-priced stocks is also worthy of note: the way in which brokers are compensated and what grabs or loses their attention, which directly affects sponsorship for a stock.

Brokerage firms are becoming increasingly sensitive to legal risk, so they are taking more action to reduce exposure. One defensive brokerage weapon is the method by which firms pay their brokers. Some firms have become so risk-averse and image-conscious they do not pay brokers any commission on buy orders for stocks under $2.00 per share. (An exception is made in the rare instance when the research department is recommending the stock.)

Obviously, brokers would rather have clients invest in a stock that pays buy-side commissions. Needless to say, if brokers are not paid for buy orders in unlisted stocks below $2.00 per share, those issues have little sponsorship in the market. If and when the price slips below that magic level, there could be further erosion caused when demand dries up. After that point, it may take an unusually large amount of positive news to get the stock to move up. So keep the $2.00 level in mind as a mental quitting point on stocks, especially when the overall market tone is negative and cautious. In fact in a fear-driven market, bail out earlier and beat the crowd.

The $3.00 and $5.00 critical levels both derive from the same basis. These price levels have considerably more significance in terms of price effects because of the way brokerage rules work. The reason is that while the $2.00 level affects a stock's market "respectability," the $3.00 and $5.00 levels determine marginability. And marginability is very important to a stock.

The unsolicited-letter effect is mostly psychological, but the effect of margin requirements is very real and urgent. It definitely moves stock prices, mostly to the downside — an important effect to factor into selling and holding decisions.

Margin Loans

The ability of a brokerage firm to make margin loans to purchasers of securities is governed under Regulation T of the Federal Reserve Board (under Regulation U for margin loans from commercial banks). The Board can change the rules of the game whenever necessary, although in recent years there has been less tinkering with margin requirements than in the past.

Basically, the Board sets as a policy the percentage of a purchase price that a brokerage firm (and, technically, a member bank) can loan to the customer. For historic reasons, this power has been used to regulate speculation and to allocate credit within the economy.

For many years, the going percentage has been 50 percent. If an investor wants to buy $10,000 worth of stock, he can do so with only $5,000 of his own equity. The brokerage firm loans him the rest (and charges interest on the borrowed balance). This is a very convenient type of loan because it requires no credit check or qualification, and it does not require monthly payments against principal.

As long as the value of the collateral (i.e., the stock bought and held by the brokerage as security) is not badly impaired, the brokerage firm allows an investor to continue carrying the loan as long as he holds the stock. When the stock is sold, the loan gets paid off out of the proceeds. (See Table 21-1.)

Maintenance Margins

The level called "maintenance margin" is generally the 40 percent. That means the brokerage firm can let the investor's margin of equity shrink to the 40-percent level before it is forced to call him for more cash (margin call).

Here is how the 40-percent maintenance-margin rule works in practice. Suppose that an investor buys 1,000 shares of XYZ common at $10 per share and puts up the minimum 50 percent required. (Commissions are ignored for the sake of simplicity; but the commis-

Table 21-1. Margin Loans

	Price	Value	Less Debit	Equals Equity	% Equity
Situation #1					
Just Bought					
1000 at $10	10.00	10,000	5,000	5,000	50%
Borrowed $5,000					
Situation #2					
Stock Drops					
to $9	9.00	9,000	5,000	4,000	44%
Situation #3					
Stock Drops					
to $8.50	8.50	8,500	5,000	3,500	41%
Situation #4					
Stock Drops					
to $8.25	8.25	8,250	5,000	3,250	39%

sion is allowed as part of the gross amount, so he can borrow half of it, too.) He borrows $5,000 from the brokerage firm and sends in the other $5,000. If the stock stays steady at $10 per share, obviously his equity stays at the 50 percent level (before the monthly subtraction of interest charges).

But if the stock declines, his percentage of equity in the position decreases. Assuming that interest charges have not been taken yet (which increases his debit balance and thereby reduces equity), his equity will fall to the 40-percent level when the stock has declined to $8.33 per share.

To calculate, take the amount of the debit or loan balance, and divide by 60 percent (the complement of the 40 percent), to get the minimum market value allowed. If the stock is worth $8,333 (1,000 shares times $8.33 each) and the loan is the original $5,000, the remaining equity is now just $3,333, or the difference between the gross market value and the loan balance.

Below that point, the broker must demand that by the next business day the client add more money to his account to reduce the loan balance. If the investor fails to do that, the broker is required to sell sufficient stock out of the account to restore up to at least a 40-percent position.

For the sake of simplicity, the account shown consisted of just one stock. In actual practice, all of the stocks in the account are valued together, and the total loan balance against the stocks is calculated as a single figure. The effect of one stock dropping from 10 to 8 ¼ is softened by the likelihood that other stocks in the account stayed steady or rose in value. Most brokerage firms produce analyses of all accounts every night; brokers get notified in the morning if any accounts need a call. The compliance department makes sure that the brokers enforce the rules and get clients to pay margin calls promptly. The alternative, to stay within the rules and to protect the firm's capital, is to sell out some of the stocks. If a client does not choose which to sell, the firm does it for him — without delay.

Not-Marginable Stocks

There is one other critical aspect of margin rules that directly affects the calculation of equity margin: the marginability of specific stocks. The Securities & Exchange Commission or the listing exchange sometimes designates certain securities as "not marginable," usually because their price behavior has been highly erratic. With sharp fluctuations in prices, values in margin accounts gyrate daily, causing margin calls and adding to market instability. To avoid this, highly-volatile stocks are declared nonmarginable. This, in itself, tends to dampen their volatility because some speculative purchasing power is voided.

Any stock can, regardless of volatility, become nonmarginable for another reason that is the focus of an important warning: price alone can get the stock in marginability trouble. In the past, the standard rule was $5.00 per share. In recent years during the trend toward less government regulation, price level has been left to the discretion of brokerage firms. Many have retained the traditional $5.00 rule, while others have adopted $3.00; both have implications for the price behavior of stocks.

The $5.00 and the $3.00 levels can signal danger for stocks in a declining market. When a stock falls through either of those levels, its decline is likely to accelerate because of margin rules. First, the stock immediately becomes 100 percent worthless for calculating margins. That, in turn, causes the brokerage firm to send out margin calls to clients who own the stock in margin accounts, and whose calculated equity has been impaired by the sudden exclusion of the stock from the margin formula.

To illustrate, suppose an investor's account consists of 2,000 shares of a stock bought at $5 per share. He puts up the minimum 50 percent or $5,000, and borrows the other $5,000 from the firm. (His broker is irresponsible to allow this, knowing that a serious problem lurks just ⅛ point away.) As soon as the stock declines to close at 4 ⅞ or lower, a printout is placed on the broker's desk. The entire portfolio has dropped below the marginable level.

Per the house rules, the investor has a loan of $5,000 outstanding and no allowable collateral behind the loan. He has not been wiped out because at 4 ⅞ the stock is worth $9,750; equity is $4,750 after subtracting the loan. But the rules say that the stock is now worthless for margin calculation. He is not broke, but his credit line has been pulled.

The investor has four choices; unfortunately, none of them is to call for a time-out. First, he can send the broker $5,000 to pay off the loan immediately. Second, he can send in stock certificates of other companies that are marginable. But those certificates must equal $8,333 in market value of marginable stock. This strategy leaves $8,333 in countable assets to secure the $5,000 loan and a countable equity of $3,333 after the loan is subtracted; it thus restores the minimum 40 percent maintenance margin level.

The third choice is to sell without delay at least $5,000 worth of now nonmarginable stock, or a little over half of the total, to satisfy the compliance department and federal regulators. A fourth option is to sell from the account at least $10,000 worth of stocks that are still marginable, if any such are available.

Whenever maintenance calls occur, at least some stockholders sell part or all of the stock, which creates a sudden avalanche of shares coming into the market for sale at quickly declining prices. Because knowledgeable market players see the situation plainly, very few people bid to buy the stock. If it is an over-the-counter stock, market-making firms lighten inventory to the minimum to control their loss exposure. In a listed stock, the specialist is less willing to take stock unless it is at a price concession.

The psycho-mechanics of the market dictate that this process unfolds a fraction above the key $5.00 level. Knowing how margin rules work, few investors are willing to buy a stock that has fallen from $6.00 or above to near $5.00, creating a weak market.

There are three refinements in this example. First, most investors own more than one stock in their margin accounts. So the decline of one stock below $5.00 does not wipe out their marginable assets. Second, not all margin accounts are down to minimum equity, so a drop in one stock — even from $5.00 to a countable zero — may not cause an immediate problem. And third, when one stock causes a problem in a margin account, there is no rule that says this particular stock must be the one singled out for sale to satisfy the margin call.

In practice, of course, the offending stock often is thrown overboard for psychological and financial reasons. First, when the broker says there is a margin call on XYZ stock, the investor examines his options and discovers that selling any other stock generates half its dollar value toward equity and the rest toward the loan. This is because of the 50-percent rule and the fact that once the stock is sold, it is no longer an asset in the account against which to borrow.

But selling the offending stock, which suddenly has zero loan value, nets full, dollar-for-dollar relief. Since this is the troubled stock, the broker is quick to point out that this stock is likely to feel pressure as other people sell it to meet their margin calls. The investor is wise to sell as soon as possible to get the best price.

Against these forces, he must be extremely stubborn or highly convinced that the intrinsic value of XYZ makes it worth holding through the storm. While there is no rule that this stock must be sold, it is clearly the top candidate for dumping.

All facets of the $5.00 level apply equally at the $3.00 level for the market and for some brokerage firms. Some investors do not face a margin call generated by the $3.00 scenario until their stock slides below $3.00. But there are dozens of other brokerage firms that still adhere to the $5.00 rule, so their clients sell stock at that level, driving the price down. These price declines at both margin call levels have an equal effect even when an investor does not have a margin account. Foregoing a margin account certainly protects him from margin calls, but it does not protect against the downdraft in prices when *other* investors get *their* calls.

Remember also that in a general bear market — as opposed to a situation in which one stock is distressed due to specific news — the effect is intensified. Players are apprehensive, so fewer come up with added cash to meet their margin calls. The instinctive reaction is to sell out now. In addition, the weakness of unrelated stocks can cause derivative selling in the issue to help other investors meet their margin calls.

There is no converse side to this $3.00 and $5.00 phenomenon. The only benefit of having a stock trade a safe distance above $3.00 or $5.00 is that it is safely marginable. So some buyers may buy extra shares using credit. But there is no automatic surge in price when the stock edges through $5.00 on the upside. Players know that using margin then is fraught with peril because the stock easily could slip back to 4 ⅞.

The bottom-line lesson is to draw a red zone at all times around stocks if they slip toward the $5.00 or $3.00 levels. Use perhaps a half-dollar safety zone in a normal market and a wider buffer in a bear market, particularly if it has gotten violent. Be realistic and expect the worst; anticipate trouble before it starts. Getting out at 5 ½ can prevent a quick slide to 4 ½ or 4. And regardless of the fundamental merit of a low-priced stock, it is in imminent danger at the $5.00 and $3.00 levels because of marginability problems.

CHAPTER

22

Sell Smart on Good News

KEYS TO INVESTMENT SUCCESS

- Great News vs. Huge News
- Acting on News

The prior chapters dealt with technical phenomena like volume and price as clues to finding market tops. Fundamentals like the publication of positive news also accelerate market tops. So good news can be a signal to sell, ironic as that may seem.

There are three kinds of positive news that act as clues. One is such unsurprising positive news as on-target earnings estimates or the declaration of moderately higher dividends on schedule, which are irrelevant to this chapter. These events typically have no effect on stock price, although if they are expected their *absence* causes a drop. And these expected events seldom coincide with an interim price peak unless such a high proves to be reversed by a general market retreat.

The two other types of positive stock news — or impact news — are important to price behavior in the short term. These are events that are big or surprising enough to have an immediate effect on stock price. Within the impact category, also, the two types of news must be distinguished accurately by the alert market player, in real time, in order to determine proper action.

Great News vs. Huge News

The factor that determines impact is the true, long-term importance of the news. So impact news includes "great news" and, by contrast, "huge news." Great news refers to positive developments that have no major fundamental long-term significance to a company. Examples are a quarterly earnings report that comes in well above expectations, or the award of a major contract.

Sometimes a contract award has long-term impact by signalling superior technology or a series of follow-on contracts. Sometimes the directors' declaration of an unexpectedly large dividend is "great news" that has a short-term positive effect on a stock's price.

Any of these events is welcomed by investors and usually causes a near-term rise in the company's stock price. However in judging their significance, be coldly objective to compensate for the stockholder's bias. Remember, also, that a holder generally is in a positive mental state about owning the shares because the current price action is rewarding. Do not let the prospect of success for the company or portfolio value impede a realistic analysis.

To make an accurate and meaningful judgment about a current piece of positive news, take an imaginary look back from the future. Move forward 10 years in time, and then look back at company and industry history over that period. The key filter is the true importance — in a *long-term* context — of the news that looks so positive today. Is it certain that today's event will be judged one of the two or three most significant events in a decade for the company, or is it among the top dozen events in its industry? By definition, the answer in virtually every case is negative.

So the news today is great but not huge. By contrast, what *is* a huge news event? These are developments or announcements with true long-term fundamental and strategic importance to the company: usually management, technology or strategy issues rather than current financial results or growth rates.

Changes in these nonfinancial areas have much greater long-term significance and generally fall into the categories of blockbuster events or major unexpected changes. Examples of huge news in management are items about key individuals and shifts in types of corporate governance or management: Lee Iacocca's appointment in 1979 as head of Chrysler Corporation was a crucial turning point in the survival and revitalization of the number three U.S. automaker, as an example.

A key transition in management is often necessary as a company built on entrepreneurial spirit reaches maturity. An excellent example occurred in 1983 when Apple Computer founder Steve Jobs — a technology genius — was replaced as chief executive officer by a veteran marketing executive, John Scully of Pepsi Co.

Sometimes the retirement or death of a company officer and major stockholder proves to be huge news: management power changes, and a block of stock transfers control, triggers a merger or signifies a significant change in corporate direction. Dr. Armand Hammer's death in December 1990 began a new era at Occidental Petroleum. Critical technological advances can also constitute huge news: an example is the issuance of an early patent on a test for AIDS to Cambridge BioSciences.

Finally, strategic changes in a company's direction can be huge news: abandoning a money-losing or highly competitive business, halting acquisitions in a debt-laden firm, selling off assets, working existing businesses harder and paying down debt.

A strategic acquisition that creates vertical integration, a broader product mix or strong distribution overnight are other examples. In 1988, Georgia-based Colorocs — which had developed an inexpensive, high-quality color photocopier — made what appeared to be a critical positive move by acquiring control of Savin Corporation instead of risking time and capital in the creation of its own distribution infrastructure. That decision removed a major risk factor for investors and, therefore, was huge news.

Acting on News

The critical distinction between great and huge is important because it indicates the proper tactical action to take: whether and when to sell on strength. Great news is usually good for two or three days of rising stock quotes, assuming a reasonably hospitable market climate at the time. Because the nature of great good news is not long-term in significance, a good short-term rally triggered by such news often provides an attractive opportunity to cash in on strength by selling.

This is especially true if a significant trading-volume buildup takes place following the news. Remember that a rising pace of volume is required to sustain a further price increase. Given surprising great news, how much more can be expected realistically? Where will even higher trading volume and more excitement come from?

The mechanics of news dissemination and the timing of broker and investor reactions help create a typical two- or three-day pattern of rallying prices following great news. The day news is announced, assuming it is during the market session and receives prompt newswire treatment, professional traders and boardroom ticker watchers act virtually immediately, as do a few other investors whose alert brokers call to relay the developments.

That same news is printed the next day in most daily newspapers and in the national financial press. Now more people can and do react. By the third day, those who got the news late or who typically are slow to act finally jump on the bandwagon. Beyond that, there is little left in the short term. If an investor cannot imagine being a buyer *after* the run-up, it is a good idea to sell.

The occurrence of huge news poses more of a tactical challenge for the stockholder because there are likely to be two positive reactions in the stock price. In addition to judging the possible strength of the two price moves, the savvy investor confronts a psychological test: he is so pleased by the enormity of the positive development that he is in danger of losing perspective and cool judgment.

The first price reaction is a short-term burst, similar to that from great news. But there is also likely to be a second, less dramatic effect. Because of the true import of huge news, the company, in effect, rises to a new and higher level of esteem among investors — particularly among those professional money managers who look at the big picture rather than the short-term reaction.

Even if the stock continues to exhibit gradual further price strength after its initial upside burst from the huge news, the tactical problem is to make a judgment about *when* the second effect has run its course. Again, this is an art rather than an exact science.

In general, remember that the occurrence of huge news should cause an investor to ease back on the selling trigger. And once the stock takes a rest and declines, expect it to decline less deeply than before the huge news. Not only will there have been, in effect, a one-time markup for the new information, but there will be some institutional investors who did not jump in right away, waiting for a correction before accumulating their positions. These investors provide the buying support for future basing and rallies in the stock.

If the stock develops a classic volume mountain and an extended string of consecutive daily rises after great or huge news, it is advisable to sell on the crescendo in trading. (Review Chapter 18.) No matter how fundamentally important or long-term significant the news is, the stock cannot be expected to rise uninterrupted for an indefinite time. The formation of a flagpole advance on a volume mountain is a signal that the strength is unsustainable for at least the short-term and the stock should be sold on the rise. It can always be bought back, probably lower, at a later time.

CHAPTER

23

Understand How Bad the Bad News Is

KEYS TO INVESTMENT SUCCESS

- Specific Types of Bad News
- Reacting to Bad News

Bad news travels fast in the computer age and this has important price implications when a company's news is unexpected or highly disturbing. Too often, investors give in to emotional market swings by selling out when all seems lost, only to find later that they were part of a selling-panic bottom.

Before describing bad-news selling tactics, it is necessary to identify the "bad news" characteristics covered in this chapter:

- Relates only to company-specific news, not to market trends as measured by averages.
- Concerns sharp price declines driven by negative news, not routine price declines that are merely technical corrections.
- Excludes acquisition stocks, in which the ongoing sequence of news is highly unpredictable, and events and emotions are dramatic.
- Excludes situations driven by continuous (non-discrete) outside influences, including commodity-price collapses (for mining companies) which have a life of their own and, therefore, are not discrete, one-day news items.
- Applies in context of a sideways or higher market environment in which reactions are worse in total, but not initially as severe as during bear markets.

Specific Types of Bad News

This chapter explores material, unexpected and discrete bad news for a company. "Material" and "unexpected" are important qualifiers because other negative information does not tend to move stock prices.

News discreteness is important conceptually because it affects the validity of certain ideas. (Discrete news developments are one-time items which do not breed the suspicion of further negatives to come.) Usually discrete bad news causes 2 to 3 days of sharp declines. (See Exhibit 23-1.) Sometimes an apparently discrete negative item is

Exhibit 23-1: 2-Day and 3-Day Drubbing on Bad News

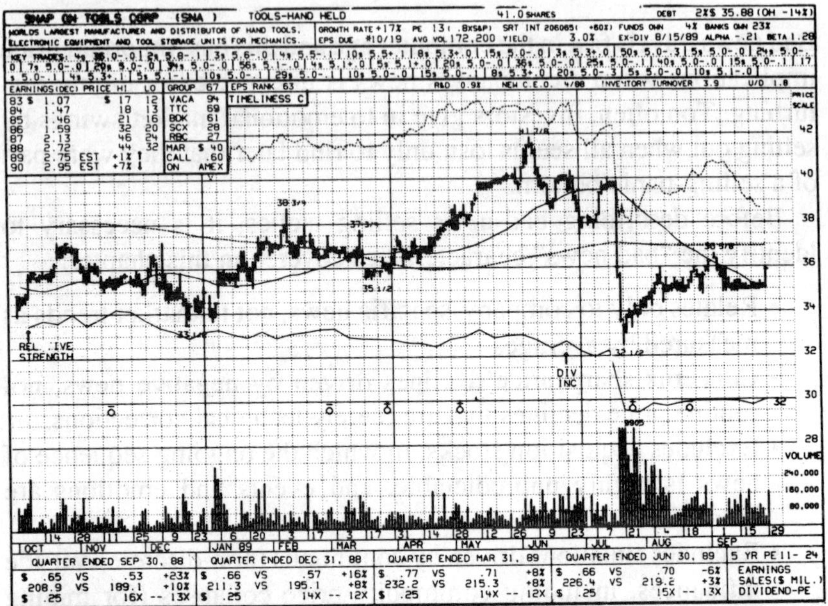

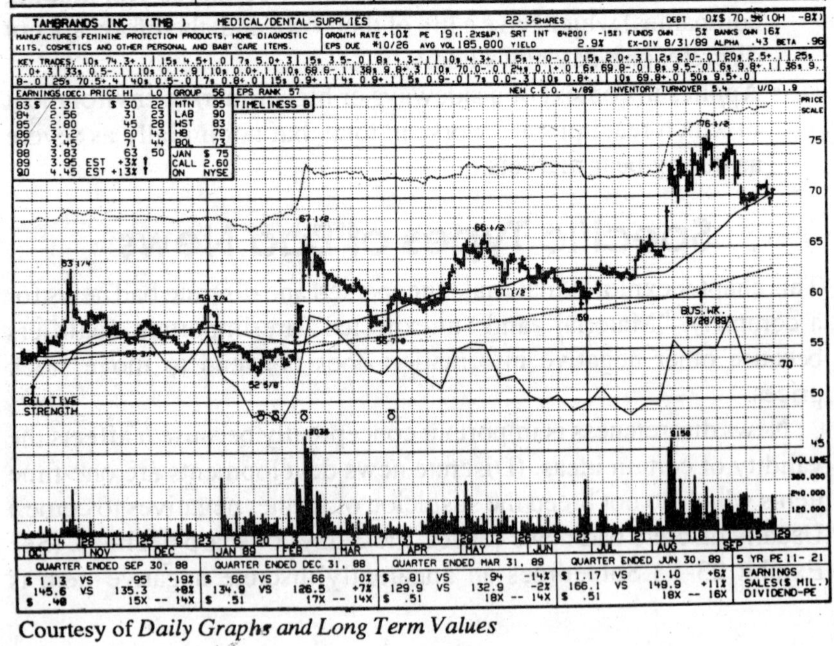

Courtesy of *Daily Graphs and Long Term Values*

Exhibit 23-1: 2-Day and 3-Day Drubbing on Bad News (cont.)

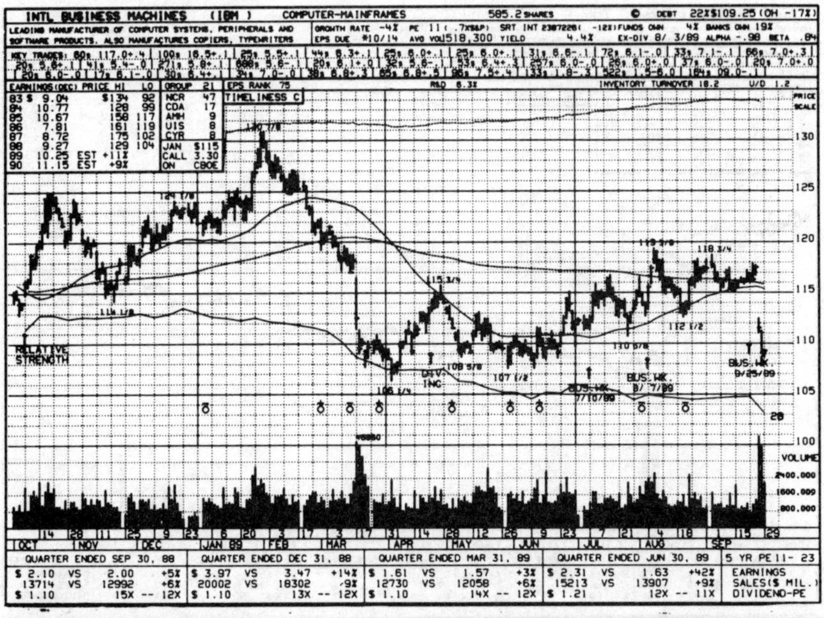

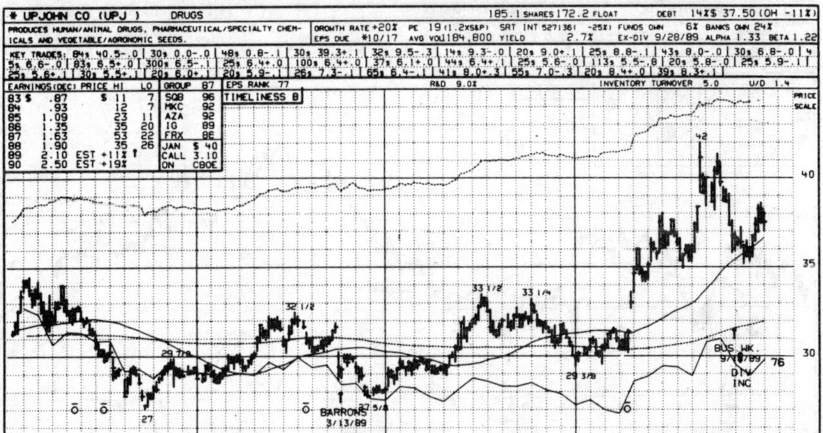

Courtesy of *Daily Graphs and Long Term Values*

Exhibit 23-1: 2-Day and 3-Day Drubbing on Bad News (cont.)

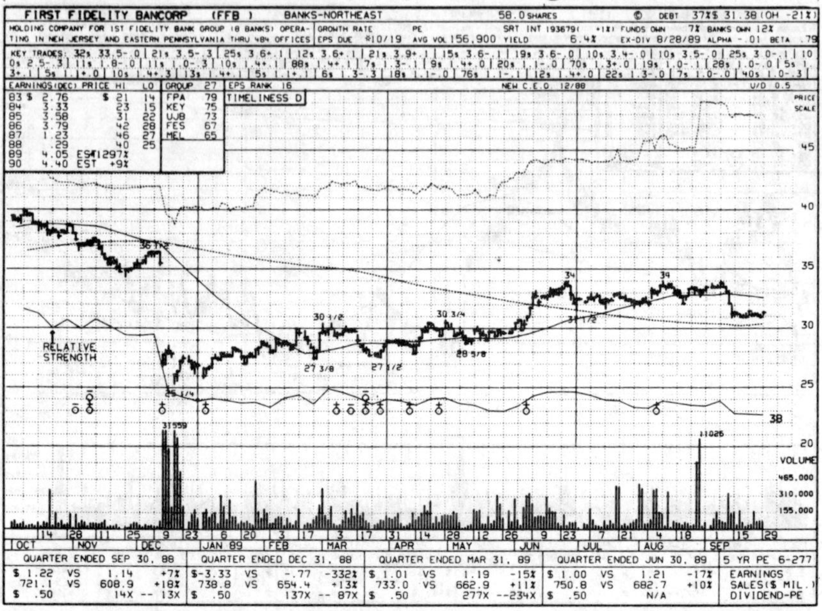

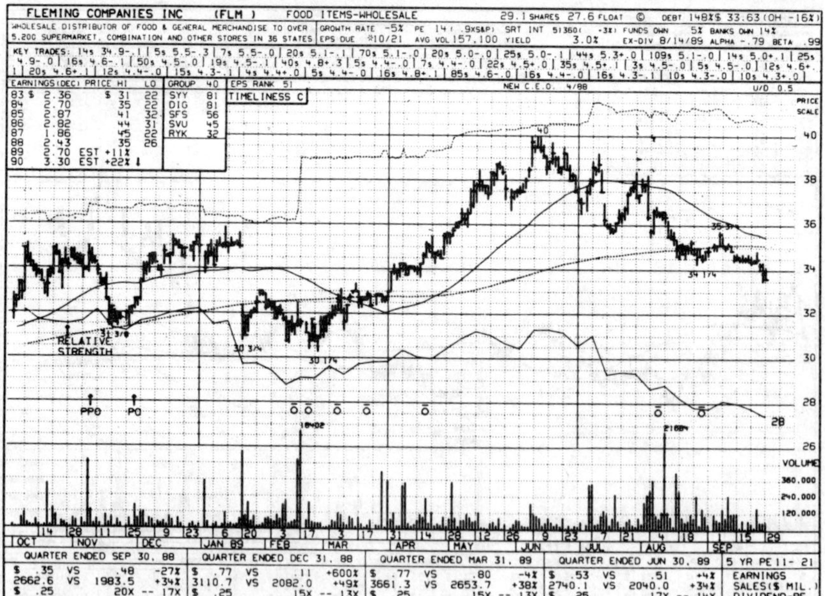

Courtesy of *Daily Graphs and Long Term Values*

Exhibit 23-1: 2-Day and 3-Day Drubbing on Bad News (cont.)

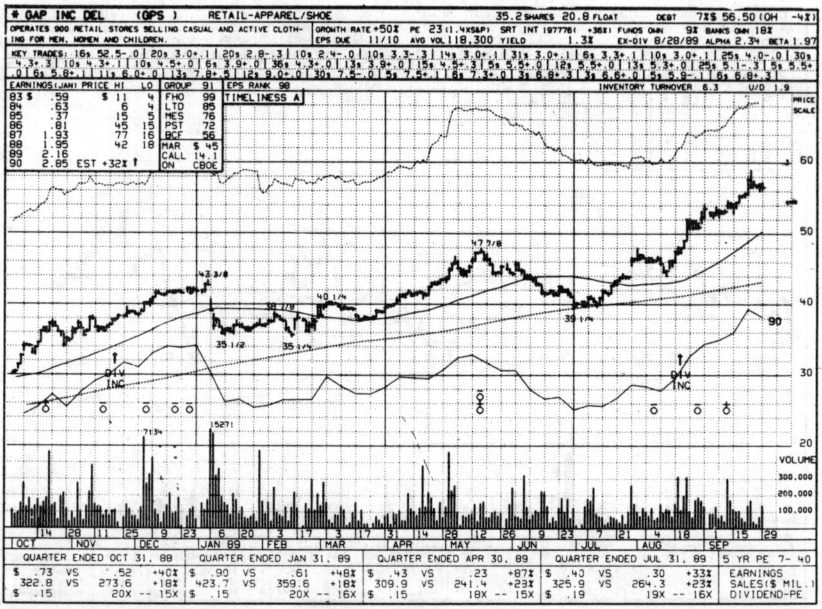

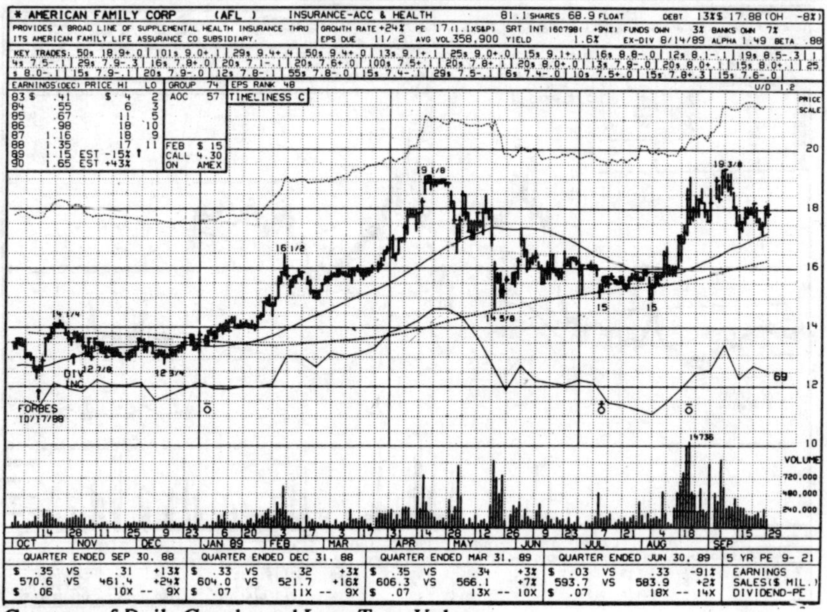

Courtesy of *Daily Graphs and Long Term Values*

Exhibit 23-1: 2-Day and 3-Day Drubbing on Bad News (cont.)

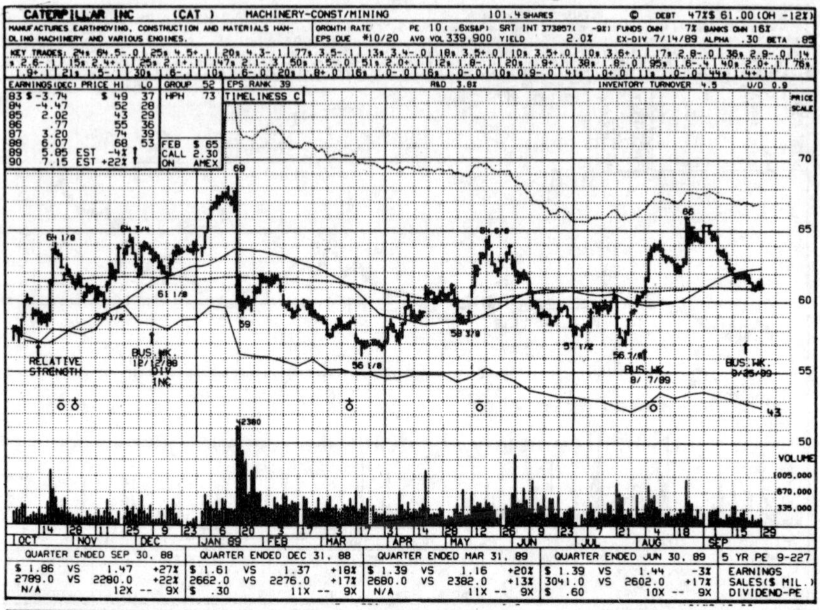

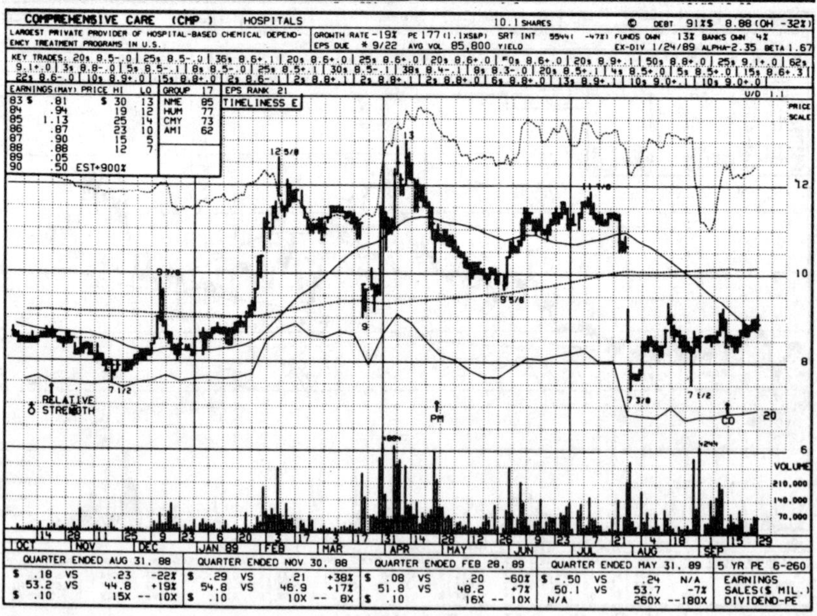

Courtesy of *Daily Graphs and Long Term Values*

followed quickly by another piece of bad news. In this situation, the clock starts running again in reaction days. And quite often the newly-emerging pattern of clustered bad news means the stock will act like it would to a non-discrete piece of bad news because suspicions have been kindled.

Some examples of material, unexpected and discrete bad news (or MUD for short) are:

- For an insurance company, a major natural disaster that raises loss expense beyond normal expectations.
- For a high-technology company, the resignation or death of a key scientist or inventor.
- For any small company, the death of a senior officer, especially the founder or other person whose identity is central to the investment community's concept of the company.
- For a fast-growth company, the announcement of a competitor's major new product or technology that reduces the lead time or exclusivity enjoyed by the first company.
- A one-quarter earnings surprise caused by non recurring factors such as a supplier's strike or storm damage, or by write-offs that are not part of an established company or industry pattern.
- A dividend reduction (or in rare cases, an omission because it usually follows other bad news).
- Damage to plant or other assets clearly caused by an outside force such as a storm or the explosion of a nearby plant — a case in which no fault is likely to be attributed to the company.

In contrast are non-discrete negative events:

- For an insurance company, a new law or court ruling that creates broader concepts of liability with true costs that cannot yet be calculated.
- Issuance of a qualified opinion by independent auditors.

- A major workplace or ecological accident in which the company will probably be found, at least in part, at fault.
- For any company, the unexplained resignation of a very senior executive or financial officer with any hint of mystery or scandal.
- For a high-tech company, failure to secure a patent on a device or technology that was presented as critical to success.
- For a high-tech or fast-growth company, delayed or cancelled introduction of a new product previously announced or expected.
- Announcement (or the expectation) of a decline in earnings for reasons that reflect management weaknesses (poor control) or unrecognized competitive pressures in the business (lack of foresight).
- Government probes of the company for possible antitrust violations, bid rigging or false documentation.
- SEC investigation into possible securities violations on the part of the company, or one or more officers.
- Disclosure that one or more past financial statements were inaccurate and that it will take some time to investigate before issuing revised reports.
- Announcement that the company's board is considering or will consider reducing or omitting the dividend or declaring bankruptcy.
- A news announcement which, while appearing to be discrete, represents a contradiction of previous management representations to analysts or the press.

The key difference between these groups of examples is the apparent degree of closure versus uncertainty on the bad news. There is an old traders' cliche that the market can handle good news, and it can even handle bad news; but uncertainty drives it crazy.

Reacting to Bad News

The difference between finite, known bad news and uncertain but bad-portent news is reflected in the way investors react to it. The market's reaction to open-ended news with bad implications is painfully drawn out because uneasiness creates less severe selling pressure at first and leaves a psychological dark cloud lingering for a long time afterward. When the bad news is discrete, the reaction is usually sharp but relatively brief.

MUD bad news typically imposes a two- or three-day price drop on a stock which is often quite sharp in percentage terms. In effect, it is a private crash. There are psycho-mechanical reasons for this pattern of typical duration, and they concern news dissemination and absorption. The sharpness of the price reaction has been compounded almost certainly in recent years by the twin demons of short investment horizons and the high concentration of institutional holdings.

When news is announced, it typically has a two-day life in the media unless it is so major that prolonged follow-up coverage ensues. Major examples are Three Mile Island, the Bhopal chemical disaster, the Exxon Valdez accident and various spectacular plane crashes. On the day of the announcement, unless the company arranges to have the news released after the market closes, the item runs on the wire services and perhaps on stock market shows (for example on Financial News Network) televised during the session.

Some investors and traders react immediately. Then the next day, the story is run — perhaps in greater length and detail — in daily newspapers. Then even more people react. So on any meaningful negative news, generally expect a two-day price reaction at a minimum.

If the bad news occurs on a Thursday or Friday, a three-day reaction is likely. This is because weekend researchers/investors react on reading the stock quotations in the Saturday and Sunday papers. They call their brokers on Monday and ask what caused the big drop the prior week, often creating a minor third wave of selling pressure.

In cases when major bad news occurs on Friday, the three-day rule emerges if the market happens to take a serious dive (related to the company's news or otherwise) on Monday. This is followed by a Tuesday morning rout that lets further air out of the stock that has suffered the bad publicity.

An important issue in the two- or three-day reaction to MUD bad news is the extent of the damage, specifically during the period of sharp price decline before stabilization takes place. There is a period of time — perhaps two days to a week or longer — during which the stock steadies and sometimes tries to rally.

Later there is also a renewed price decline, but it is usually less dramatic than the first. (See Exhibit 23-2.) The second decline occurs, typically, because the stock has run out of gas from bargain hunters attracted by the first crack, because the technical chart pattern looks weak (probably a rally on low volume or a rise into supply), or because the general market weakens and this particular stock cannot hold in the face of a widespread decline. With all these caveats, selling seems obvious if not easy; a self-drawn selling scenario provides necessary guidance on specific selling tactics in this environment. For an effective sale:

1. Distinguish carefully between discrete bad news and non-discrete bad news — which have very different longer-term implications for the hold/sell decision.
2. Create expectations about the decline and stabilization. It is useful to know that, while the price probably will not recover to its pre-news level soon, it will stop declining shortly to provide at least two days' stability during which a better sale can be executed. If due to inattention, lack of broker service, indecision or denial an investor has not sold the stock on the first day of bad news, he will know that by the third day's arrival it is

Exhibit 23-2: Crash, Stabilization, Decay

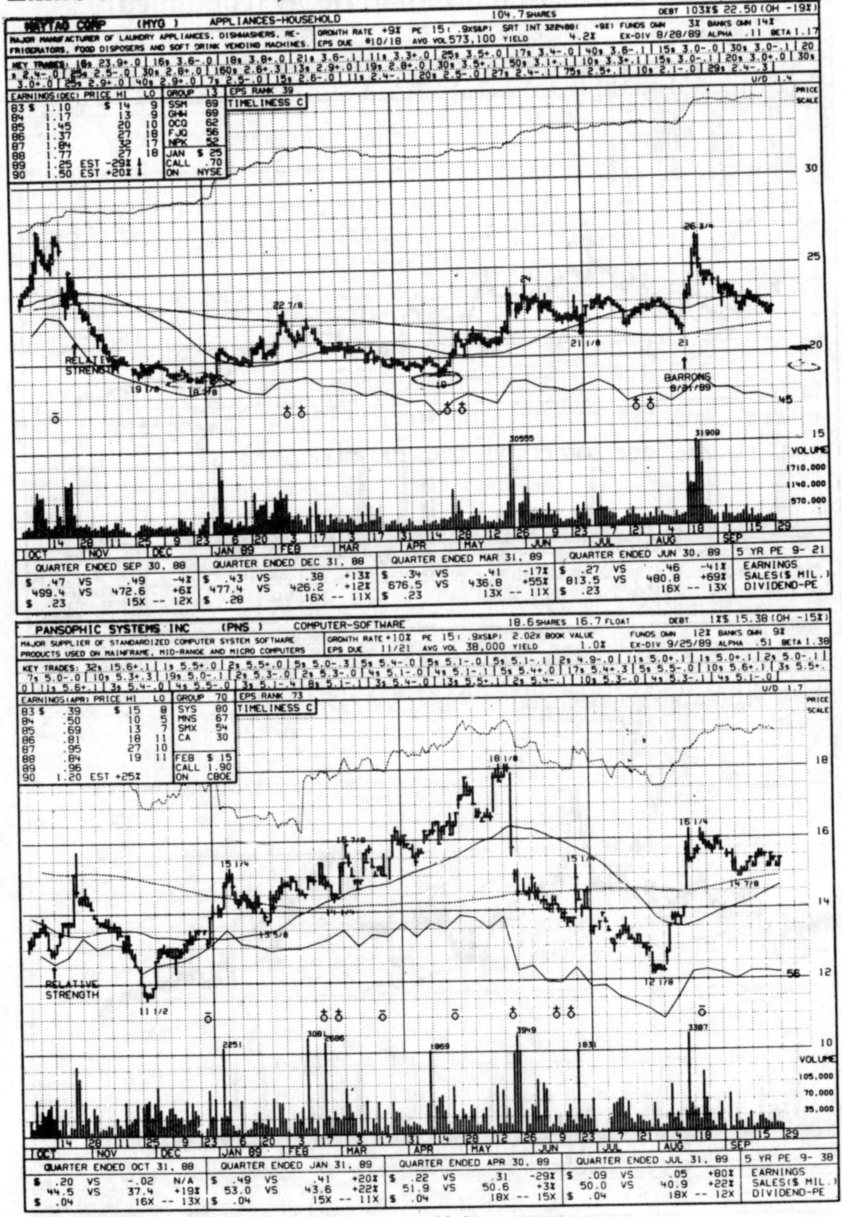

Courtesy of *Daily Graphs and Long Term Values*

Exhibit 23-2: Crash, Stabilization, Decay (continued)

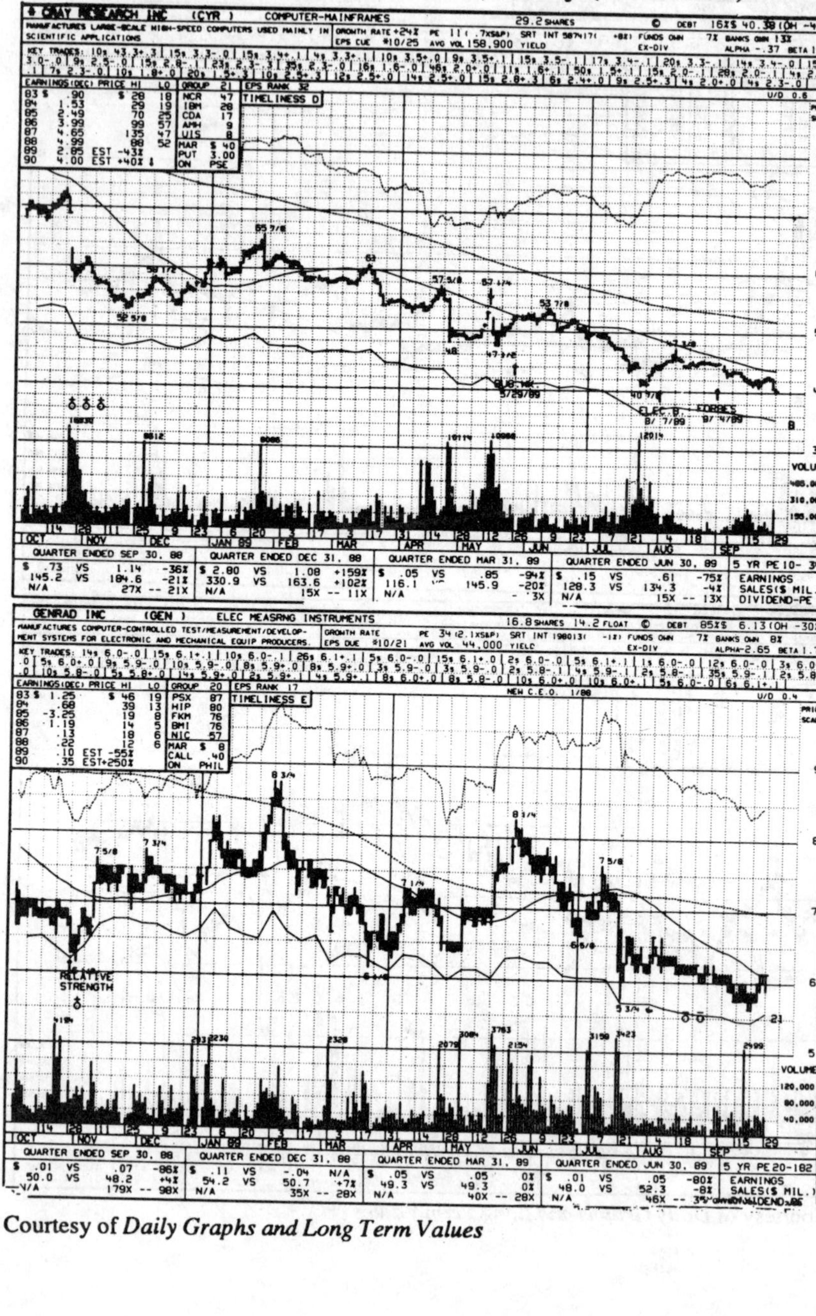

Courtesy of *Daily Graphs and Long Term Values*

Exhibit 23-2: Crash, Stabilization, Decay (continued)

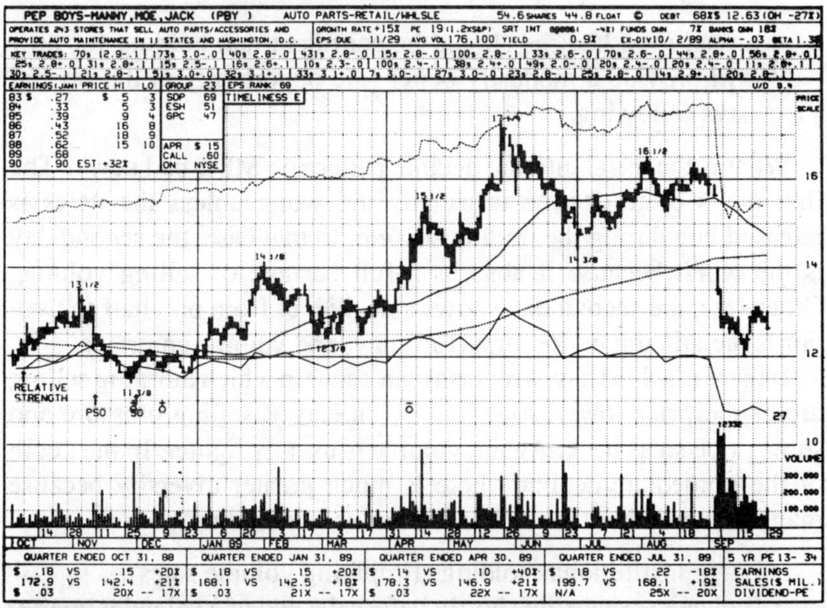

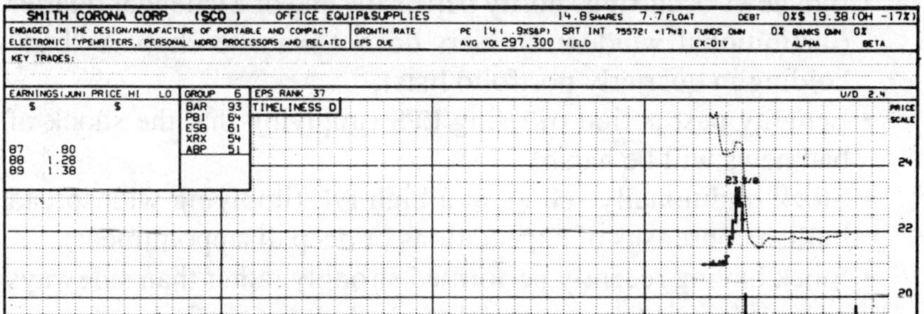

Courtesy of *Daily Graphs and Long Term Values*

already too late; he should be confident that holding for now will provide a modestly better sale opportunity in the several days following.

What is the usual internal decline pattern on MUD bad news? The first day's price decline is usually the worst unless the news is released late during the trading session. In that case, the second day is the worst because it absorbs a full barrage of selling volume. Otherwise, the second day shows a decline of from one-half to two-thirds the amount on the first (full) day, and volume contracts.

If there is a third day, a reversal can occur in which morning selling drives the price lower, followed by an end of selling pressure and some price snap-back. Again, volume is usually lighter. In the depth of the immediate decline, there is much greater diversity because many factors other than time are involved, including:

- Large institutional holdings (implying volume sales),
- Bad news occurring shortly before the end of a calendar quarter (institutional window dressers do not want to show a "bad" holding in quarterly portfolio lists),
- Lengthy past period of rising EPS (implying that the shock of bad news will be harsh),
- Stock traditionally selling at a high P/E (implying widespread bullish consensus of expectations or deep disappointment),
- Stock having recently performed strongly rather than sideways or lower (implying a scramble to lock down profits),
- Coincidence of a sharply weaker market at the same time company-specific news hits the stock itself (bargain hunters standing aside),
- Stock price fall creates a technically significant chart flaw such as a breakdown from a channel bottom or the downward resolution of a triangle (bringing in technician sellers as well as fundamentally disappointed sellers),

- Bad news smacks of a currently sensitive subject such as insider trading, ecological problems, health scares or other hot news.

When seemingly discrete bad news is followed by a second news item, either the clock starts running again for two or three days, or the situation must be considered an erosion problem in which investors see the announcement as no longer discrete. It begins to look like a process of going from bad to worse.

A good example occurred in 1989 when Phoenix-based Pinnacle West Capital, the parent company of MeraBank and Arizona Public Service, announced a dividend omission late one afternoon. The stock moved fractionally lower to the close and broke sharply the next day. The second full day of post-news trading brought a further drop on lower volume.

Normally, a stabilization and a bit of a snap-back rally could have been expected. But then a major newswire interviewed a company spokesperson, who mentioned the possibility of a Chapter 11 bankruptcy filing to rid Pinnacle West of its troubled thrift unit. This second piece of bad news lengthened the period of sharp price drop for another two days. It was arrested only when an 80-point morning smash in the Dow Jones Industrials reversed to a four-point drop by the close.

For anyone not already familiar with the Pinnacle West story, the second item created a new cloud of ongoing uncertainty: so the stock was no longer in the discrete-bad-news category and, subsequently, the news continued to worsen.

The bottom line is that a two-day (three-day if over the weekend) price crack is to be expected, followed by calmer trading and probably a slight recovery from panic lows. A different response is called for if the bad news is open-ended or if it supports a pattern of deterioration. Without hesitation, sell when the news indicates general corporate decay.

CHAPTER

24

Sell on News Delays

KEYS TO INVESTMENT SUCCESS

- Scheduled Announcements
- Dividend Declarations
- Earnings Reports
- Other Delays

No news in the investment arena is usually *not* good news, and expected but delayed news often falls into this category. There are three categories of expected news from a company:

- Dividend declarations
- Earnings reports
- Scheduled announcements

Scheduled Announcements

The smallest and most unusual category is scheduled announcements. The managements of most companies do not box themselves in by committing to an announcement on a predesignated timetable because too much can go wrong that might require delay. Most managements say only that they are "preparing a statement and will release it as soon as possible under the circumstances."

An expected or anticipated announcement (other than periodic dividend and earnings news) usually occurs when the company is under some pressure. Something has gone awry and a response is needed. Occasionally, under such pressure, the company attempts to control the public relations damage and to ward off further telephone barrages by saying it expects to make a statement on the matter by a certain date.

When a company makes this commitment, it has put its reputation on the block; if the deadline passes with no further announcement, presume that the situation is more difficult, or that the response will be more drastic or far-reaching than shareholders would wish.

Suppose a corporate treasurer suddenly resigns and the audit committee of the board suspects foul play. The company makes an announcement of the resignation. Under generally accepted standards of full and prompt disclosure, the fact that an internal investigation exists is considered material, so the company most likely feels obliged to release this information at the same time.

If management announces that it expects the investigation to last for a certain number of days and will issue a statement at that time, expect it to make good on the announcement unless the problem turns out to be particularly thorny. A delay past the appointed time without a timely and specific announcement is a danger signal.

What requires extra time? Management may have had to call in independent auditors or a legal investigative agency to uncover the full extent of a problem. Or there are legal subtleties that require careful review because of potential litigation. Or the situation is so significant that management wants to complete a Form 8-K filing for the SEC covering the news before making a statement.

Whatever the cause of delay, the outcome is much more likely to be bad rather than good news. Because money has a time value and because avoiding losses is very important in investing, lean to the cautious side and anticipate bad news by selling out on the delay itself instead of waiting for the other shoe to drop.

This is an occasion when commission phobia can get in the way. If an investor is proven wrong and the late news is no worse than expected, the stock is unaffected. So the investor is out a round-trip commission as the cost of insurance to be safe rather than sorry. If the news only gets worse as it emerges, he may see a gap opening of several points down (dwarfing a commission), followed by further erosion. If the news is bad, management credibility is tarnished, delaying price recovery.

The caution to be safe rather than sorry is even more forceful when the stock is widely-held by institutions. In today's short-term money management culture, there is a rush to exit with huge sell orders when the news is bad.

When the time period of news uncertainty is open-ended, the market collectively is prone to suspect the worst and to invent or listen to rumors. While the delay for clarification is in effect, the stock price is likely to erode anyway. So the delay in releasing follow-up news quite often means a lose-lose situation for stockholders: continued holding simply puts money at unnecessary risk.

While not all investors should take a short-term approach to the market, it is nearly always true that the first loss is the best loss. Therefore, when something goes wrong it is most prudent to exit and reexamine the situation from a distance. If an investor holds hoping that the bad news will not be too bad after all, he is (1) playing a game for minimized loss and (2) exposing himself to the heavier emotional baggage that will accrue if the stock takes a big dive.

Dividend Declarations

The second category of news delays involves dividends. Not all delays are dangerous, so it helps to do some homework and have references available to know the difference between alarming and forgivable delays in time to take action.

Corporate boards of directors usually meet on a predictable schedule, especially for dividend declarations (boards usually meet more than four times a year, even though shareholders do not see any evidence of most non-dividend meetings). As a courtesy to the board members, a company schedules board meetings on a standing basis so members can anticipate travel well in advance. Examples are third Tuesdays or fourth Mondays of the month.

How does an investor know when the board meets? If he is concerned — and generally there is little cause to be worried if the latest earnings reports have been favorable and there is no pattern of trouble elsewhere in the industry — he can call the company. Or there are three sources of accessible information. One is Standard & Poor's individual stock reports. For dividend payers, there is a table, usually on the back side, showing the date of meeting, stock-of-record date and payable date of the last four quarterly dividends.

Be aware of two wild-card factors, however: the meeting after year-end is often further into the quarterly cycle than other meetings;

and in the summer, meetings are less regular due to travel for vacations. So use the spring and fall meeting dates for the best guidance in the case of a company using the calendar year.

A second source that is widely available is *The Value Line Investment Survey*, although its coverage is narrower at only about 1,800 companies (most public libraries subscribe, as do many brokerage offices). For each stock covered by Value Line there is a notation in the lower left corner of the page, or sometimes at the lower center, indicating the date of the next expected board meeting.

A third and highly comprehensive source is Standard & Poor's *Dividend Record*. Fewer libraries and brokerage offices subscribe, but give it a try and become familiar with it. This service tracks and reports declarations on both preferred and common stocks. There are annual soft-cover, 8 ½ x 11" volumes that give the same data as the S&P sheets described above. The monthly and weekly update supplements track the most recent declaration dates. These sheets are looseleaf and usually filed in front.

The reason for looking at delays in dividend meetings is cautionary. Although a delay can be innocent, it more often results from problems. Before calling the company, check with a broker; ask to have the day's news headlines scanned. If a news release got out too late in the day yesterday, it will miss the morning papers and appear a day late. The dividend item will run on the ticker as soon as possible.

To call the company, try the corporate secretary's office rather than the public relations or stockholder relations department. It is an official duty of the corporate secretary's office to schedule board meetings and notify members, so it has the timing information readily at hand.

Earnings Reports

By far the most perilous reason for delayed reports is bad corporate earnings. This delay most often means trouble; but before concluding that a suspicious delay is occurring, check the facts and remember seasonal exceptions. Note that after the end of the fiscal year it takes longer to release earnings than after the ends of the first three quarters.

Quarterly numbers usually are unaudited. And small adjustments can be pushed from one period to the next between quarters in case something slipped by earlier. But the year-end numbers are audited, and there is no way of taking back a year-end number once it is released without embarrassment and loss of credibility. So expect those releases to come more slowly.

How does an investor find out when to expect earnings? A majority of brokerage firms capture and store the last 90 days' headlines from the Dow-Jones wire on their quotation machines. To anticipate the release schedule rather than waiting until the news is out, call just after the end of the quarter and ask for the date of the prior EPS announcement. Add three months and mark the calendar. After more than 90 days have elapsed, the prior headline and its date are wiped off the quote machine.

Another free source is *The Wall Street Journal* Cumulative Index, which often can be found in a public library. It cross-indexes the past year's articles in *Barron's* also, giving headline, date, page and column. The release runs on the wire the prior market day. This source saves the amount of time it takes to look at every day's back issue in the month of the prior report.

Another handy source is a chart service, for example, Daily Graphs by William O'Neil (see the reference list at the end of the book for addresses). In the small print in the narrow lines above the charts are the words "EPS due" and a date. The chart service monitors past news release dates and adds three or 12 months to give due-date estimates.

A computer-based news service such as Dow-Jones News/Retrieval or Compuserve provides the dates of past quarterly reports via personal computer, but the information is not free. Why does a company delay the announcement of earnings? For example if the company made an acquisition or divested a business in the last one or two quarters, the accounting department is very likely still in scramble mode putting together revised numbers. On rare occasions, the summer vacation season might be a real excuse. Another legitimate delay is the imposition of new accounting requirements by the SEC or by the Financial Accounting Standards Board (it takes a lot less time to change the rules than it does to comply with new rules). If many companies are noting the effects of new reporting rules, some delay is tolerable.

Other Delays

Other delays are harbingers of trouble. A new computer system may have been installed, which can bring a company at least temporarily to its knees. Sometimes records get lost and management loses control of operations until the loss is rectified. If it is not a new computer, it could be a new accounting treatment that the company has decided voluntarily to adopt.

Analysts usually greet such news with suspicion; sometimes the revised methods of accounting are more liberal or allow the company to cover poor performance for awhile due to lack of comparability. A delay due to new standards voluntarily adopted usually is a cause for concern.

There can be really serious problems: a cash or inventory shortage is discovered, accounting records are falsified, or operating problems occurred and management is assessing how to explain what happened. Another possibility is a write-off or write-down of assets. That can take extra time when independent auditors are called in to give advice and/or approve the charges.

Finally, be aware of the regulatory deadlines for filing SEC reports. Public companies are expected to report quarterly results no later than 45 days after the period ends; annual numbers are due not more than 90 days after year-end. In practice, the SEC is understaffed and has more pressing matters to police than late reports. However, company managements, lawyers and auditors are well aware of the rules; failure to meet the deadline is usually a sign that something meaningful is wrong.

Another source of concern is not an actual delay: a few companies routinely report results at the last possible date (the SEC deadline). Typically, they are extremely secretive and report only what is required and when it is required — neither more, nor sooner. They tend not to give much or any useful interim information to analysts, so there is greater potential for surprise.

However, if AT&T can get its quarterly data out in 10 days or sooner, surely a small company can do it in fewer than 45 days. If not, their accounting function is dangerously understaffed, and management is at risk of not being in the know and in control.

CHAPTER

25

Selling Versus Holding in a Crash

KEYS TO INVESTMENT SUCCESS

- Weathering a Panic
- Stocks That Don't Fare Well
- Panic-Resilient Stocks

In any discussion of holding versus selling stocks, the circumstances under which it is best to sell should be outlined first. *Holding should occur only if no tests for selling are failed.* The company-related reasons to sell are:

- Sell if the news cannot get any better.
- Sell if things did not go as planned.
- Sell when the broker's advice goes from "buy" to "hold."
- Sell if company fundamentals are getting sick.
- Sell on the rebound in the aftermath of material, unexpected or discrete bad news.
- Sell in certain cases when expected news is delayed.

The market-action reasons to sell are:

- Sell when the stock reaches the target.
- Sell on an unsustainable upward price spike on big volume.
- Sell when a portfolio shows all gains.
- Sell if the stock is lazy money and likely to stay that way.
- Sell using above-market limit orders, letting the market come to the investor.
- Sell with a stop-loss order, but never remove or lower it.

Investor-related reasons to sell are:

- Sell if the stock would not be bought again today.
- Sell after gloating or counting the chips.
- Sell rather than hope against hope for a "maybe" bailout.
- Sell and step aside on a personal losing streak.

If an investor sells stocks in a disciplined manner using the signals above, he is likely to end up with a good deal of cash before the market moves into a bear cycle. Relatively few of his holdings will fail to hit one of the 16 triggers noted in those lists. Those stocks that do survive will tend to be high-quality growth issues that have continued to perform fundamentally and have not run up to unreasonable price levels. Some experts refer to these as core holdings or "businessman's-risk" foundation stocks. They are stocks that have given consistent indications they can be held through good and bad in the market.

All other stocks will have become sales before a panic bottom because:

1. They worked as planned.
2. They acted too well for a brief period of time.
3. They got unreasonably priced.
4. They were wasting the time value of money by going nowhere.
5. They developed significant fundamental problems.

Very few stocks can escape all those screens for a long period. So if an investor is cashing in as prescribed and if his buying discipline rejects new positions when valuations get too pricey, he ends up still holding very few stocks as the market gets toppy. That, of course, protects his capital.

To understand the big-picture perspective, review the descriptions presented earlier in the book of the mechanical supply/demand processes and factors like sponsorship that make stock prices rise. Recall that if these processes and factors are absent, the investor should not hold because the stock will not go up.

Looking now at stock-price trends not from a mechanical viewpoint but from a big-picture perspective, there are two major price-driving forces: fundamentals (which control the long term) and psychology (which rules the short and medium term). Review Exhibit 6-1 in Chapter 6.

The fundamental and psychological factors affect stocks in both directions. And as an overlay, understand that they can affect a stock either directly (because of the company behind the stock itself) or indirectly (because the market trend is so strong that virtually no stocks can buck it). However,the indirect effect is much stronger on the downside than on the upside: fear is a more powerful driver than greed.

Weathering a Panic

The central concept in this chapter is the occasional need to play when it is painful. But this concept specifically and only means to hold stocks that are being affected just by the overwhelming negative psychological forces that occasionally cause selling routs or panics in the whole market.

To put this very important limiting caveat another way: when a crash or panic occurs, stocks should be held only if they are going down because of market factors and not if they are being affected by company factors. This should relate to only a few issues, however, because investors following the suggestions in this book already should have weeded out the bad performers and taken profits on the stellar performers well before a bear market reaches climax proportions.

So when appropriate selling has left an investor with only a few, high-quality stocks, he can and should hold onto the gems and play through the difficult experience of a panic or crash. He will be holding only a relatively small portfolio (having followed the other cashing-in suggestions well before the bottom nears), so his level of pain will be no worse than moderate. And his cash holdings will give emotional comfort and provide the resources for acquiring stocks advantageously when prices get really low.

Some investors may see a contradiction in this advice because earlier they were counseled that avoiding losses is the first priority and the best reason for selling. But taking a short-term dose of paper losses in a crash — by holding quality issues — is a lesser risk than selling out during the fury, and hoping to have the courage and good executions to get back in at lower prices shortly afterward.

If an investor is down to just a few core holdings anyway, he is better advised to tough it out. The very experience of playing in pain through a temporary crash (think of the October 1987 and October 1989 bashings) is of enormous instructional value despite the modest monetary cost involved. The process of crisis-thinking and the need to make wrenching decisions that prove valid in short order will serve him well for the rest of his investment career.

Once he has successfully navigated the worst of the choppy investment seas, he will have learned survival lessons and will have internalized feelings and taken in an experience that will be forever his. That experience deepens his understanding of the way the market works. Probably most of all, having won at a difficult game, he develops the wisdom and courage to succeed in similar circumstances in the future. And that provides the opportunity to make big profits in the handful of similar opportunities that will occur throughout the rest of his investing career. He will know beyond any shadow of a doubt that the contrarian philosophy of investing works.

When caught in a panic, the central question is whether capitalism in the United States and major Western democracies will continue to function after the panic ends. If the answer is yes, then there is no reason to sell at foolish levels. In fact, the only rational thing to do is take courage and make buys. Being gutsy enough to act on the contrarian test — refusing to sell good stocks cheap because Wall Street and Main Street have lost faith for a few days — insures appropriate selling. It is difficult to buy in a panic. Those who can do so are rational enough to sell with discipline as highs approach.

There is one more qualifier on whether to hold or sell after a panic has passed. Once the panic subsides, there is a lift in the market. But the effect is significantly different on various kinds of stocks. For some issues, there is a sharp snap-back rally; for others, there is very little improvement. Just as it is not advisable to sell into the panic, it is prudent to reassess positions after the selling frenzy has subsided and the lift in prices has begun.

The object, as always, is to decide what to sell and what to hold. Selling should not be urgent because pre-bear-phase tactics will have raised a lot of cash, so there's no need to sell to raise cash for margin calls or buying. But because the goal is always to maximize return on capital and to take advantage of the time value of money, look closely at what to hold and what to sell after the panic has cleared.

Stocks That Don't Fare Well

Stocks that tend to be sub-par performers in a post-crash environment are:

- OTC issues
- Low-priced stocks
- Small total-capitalization issues
- Thinly-traded, under- or non-covered stocks
- Industry laggards
- Recession-sensitive by industry
- Discredited groups
- Panic-trigger related groups

Because of fear, nervousness and lack of speculative appetite after a crash or panic, the first five groups (some of which overlap) lack sponsorship. In addition, because market panics generate immediate scare headlines in the media, there is talk of recession and parallels drawn with 1929. So recession-sensitive stocks by industry do not bounce back much for a period of time.

There may, in fact, be no recession following the market's downmove (as in 1988), but perception and expectation drive prices near-term more than facts do. So cyclicals like steels, chemicals, paper and capital-goods producers are not solid choices for participating in the bounce. Similarly, vacation and luxury stocks fare poorly.

The discredited groups vary from one market period to another. Their identity depends on what was in the headlines in recent months.

Basic industry stocks were taboo in the early 1980s, known as the "rust-belt" period. High-tech stocks suffered through a private, one-industry recession in the mid-1980s. Banks were whipping boys in the early era of bad third-world loans. Most recently, savings and loans have been in the doghouse due to bailout legislation and highly-visible failures and scandals.

Again in a longer-term perspective, the facts may prove that the fear about leading companies in discredited groups was unfounded. But in the short term after a crash, there are few who have the courage to sponsor tarnished-image stocks with either money or written advice. Such issues are early recovery laggards.

The final category should be off the hold list for similar reasons. Sometimes there is an industry or category of stocks related to the news that triggers the panic selling. In 1962, it was steel stocks sensitive to pricing confrontation with the Kennedy administration. Brokerage stocks would have been poor choices to hold after the 1987 crash because of all the controversy surrounding program trading. The 1989 crash was triggered by the collapse of the proposed buyout of UAL, Inc., so airlines and other proposed leveraged buyout candidates were identifiable as the trigger-related group at that time.

Panic-Resilient Stocks

There are, by contrast, several groups that tend to act well in a post-panic environment, especially if the crash itself drives prices to incredible levels. Of course, the more unusual the values created, the quicker is the upside correction. Some of the groups most likely to snap back are:

- Recession-resistant industries (foods, drugs, utilities).
- Noncyclical blue chips driven well down (oils).
- Big names with corporate staying power (AT&T, Exxon, General Electric and General Motors).
- Fortune 100 and similar companies with good yields.

- Trade-down concepts like low-cost restaurants and discount retailers (recession "beneficiaries").
- Companies with low P/Es or low price/cash flow ratios not in the first list above.
- Companies selling below book value and with positive earnings estimates for the coming year (implying credibly sustainable book values).
- Companies with low debt/equity ratios.
- Unleveraged closed-end, non-junk bond funds.
- Panic-trigger *beneficiaries* (e.g., oil-service and insulation stocks after OPEC raised oil prices in 1973).

All of these stocks are recession-resistant or perceived as among the most likely to survive hard times. They retain market sponsorship and regain enthusiastic buyers soonest. Related positively to the trigger event, they have high visibility because investors remember the concept vividly.

It is important to make hold/sell calls in the light of prevailing market expectation and not personal judgment of what may happen. If the (correct) bet is no recession, the reward is smaller and slower than if the (correct) bet is market *expectation* of a recession (whether it comes or not). The investor must subject his ego to the realities of the emotional climate. It is better to be rich than to be vindicated slowly.

CHAPTER

26

The Hold/Sell Decision Checklist

KEY TO INVESTMENT SUCCESS

- 20 Questions to Focus the Hold versus Sell Decision

This chapter contains a list of questions that summarize in short form the points developed in this book to help investors create a selling strategy. The questions are adapted from a training session developed for brokers in a regional retail brokerage firm and have proved useful for two reasons: they deal with a relatively unfamiliar facet of the investment process (i.e., selling stocks) and they help brokers focus investor thinking in ways that encourage rational decisions and (not incidentally) sometimes free up lazy funds for re-use.

Investors are encouraged to photocopy these pages of the book and to keep copies in three places: in the office, where broker conversations tend to take place; at home, where market studying and decision-making tends to take place; and in a broker's office so that *he* will spend time thinking about these issues and will help the investor back onto the path should he stray from logic.

20 Questions to Focus the Hold versus Sell Decision

At the Time of Purchase

1. Date stock bought?
2. Price paid? (For reference, what was the DJIA on that date?)
3. Price target?
4. Target date to sell the stock? (Calculate projected return in percent/year from numbers 1, 2, 3 and 4.)
5. Specific expectation of what would make the stock go up?

Reviewing the Position at a Later Date

6. Currently more, less or equally excited and sure about the company versus when stock was bought?
7. Has the story expected in number 5 played out yet? If no, is there still a concrete chance the story will play? If yes, did the stock go up at all on the news? If yes, did the stock reach the objective in number 3?

8. What is the price now? (Compare with number 2 and number 3; note number 6.)
9. What is expected to happen fundamentally now? (Compare to number 5.) If discussed originally with friends, relatives or colleagues, would the stock be discussed enthusiastically now and be purchased today?
10. Due to number 9, what price is expected now? (Compare to number 3.)
11. When is the price in number 10 projected? (Compare to number 4.) Projected annualized percent return from numbers 8, 10 and 11?
12. What is the downside price risk from current prices if nothing happens? If the story or concept in number 5 or number 9 proves false?
13. Is the risk/reward balance favorable from current prices? (Compare number 10 and number 12 with current price.)
14. Where is the DJIA now? (Compare with DJIA level in number 2.) Is the relative performance of the stock surprising?
15. Have there been negative surprises from the company or its industry since purchase?
16. Since purchase, has there been a near decision to sell, only to hold on for a little more? Was a mental or actual stop-loss point set, and then reduced or removed as the stock weakened?

Analyzing Whether to Hold or Sell Now

17. Why, specifically, should the stock be held now?
18. With current knowledge, should this stock be purchased right now at today's price?
19. Have significantly better opportunities been identified for purchase right now?
20. Does the answer to number 17 square with answers to numbers 3, 18 and19?

Written responses to these questions are recommended for two reasons: the discipline of thinking through the exercises in detail and the creation of an archival notebook record that can be used for later reference, comparison and learning. Number a sheet from 1 to 20, put a blank for the stock's name on the top and photocopy this answer grid for future use.

Start by filling out the sheet at the time of purchase by answering numbers 1-5 immediately when the buy order is made. Then there is no need to search back for data for number 1 and number 2 and, most significantly, there is no fudging of responses to numbers 3, 4 and 5.

Later, answer numbers 9, 10 and 11 with numbers 3, 4 and 5 covered up: no copying or the exercise is useless! The quality of investment decisions is enhanced by the rigor of responding to this process.

Note that there is a built-in bias toward making the respondent feel a bit defensive about holding a stock. This creates a presumption in favor of selling when things have not gone as planned. If a holding is not working, it needs to be fixed.

For starters if it is no longer the time period indicated by number 4 or if the stock actually has traded at or above the answer to number 3, something has gone wrong with the plan or the execution. If there are differences between the answers to numbers 3, 4 and 5 and numbers 9, 10 and 11, study them again.

And a positive answer to number 15 or to either part of number 16 indicates less decisiveness or consistency in dealing with this situation. Either greed arose when things went well or denial arose when things turned sour. It is only human to shift ground (rationalize) in an effort to be tolerant of the stock's performance (one's own judgment) or of less-than-perfect strategy and execution. Learn from past executions and make a special effort to avoid falling into this pattern again.

The key question is number 18. If this question cannot be answered in the affirmative with total honesty and enthusiastic conviction (use the sub-part of number 9 as an acid test), sell. If the investor would not buy today, why should others be expected to do so? If other investors are not expected to be buyers, lower prices are forecast by implication.

How soon or how often this exercise should be conducted for each stock held is a reasonable question. It is advisable to create a tickler file in which to place each sheet for review 90 days from the buy date (or at the date noted in number 4, if that is sooner). If the review results in a hold decision, file the page for re-review at the date in number 11.

The use of this questionnaire is not guaranteed to be a cure-all. Nor does its use automatically make every position profitable. It does help to impose closure on situations that are not working out as expected, to generate urgency by imposing the time value of money and by serving as a reminder that a decision to hold should be an active and reasoned act of the mind, not a lazy default. A decision to hold should be every bit as active as a decision to sell, short of the need to pick up the telephone and dial the broker's number.

To be successful, an investment must not only be bought right, it must be sold right. Until the sale occurs, the outcome is only a temporary paper result; a handsome profit can still melt away unless it is actually closed out. This questionnaire should be used as a reminder, guide and prompting tool to sharpen decision-making skills and sale executions.

Index

2

INVESTMENT BASICS

Order No. 482-1

Price: Rs. 190/-

Investing for Beginners

Kathy Kristof

This book is simple. It's straightforward. It skilfully guides you step-by-step to investment success. Highlights: ■ Investment Risks and Rewards ■ Your Starting Point ■ How to pick stocks ■ Investing in Bonds ■ Mutual Funds Primer.

"Smart, sensible advice . . . a road map to financial success without gimmicks or secret formulas."

Los Angeles Times, USA

Order No. 394-9

Price: Rs. 145/-

How to Manage Your Investment Risks & Returns

An Essential Self-teaching Guide for Every Investor

David L. Scott

The secret of successful investing lies rather in understanding and controlling the risk involved in any investment. Step-by-step this book shows you how to control your investment risks.

"An object lesson." *The Economic Times*

INVESTMENT OPTIONS

Order No. 573-9

Price: Rs. 145/-

Profitable investment in shares : *A Beginner's Guide*

S. S. Grewal & Navjot Grewal

This hugely popular book tells you the basic principles and guidelines of profitable investment in shares. It also highlights the basic rules to follow in order to ensure reasonable safety of your capital. And it does all this in simple, clear language without resorting to jargon or technicalities. So, if are you one of those who wants to invest in shares but doesn't know quite how to go about it, then you can't do much better than starting with this book.

"Positively rewarding." *Financial Express*

The Basics of Investing

Gerald Krefetz

Order No. 446-5

Price: Rs. 225/-

The rapidly growing number of investment avenues often lead to confusion. In this book, an investment expert offers you the must-know principles, expert guidance and sensible solutions to invest your money profitably.

The Basics of Stocks

Gerald Krefetz

Order No. 448-1

Price: Rs. 225/-

You probably need to invest in shares to achieve long-term capital appreciation. What you also need to do is to do it right. In simple, easy-to-follow steps, a Wall Street expert offers you solutions for making the most out of investing in shares.

Order No. 447-3

Price: Rs. 225/-

The Basics of Bonds

Profitable Fixed-Income Investing

Gerald Krefetz

The lure: bonds and other fixed income investment avenues offer relatively greater safety of capital with predict-able returns.

This book by a U.S. investment expert will assist you in making intelligent decisions about your fixed-income investing.

Order No. 449-X

Price: Rs. 190/-

The Basics of Speculating

How to Speculate Most Profitably with Your Hard-Earned Money

Gerald Krefetz

This book tackles in detail the most popular financial instruments used for speculation: stocks, bonds, options, futures, commodities, precious metals and foreign exchange, etc.,

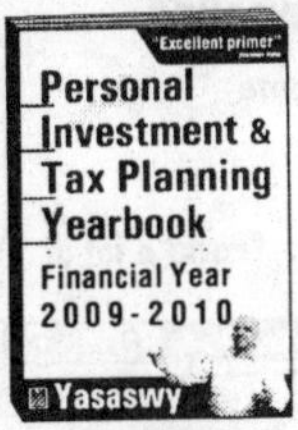

Order No. 752-9

Price: Rs. 295/-

Personal Investment & Tax Planning Yearbook (A.Y. 2009-10)

How to Invest Your Money Most Profitably This Year

N. J. Yasaswy

Are your savings invested profitably enough to buy you a house, provide the best higher education for your children, take you on a vacation abroad or ensure a fail-safe retirement income? Whether it is Rs 10,000 you want to invest or Rs 10 lakh, *Personal Investment & Tax Planning Yearbook* shows you the most profitable ways to do so, combining the best investment options and the latest tax incentives offered in the 2007-2008 budget.

WHERE TO INVEST YOUR MONEY THIS YEAR: ■ The investment scene and Budget impact ■ The 50 best equity shares for aggressive investors ■ The 50 best stocks for conservative investors ■ Corporate debentures and public sector bonds ■ Safe company deposits ■ Where not to invest ■ Performance analysis and long-term outlook of mutual funds ■ *Also,* 10 readymade investment portfolios for you to pick from.

HOW TO SAVE TAXES THIS YEAR ■ Sensible, practical guidance on tax planning, including income tax and wealth tax ■ How to lower your tax rates through long-term capital gains from growth shares ■ How to achieve a zero-tax status ■ Tax planning for your whole family ■ Tax deduction, tax-exempt incomes and other tax benefits ■ Your tax calendar for the year ■ *Plus,* how much investment risk you should take.

"Annual ready-reckoner for the investor." *The Hindu*

MUTUAL FUNDS

Order No. 683-2

Price: Rs. 395/-

Indian Mutual Funds Handbook: *A Guide for Industry Professionals and Intelligent Investors*

Sundar Sankaran

This comprehensive handbook by an expert lays out the working of Indian mutual funds, their operational and regulatory mechanisms, the advantages and limitations of investing in them along with suitable approaches to personal financial planning. The author's experience of handling hundreds of training programmes ensures an engaging and easy to understand approach to mastering the subject.

"I recommend this book to everyone who wants to make informed investment decisions"

Shekhar Sathe, Kotak Mahindra

"The best book for understanding (Indian) mutual funds"

M. Subramanian CEO India, Barclays Bank, plc.

"If you think you know everything about mutual funds, read the book to find out how much you don't know!"

Prof. G. Sethu, Dean, UTI Institute of Capital Markets

Order No. 479-1

Price: Rs. 280/-

The New Commonsense Guide to Mutual Funds

Mary Rowland

In this top-selling book, one of America's pre-eminent financial journalists, cuts through the hype and confusion surrounding mutual funds and tells you exactly what you need to know.

"Remarkable! " *John C. Bogle*

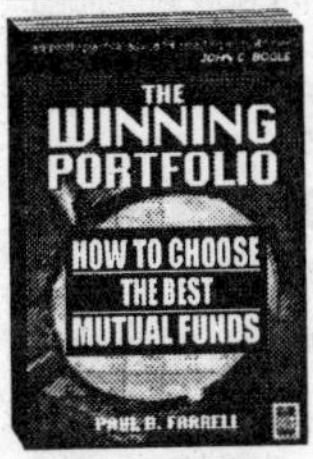

Order No. 481-3

Price: Rs. 190/-

The Winning Portfolio

How to choose the best mutual funds

Paul B. Farrell

Farrell's strategy is easy-to-follow and will help diversify your portfolio while shielding your investment from market downturns.

"An easy-to-follow roadmap for maximizing your mutual funds profits. . . both rational and intuitive" *Brian Murray*

STOCK MARKET KNOW-HOW

The Indian Securities Market

BEST SELLER!

A Guide for Foreign & Domestic Investors

Tadashi Endo

"The best book on India's securities industry. . ." *Business India*

"Brilliant." *Business Standard*

No. 386-8 Rs. 395/-

The Stock Market Dictionary

BEST SELLER!

Guide to Dalal Street Money-Talk

Praveen N. Shroff

Nearly, 2,000 stock market terms clearly defined and explained. **"Well worth possessing."** *Financial Express*

No. 436-8 Rs. 190/-

Intelligent Stock Market Investing

How to Win the Dalal Street Game

N.J. Yasaswy

Framework for intelligent investing. "Packs a lot of substance." *Business India*

No. 695-6 Rs. 280/-

Stock Market Logic

A Sophisticated Approach to Profits on Wall Street

Norman G. Fosback

Hundreds of sophisticated investment techniques. "Classic." *Joseph Granville.*

No. 440-6 Rs. 280/-

Fundamental Analysis for Investors

Raghu Palat

"A masterly introduction to fundamental analysis." *Times of India*

No. 569-0 Rs. 250/-

Balance Sheets

Contents, Analysis & Interpretation

Hemant R. Dani

How to interpret and analyse financial statements . . . of great value for investors

No. 476-7 Rs. 250/-

STOCK MARKET STRATEGIES

The Tough-Minded Investor: Pistolese

This book will help you understand how emotional decision making may be hurting your chances for success. It outlines long-term strategies to help you avoid the emotional stress of sharp, short-term price fluctuations.

No. 219-5 Rs. 125/-

Value Averaging

Systematic investment techniques for fail-safe stock market returns

Michael E. Edleson

How value averaging helps you automatically buy low and sell high — without market timing and stock-picking techniques.

No. 228-4 Rs. 125/-

It's When You Sell That Counts

It's Not What Stocks You Buy. . .

Donald L. Cassidy

You haven't made your profits until you have the money in hand — and that doesn't happen until you sell your shares.

"Just as Peter Lynch stripped away the mystique of buying stocks... Don Cassidy successfully answers the question, 'When do I sell?'" *R. Jerry Falkner, CFA*

"Should be required reading for all investors." *Phoenix Balance Fund, USA*

No. 561-5 Rs. 325/-

100 World-Famous Stock Market Techniques: Richard J. Maturi

BEST SELLER!

One-of-a-kind, handy reference that provides concise descriptions of one hundred of the most important stock market investment methods used worldwide. . . describes how each method works — and how and when it can be used to best advantage.

"The best book of its kind." *Business Standard*

No. 562-3 Rs. 250/-

Order No. 682-3
Price: Rs. 395/-

How to Make Money Trading Derivatives: *An Insider's Guide (2nd Edition)*

Ashwani Gujral

This is a pioneering book on trading derivatives in the Indian market.

The book focuses on: ■ Technical tools for traders ■ Profitable day trading ■ Cash and futures arbitrage to make profits from idle cash ■ Futures trading strategies ■ Option trading strategies ■ The high returns ■ Covered call writing strategies ■ Trading during special events, such as elections, company results.

"Gujral has cemented himself as a pioneer in this field" *James Holter, Editor, Futures Magazine, USA.*

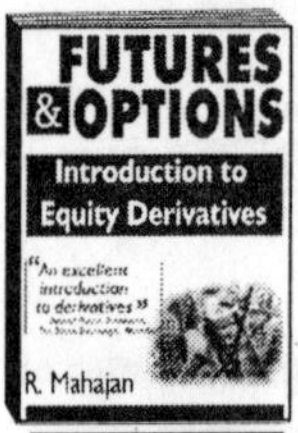

Order No. 691-3
Price: Rs. 295/-

Futures and Options

Introduction to Equity Derivatives

R. Mahajan

How derivatives work and how you can benefit from them to protect your stock market investment is the thrust of this book.

The book lays particular emphasis on stock index futures — the first risk-proofing tool available to the Indian investor. The author explains both the underlying concepts and procedures in a straightforward manner. Assuming no prior knowledge, both the beginners and market operators will find this an easy-to-understand book to get started in futures and opetions.

"An excellent introduction to derivatives"
Anand Rathi, President, The Stock Exchange, Mumbai

Order No.520-8
Price: Rs. 395/-

Profit in the Futures Markets!

Insights and Strategies for Futures and Futures Options Trading

Jake Bernstein

Filled with practical tools and techniques for understanding and prospering in the world of futures trading, *Profit in the Futures Markets!* shows how to use such information to your best advantage.

"One of best books I've ever seen on the futures markets" *Rick Bensignor, Chief Technical Strategist, Morgan Stanley*

"Jake Bernstein is one of the best at putting together the emotions and mechanics of trading"
Futures Magazine, USA

Order No. 555-0
Price: Rs. 395/-

New Insights on Writing Covered Call Options

The Powerful Technique that Enhances Return and Lowers Risk in Stock Investing

Richard Lehman and Lawrence G. McMillan

In this pioneering, easy-to-understand book, leading options experts, give a complete guide to covered call writing and the increased control and lowered risk it affords. They detail the basics and beyond, from the mechanics of implementation to developing strategies that are best suited to your investment goals.

"This book makes a great case for basic reading and writting — reading stock charts and writing covered calls" *John Murphy*

"This was a definite eye-opener and one of the soundest approaches to stock investing I've seen. It makes you wonder what else Wall Street has been keeping from us" *Brian R. Workman*

Order No. 331-0
Price: Rs. 325/-

Dictionary of Futures and Options

Over 1,500 Terms Defined and Explained

Alan Webber

The *Dictionary of Futures and Options* is a comprehensive reference source of essential information for any investor involved in futures and options. Both the complete beginner and the seasoned professional will find this book invaluable. It contains all the basic terminology.

"Reference book on futures and options" *The Hindu*